A Guide to Mooting in Ireland

A GUIDE TO
MOOTING IN IRELAND

By

Dr EDANA RICHARDSON

Published by
Clarus Press Ltd,
Griffith Campus,
South Circular Road,
Dublin 8.
www.claruspress.ie

Typeset by
Gough Typesetting Services,
Dublin

Printed by
SprintPrint
Dublin

ISBN
978-1-911611-18-9

A catalogue record for this book is available from the British Library

Disclaimer
Whilst every effort has been made to ensure that the contents of this book are
accurate, neither the publisher and/or author can accept responsibility for any
errors or omissions or loss occasioned to any person acting or refraining from
acting as result of any material in this publication.

Foreword

Many lawyers go through their professional lives without ever seriously engaging in courtroom work. They see litigation as 'the dark side'. But every lawyer who 'does' litigation remembers the first time they stood up in court to present a case. Not all of those recollections are comfortable. Some neophytes are overcome by the occasion and become lost in a welter of hesitation and confusion. But every lawyer, whether working in the field of scholarship, or in a law practice — they are not, of course, mutually exclusive — acknowledges that there are significant differences between the 'pure' study of law and its practice. Legal scholars and students do not, for example, have to deal with clients, mounting files of documents going back decades, the gathering of witnesses, and adducing evidence — not to mention judges and deadlines. In fact, in many cases which come to court, the facts themselves are determinative; the legal principles well established (the vicissitudes of academic life are perhaps different in some respects, but, I am sure, no less stressful). What is refreshing is that, in the last 20 years, both law schools and legal professional teaching bodies have recognised not only that litigation is central, but that there is a real necessity to take advocacy seriously.

As a consequence of this recognition, mooting has now become an established part of the curriculum in many, if not all, Irish law schools. Not only are there many national competitions, but, each year, Irish law students go abroad and participate in international moots, thereby gaining valuable experience which will stand by them for the rest of their lives. Mooting can also be an enlivening social experience; an opportunity to meet law students from other law schools, at home and abroad. I learnt from this book that the young Hilary Rodham first met Bill Clinton at a law student mooting competition (see Donald Baer: 'Man-Child in Politics Land', US News and World Report, 14 October 1991, at page 40). I leave it to the reader to find the footnote in this book from which I found out this interesting fact. I will give one hint, it is in an article written by a prominent, colourful, if not controversial, United States Appeals Court judge, recently retired.

It is truly an honour to write the foreword to this excellent work. It genuinely does bridge that gap between principles and practice. Some 'practical' books have mind-numbing titles, like *Everything you need to know about woodwork*. Many readers will leave such unilluminating works unenlightened. But this stimulating and concise book could justly be entitled *Everything you* really do *need to know about mooting and never asked*. By the end, an attentive reader will have, genuinely, learned everything that is necessary to know about the subject. This includes issues from vital 'arcana' like the proper citation of cases; and the hierarchy of legal precedents; down to how to address a court; even what to wear. The book covers every angle of the subject. The author gives truly useful advice and information about mooting preparation, presentation, teamwork, and even the under-estimated and difficult task of setting moot problems. The work contains a number of excellent problems in Chapter 8.

Of course, one can cavil that moots tend to emphasise legal *principles*, rather than addressing the *facts* of a particular case. In the real world the opposite is often the case. But, as one goes up the legal food chain, legal principles become an increasingly vital part of advocacy. In the 'real world' of ordinary day-to-day litigation, of course, cases are often about people, human nature, facts and credibility. The true art of advocacy, at whatever level, not only involves a clear exposition of the applicable law, but the identification of how legal principles apply to the facts of the case at hand. Mooting helps a student really *understand* cases and principles, and how the law really works in theory, practice and as a *praxis*.

Whether you are a lawyer, a law student, or a general reader, reading this foreword in a bookshop or on a website, I would like to pose a challenge to you. Open any random page of this book and I promise that you will find there genuinely useful advice and information. This sort of material is not only applicable to students, but even to young qualified advocates.

Just prior to writing this Foreword I engaged in just such an exercise. Each random page I opened dealt with the issues which I identified above, from 'arcana' to 'clothing'. All useful. But, as well, there are the other *sine qua nons*. Prepare, prepare, prepare. Practice, practice, practice. Be early. Know where you are going, and how you are going to get there. These simple things form part of the lawyer's life and discipline.

The late Mr Justice Niall McCarthy, one of my great predecessors, once observed that every foreword penned by a judge should contain some element of judicial 'axe grinding'. I confine myself to pointing out to mooters that, when presenting a case, they will do well to avoid the dreaded verbal jargon formula '*it is submitted*'. This phrase, in itself, makes any submission sound like a dry legal treatise, and will induce instant narcolepsy in a mooting judge. Advocacy is about principles, facts and *persuasion*. It is *the judge*, or judges, you are trying to persuade.

While the book is primarily tailored for use in Ireland, in fact, the advice and material contained here could equally be used internationally. I can say with personal knowledge that a copy of this book will soon be winging its way to one of the pre-eminent Indian law schools. There it will, doubtless, be devoured by a ready audience of new mooters. The advice which is contained in this book is as applicable to international participants, as national. I am sure this work will attract readers from many other jurisdictions: it deserves to. What is contained here is, in fact, universally applicable. The book not only provides 'Everything you need to know': it does so for every jurisdiction, where mooting is carried on.

Some books are scholarly, some books are practical, a few are both. This book is one of that few: it is both entirely scholarly and utterly practical. I heartily recommend it.

Mr Justice John MacMenamin
The Supreme Court
December 2018

Preface

In recent years, mooting has become an established component of legal training. In Ireland, opportunities to moot are now available in the form of modules in law degree programmes and vocational legal training courses, and on an extracurricular basis through participation in national and international mooting competitions. This growth in opportunities to moot is not surprising. Mooting can help to build important skills in research, advocacy and the construction of persuasive arguments. These are skills that are relevant to academic study and professional life, both within and outside of law. In this way, mooting complements more theoretical aspects of a student's legal studies.

A Guide to Mooting in Ireland is the first book to focus on mooting in Ireland. As a result, it has been specifically tailored for those involved in mooting in Ireland. However, as many of the skills discussed are not unique to Irish moots, this book should be of value to those participating in moots outside of Ireland. Through the use of worked examples and practical tips, this book helps to build a mooter's skills by examining in detail each stage of a moot. It addresses techniques for understanding a moot problem question, how to structure and enhance written and oral submissions, and what to expect on the day of a moot. It also discusses the organisation of mooting modules and competitions.

I am grateful to my colleagues and friends who commented on various sections of this book: Amina Adanan, Louise Kennefick, Charles O'Sullivan, Karen Petch, Fergus Ryan and Seth Tillman. In particular, I would like to thank Siobhán Buckley and Joseph Harrington for their helpful comments on drafts of this book. I would also like to thank David McCartney of Clarus Press for his guidance during the writing of this book and Shane Gough of Gough Typesetting Services for his patience during the editing process. Finally, I thank Mr Justice MacMenamin for writing the foreword, which is endlessly entertaining and extremely insightful in equal measure.

Edana Richardson
January 2019

Table of Contents

Table of Cases

Table of Legislation

An Introduction to Mooting

1.1 Introduction

A Guide to Mooting in Ireland is aimed at those participating in, or organising, moots. It covers every stage of a moot, from initial receipt of the moot problem question, to the construction and delivery of persuasive submissions, appropriate moot courtroom manner and the organisation of a moot. While the skills discussed in this book are applicable to anyone involved in mooting, *A Guide to Mooting in Ireland* will be of particular relevance to participants and organisers of moots in Ireland.

Chapter 1 introduces the reader to mooting and sets out a sample moot problem question that will form the basis of the illustrative examples used in this book. Chapters 2 and 3 address the research portion of preparing for a moot by outlining key aspects of the Irish legal system and legal research skills. Chapter 4 focuses on the preparation of written submissions for a moot by discussing the structure and content of memorials and lists of authorities, and on the legal writing skills that should be demonstrated in written submissions. Chapters 5 and 6 deal with a moot's oral submissions by considering key phrases used and the structure of these submissions. These chapters also deal with skills to help a mooter's performance on the day of the moot. Chapter 7 provides details on how to organise mooting competitions and mooting modules, and Chapter 8 sets out Irish law-specific sample moot problem questions.

The specific rules of any moot will be determined by that moot's organiser. Consequently, if you are using *A Guide to Mooting in Ireland* to prepare for a particular moot, it should be read in conjunction with the rules of that moot.

1.2 What is mooting?

A moot is a simulated appeals case on points of law in which mooters present arguments before a moot judge, or a panel of moot judges, on legal issues raised by a fictitious civil or criminal case. As a mooter, you will represent a fictitious party to the appeal. The

'Appellant' is the party who wants the appeal to be allowed; the 'Respondent' is the party who wants the appeal to be dismissed.

An appeals case: In a moot, one party (the Appellant) is challenging the legal correctness of a decision handed down by a judge (referred to as the 'trial judge'). As a result, a moot takes the form of an appeal from a decision of a court of inferior jurisdiction (that is, a court that sits below the moot court in the hierarchy of Irish courts).[1] Most Irish moots are set in the Supreme Court or the Court of Appeal (civil or criminal division), but may also be set in the High Court.

On points of law: Moots involve an appeal on points of law, rather than on the facts of the fictitious case. As a result, a moot will not involve a full rehearing of the case or arguments over what the facts of the case are. As a mooter, you must accept the facts as presented in the moot problem question—do not question or challenge these facts. Instead, your focus will be on arguing the legal merits of the appeal. If you represent the Appellant, you will argue that the decision of the trial judge was legally incorrect. If you represent the Respondent, you will argue that the decision of the trial judge was legally correct. The bases upon which these arguments are made are referred to as 'grounds of appeal'. For each ground of appeal, you will construct arguments that support your client's position.

Legal arguments: In order to be persuasive, arguments made in a moot should be based on sound legal reasoning. Legal reasoning uses legal authorities (such as law from the European Union, the Irish Constitution, legislation and case law)[2] to determine the legal principles applicable to the facts of the moot. Two methods of legal reasoning that can be used to establish applicable legal principles are deductive reasoning and inductive reasoning.[3] Using 'deductive reasoning', a conclusion logically flows from the application of a general principle (known as a major premise) to a specific situation (known as a minor premise).[4] In the context of a moot, a legal principle established by an authority (the major premise) is applied to the facts of the moot (the minor premise) in order to reach a conclusion as to the implications for the parties.

---

[1] See Chapter 2 (Section 2.4) for a discussion of the hierarchy of Irish courts.
[2] See Chapter 2 (Section 2.2) for a discussion of the sources of Irish law.
[3] Similar reasoning is used by the Irish courts. For example, in *White v Bar Council of Ireland* [2016] IEHC 406 [4], [2017] 1 IR 249, 256, Barrett J noted when referring to an earlier decision, that 'it is a decision that does not involve inductive or deductive reasoning of the type that customarily informs court judgments, but largely speculative reasoning that, again, is ungrounded in case law.'
[4] Peter Nash Swisher, 'Teaching Legal Reasoning in Law School' (1981) 74 Law Library Journal 534, 536.

> **Example:**
>
> - **Major premise** (legal principle established by authorities): In order to be valid, an offer must be communicated to the person for whom it is intended.
> - **Minor premise** (facts of the moot): There was no communication of the offer.
> - **Conclusion**: The offer was not valid.

Using 'inductive reasoning', you take one or several premises and use these to reach a conclusion. This conclusion is not certain, but is rather one that the premises *may* support.[5] In the context of a moot, this can be done either: (1) by combining legal principles established or developed in several authorities to reach a conclusion that a particular legal principle applies to the facts of the moot; or (2) by drawing an analogy between an authority and the facts of the moot to reach a conclusion that the same legal principle applies in both situations.

> **Example:**
>
> - **Premise 1**: Legislation requires a contract for the sale of land to be in writing.
> - **Premise 2**: In Case X, a contract for the sale of land was in writing, and the court also required that there be an offer, acceptance and consideration for a contract to be valid.
> - **Premise 3**: In Case Y, a valid contract for the sale of land was in writing and there was an offer, acceptance and consideration.
> - **Conclusion**: In order for a contract for the sale of land to be valid, it should be in writing, and there should be an offer, acceptance and consideration. These were not present in the facts of the moot; therefore, the contract in question is not valid.

As a way of testing a mooter's skills as a public speaker and his or her ability to construct coherent arguments, mooting shares characteristics with mock trials and debating. However, mooting is distinct. Mock trials involve a full hearing in a mock court of first instance. Participants try to establish the facts of the case through examination and cross-examination of witnesses and the presentation of evidence. The judge or jury will then make findings of fact based on the evidence adduced.[6] In a moot, the facts are settled and are not open to debate. Moots, therefore, involve neither witnesses nor juries. Reflecting these distinctions, mock trials test

---

[5] ibid.
[6] To 'adduce' something in a trial is to put it before the court.

advocates' ability to handle and present evidence, while mooting tests mooters' ability to handle and present legal arguments. Mooting also differs from debating, due to the exclusively legal nature of moots.

1.3 Why moot?

Legal professionals, whether solicitors or barristers, are expected to handle large amounts of information and to distil this information into legally correct and salient advice for clients. They are also expected to act in a professional manner and, particularly in the case of barristers, to demonstrate strong advocacy skills. By mooting while at university or while undertaking a vocational legal training course, you can practise and enhance these skills.

Whether you have chosen to participate in a mooting competition, or you are required to participate in a mooting module as part of your legal studies, there are numerous reasons to moot, including the following:

1.3.1 Mooting helps you to act and think like a legal professional

Mooting is an opportunity for you to practise acting and thinking like a legal professional. Like a solicitor or barrister, a mooter should absorb and understand relevant facts and legal principles, critically assess this information and, based on this information, construct truthful and persuasive arguments that support a particular position.[7]

1.3.2 Mooting enhances your CV and develops your transferable skills

Evidence on your CV that you have participated in mooting demonstrates commitment to your legal training and an interest in law. Mooting also encourages you to develop a variety of transferable skills, such as those relating to time management, organisation and teamwork. As you participate in moots, keep a list of situations where you have demonstrated or developed particular

---

[7] Deborah A Maranville, 'Infusing Passion and Context into the Traditional Law Curriculum Through Experiential Learning' (2001) 51(1) Journal of Legal Education 51, who noted the benefits of simulations (such as moots) as a means of engaging students in their legal education. Michael V Hernandez, 'In Defense of Moot Court: A Response to 'In Praise of Moot Court – Not!'' (1998) 17 Review of Litigation 69, 71–72.

skills. You can then discuss these skills, together with concrete examples, at interviews for internships or training contracts.

1.3.3 Mooting improves your public speaking and advocacy skills

As a student, you may have limited opportunities to practise public speaking. Mooting gives you this opportunity and lets you practise and improve your skills as a public speaker in a supportive environment. Once you begin work as a legal professional (or in many other professions), you may be expected to give presentations, to speak in front of your team and to present your recommendations to clients. If you have no public speaking experience, these tasks could be daunting.

Mooting also improves your ability to construct and deliver persuasive arguments. This ability to make your public speaking compelling and persuasive is a key skill in many professions.[8]

1.3.4 Mooting gives you confidence

Mooting can be intimidating. However, working together with your teammate, and constructing and presenting persuasive arguments, can give you a huge sense of achievement. As you practise, you will gain confidence from knowing that this is something that you can do successfully.

1.4 Mooting in Ireland

Mooting conducted as part of students' legal studies is increasingly common in Ireland, either as a standalone module[9] or embedded within another module.[10] As a result, many third-level institutions in Ireland that offer modules in law now provide students with an opportunity to participate in mooting.[11]

In parallel with (or instead of) mooting that is formally incorporated into a course of study, mooting is also informally available in Ireland's third-level institutions through students' extracurricular

---

[8]   ibid, 73.

[9]   As is the case, for example, in Maynooth University.

[10]   In Trinity College Dublin, for example, mooting is closely linked to the Private Law Remedies module.

[11]   As Higgins and Daly note, the manner in which mooting is made available to students varies between institutions, Noelle Higgins and Yvonne Daly, 'The First Annual National Moot Court Competition – An Appraisal' (2011) 29 Irish Law Times 112.

participation in mooting competitions.[12] There is a range of mooting competitions held each year. While these are primarily organised outside of Ireland, many (such as the Philip C Jessup International Moot Court Competition,[13] or the European Law Students' Association ('ELSA') European Human Rights Moot Court Competition[14]) are open to Irish students.

Within Ireland, a growing number of intervarsity mooting competitions are available to students interested in competitive mooting. These mooting competitions include[15] the *National Moot Court Competition*,[16] which is hosted by Dublin City University with oral submissions taking place in the Criminal Courts of Justice complex in Dublin. This competition is open to teams from Irish and international third-level institutions and runs in the first semester of the academic year. *Bréagchúirt Uí Dhálaigh*[17] is an Irish language mooting competition organised by Gael Linn. While this competition has no geographic requirements for participating teams, it does require team members to be fluent in Irish. It runs in the first semester of the academic year. The *Silken Thomas National Moot Court Competition*,[18] the *UCC Moot Court Competition*[19] and the *Thomas A. Finlay Moot Court Intervarsity*[20] are all intervarsity mooting competitions hosted by Irish universities (Maynooth University, University College Cork and University College Dublin, respectively). These competitions are open to teams from Irish and international third-level institutions and all run in the second semester of the academic year. *Corn Adomnáin*[21] is an international humanitarian law mooting competition organised by the Irish Red Cross that is open to teams from third-level institutions in the

---

[12] ibid.

[13] Details of which can be found at: < www.ilsa.org/about-jessup/> accessed 1 December 2018.

[14] Details of which can be found at: <https://ehrmcc.elsa.org/> accessed 1 December 2018.

[15] This is not a complete list of all mooting competitions in Ireland, but represents an overview of the different types of mooting competitions that have been run in recent years.

[16] Details of which can be found on a dedicated Dublin City University, School of Law & Government website, which is created ahead of each year's competition.

[17] Details of which can be found at: <www.gael-linn.ie/default. aspx?treeid=269&id=20> accessed 1 December 2018.

[18] Details of which can be found on a dedicated Maynooth University, Department of Law website, which is created ahead of each year's competition.

[19] Details of which can be found on the University College Cork social media channels.

[20] Details of which can be found on the University College Dublin social media channels.

[21] Details of which can be found at: <www.redcross.ie/programmes-and-services-in-ireland/corn-adomnain/> accessed 1 December 2018.

Republic of Ireland and Northern Ireland. It is hosted by Queen's University Belfast and runs in the second semester of the academic year. Finally, the *ELSA Ireland National Moot Court Competition*[22] is an intervarsity mooting competition organised by ELSA Ireland. This competition runs in the second semester of the academic year.

In addition to these intervarsity mooting competitions, a number of Irish universities and the institutions providing vocational legal training courses in Ireland (that is, the Honorable Society of King's Inns and the Law Society of Ireland) run internal mooting competitions that are not open to external teams.

1.5 Structure of a moot

A moot is designed to simulate a real court. Like a trial heard before a real court, moots are typically highly structured and stylised. Each party will perform a specific role and the moot will follow a specific format.

1.5.1 Participants

A. Mooters

A moot will typically involve two teams, each with two team members.[23] Some mooting competitions allow teams to have more than two members, although only two of those team members will generally speak during each round of oral submissions.[24]

In a moot, one team will represent the Appellant, and the other team will represent the Respondent. The party that you represent will usually be determined at random, although if the moot that you are participating in involves more than one round, you may have an opportunity to represent both parties.

---

[22] Details of which can be found at: <http://elsa-ireland.ie/index.php/activities/moot-court-competitions/> accessed 1 December 2018.

[23] Bréagchúirt Uí Dhálaigh only requires a minimum of one member of each team (in circumstances where there is one member, that member will deal with all grounds of appeal).

[24] For example, the National Moot Court Competition. Occasionally in a mooting module where there is an uneven number of students, one moot may be composed of two teams of three members.

> **Practical Tip:**
>
> In mooting competitions (particularly those in England and Wales), members of a team may be referred to as 'lead' or 'senior' counsel and 'junior' counsel. The lead or senior counsel will speak first on behalf of his or her client and may be allotted more speaking time. It is important to check the rules of the moot to confirm the speaking time allotted for each mooter. In Irish moots, both team members are usually (but not always)[25] referred to as 'counsel'.

B. Moot judges

Together with mooters, moot judges are an essential element in a moot. Every moot will be presided over by at least one moot judge, while some moots may involve a bench of three or more moot judges. Like judges in a real court, moot judges are in charge of the proceedings, they intervene with questions and comments when mooters are speaking and they deliver a judgment on the law at the end of the moot to confirm which party has won the appeal. Unlike real judges, however, moot judges will also decide which team has won the moot. A moot's winning team will be the team that most persuasively argued their client's case in light of the available facts and law.

C. Court clerk

A moot may include court clerks who assist the moot judges and the moot's organiser.[26] Court clerks may be law students.

D. Audience

In mooting competitions, spectators may be allowed to attend moots (particularly for later rounds of the competition).

1.5.2 Structure

While the periods of time allowed for each stage of a moot will vary, moots generally follow a similar structure.

---

[25] See, for example, Bréagchúirt Uí Dhálaigh, where teams include 'senior' and 'junior' counsel.

[26] See Chapter 7 (Section 7.2.9) for a discussion of court clerks and their role in a moot.

A. *Before the day of the moot*

(a) Teams will receive a moot problem question and rules of the moot in advance. The moot problem question will set out a fictitious scenario and outline the findings of the trial judge, which are now being appealed. It will typically go on to detail the grounds of appeal. The rules of the moot will explain how the moot will be run and provide teams with information about registration and timing.

(b) Teams will be told whether they will be representing the Appellant or the Respondent, or they may be told that they could be representing either party on the day of the moot (and so must be prepared to represent both parties).

(c) Between receipt of the moot problem question and the day of the moot, each team will work to construct legal arguments based on research that they have conducted.[27] These arguments, like those in a real court, are referred to as 'submissions'. All teams will be required to prepare oral submissions, where mooters present their submissions before the moot court.[28] The rules of the moot will confirm whether each team must also prepare written submissions that they will exchange with their opponents.[29]

(d) Exchange of written submissions between teams is typically simultaneous and may take place prior to, or on, the day of the moot.

B. *On the day of the moot*

(a) The moot courtroom will be set up to simulate a real court. In an Irish moot, both sets of counsel will typically face the moot judges. Counsel for the Respondent will sit at the desk on the left-hand side of the moot courtroom and counsel for the Appellant will sit at the desk on the right-hand side of the moot courtroom (in each case when looking forwards from the back of the room). If there is a court clerk, he or she may sit on either side of the moot judges' bench. Set out below is a diagram illustrating the typical layout of a moot courtroom in Ireland.

---

[27] See Chapter 3 for a discussion on researching for a moot.
[28] See Chapters 5 and 6 for a discussion on a moot's oral submissions.
[29] See Chapter 4 for a discussion on a moot's written submissions.

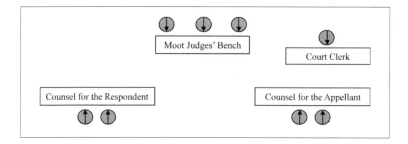

(b) Once the moot court is in session, mooters will present their oral submissions in a pre-determined speaking order and for a pre-determined amount of time. The allotted speaking time for each mooter will be determined by the rules of the moot.[30]

(c) During each mooter's oral submissions, the moot judges may intervene with questions or comments.

(d) Following submissions, counsel for the Appellant may be given a right of rebuttal where they challenge (or rebut) the Respondent's submissions. Counsel for the Respondent may also be given a corresponding right of surrebuttal to rebut points raised in the Appellant's rebuttal.[31]

(e) Once all mooters have spoken, the moot judges will deliver a judgment on: (1) the law; and (2) the winning team of the moot.[32] In a mooting module, students may also receive an individual mark for the module.

1.6 How to attend an appeals case in Ireland

The level of professionalism and style of advocacy in a moot replicate that found in a real court in Ireland. Those who are new to mooting may find it helpful to observe an appeals case in one of Ireland's superior courts, which are the Supreme Court, the Court of Appeal (civil or criminal division) and the High Court. While you can simply turn up at these courts and attend hearings that are open to the public, it is a good idea to plan your visit to the courts to observe a case.

---

[30] See Chapters 5 and 6 for a discussion of the structure, contents and skills to be demonstrated in oral submissions.

[31] See Chapter 5 (Section 5.4) for a discussion of rebuttal and surrebuttal.

[32] In the preliminary rounds of some mooting competitions, and in mooting modules, the moot judges will deliver a judgment on the law, but will not necessarily deliver a judgment on which team won the moot. See Chapter 7 (Section 7.2.8) for a discussion of the judgments given by moot judges.

Information about upcoming sittings of the courts in Ireland can be found in the Legal Diary section of the Courts Service of Ireland's website.[33] After clicking on the 'Legal Diary' link, select the court that you want to attend. For each court, you will be able to select the most recent Legal Diary, which is a list of cases scheduled to be heard in that court for the coming months. For most scheduled cases, this list provides details of:

- the parties to the case;
- the courtroom where the case will be heard;
- the time the case will be heard;
- the names of the judge or judges who are scheduled to hear the case; and
- the type of hearing. To observe a case in which there is an appeal on points of law, look for cases that are classified as 'for hearing', 'civil appeal' or 'case stated', rather than those classified as 'case management list' or 'for judgment'.

The Legal Diary for each court is updated almost daily and details of upcoming cases can change or be removed. Once you have selected the case that you want to observe, make a note of relevant timing and location information. Check this information again before your visit.

Practical Tip:

It is a good idea to make a note of other appeals cases scheduled to be heard around the same time as the case that you plan on observing. This way you can still attend a court hearing, even if the case that you had planned on observing is moved, settled or postponed at the last minute.

Make sure that you arrive at the courtroom before the time scheduled for the hearing. If you think that you will be late, do not try to enter the courtroom; instead you should select another case to observe. When you arrive at the courtroom, make sure that the public are allowed to attend the relevant hearing. In a criminal or family law case, a sign on the door noting that it is being held *in camera* means that it is not open to the public and you must select another case to observe. Once in the courtroom, sit quietly in the area reserved for the public and make sure your mobile phone is turned off and kept out of sight. If you want to keep a note of the

---

[33] See <www.courts.ie> accessed 1 December 2018. This (and other) free online legal databases are discussed in more detail in Chapter 3.

hearing, you can generally do so, but in writing only — *never* record audio or video of the court hearing.[34]

1.7 The moot problem question

Together with the rules of the moot, one of the first things that you will receive when participating in a moot is the moot problem question. Each team will receive the same moot problem question, regardless of the party a team ends up representing in oral submissions. A moot problem question will be drafted to provide mooters with the basic information that they need in order to conduct their legal research and to construct their submissions.

Practical Tip:

Moot problem questions are generally drafted so that each team should be able to construct logical submissions based on the information provided. Do not get discouraged if you think you have not found the one 'right' answer to the moot—there will be scope for making submissions on both sides of the appeal. Your job is to make your submissions as persuasive as possible.

When you receive the moot problem question, sit down with your teammate and read it thoroughly several times. If you give the text only a cursory read before you start researching the law, you may misunderstand the facts that are presented or the grounds of appeal, you may misinterpret the trial judge's findings or you may mix up the parties. Chapter 3 considers in detail the key information to confirm as you read a moot problem question.[35]

1.8 Sample moot problem question

Set out below is a sample moot problem question. This moot problem question will form the basis of all illustrative examples used throughout this book.

---

[34] Recording court proceedings 'otherwise than by written or shorthand note' is prohibited by the Rules of the Superior Courts Ord 123, amended by Rules of the Superior Courts (Recording of Proceedings) 2008, SI 2008/325, and further amended by Rules of the Superior Courts (Order 123) 2013, SI 2013/101 and Rules of the Superior Courts (Court Of Appeal Act 2014) 2014, SI 2014/485.

[35] See Chapter 3 (Section 3.2.2) for a discussion of how to read a moot problem question.

IN THE COURT OF APPEAL (CIVIL DIVISION)

Irish Sprinklers Ltd v Pete's Cabbages DAC[36]

Irish Sprinklers Ltd is a small family-run business that installs sprinkler systems on farms. The company has traditionally focused its marketing efforts on small farmers, but is currently in the middle of an expansion programme. Pete's Cabbages DAC operates a large vegetable company employing 300 people. Pete's Cabbages DAC entered into a contract with Irish Sprinklers Ltd for the installation of a sprinkler system and a follow-up network calibration on Pete's Cabbages DAC's Co. Kildare farm. This new system was designed to improve the farm's water consumption. Pursuant to the terms of the contract between the parties, Pete's Cabbages DAC agreed to pay €100,000 for the installation of the sprinkler system and the network calibration. €70,000 of this amount was paid at the time the contract was signed. The remaining €30,000 was due one week after the network calibration (although it was stated in the contract that such payment was not contingent upon the network calibration being completed).

Irish Sprinklers Ltd installed the sprinkler system, as agreed. The network calibration was scheduled to take place two weeks after the initial installation of the sprinkler system. However, between the time the sprinkler system was installed and the scheduled network calibration, Pete's Cabbages DAC lost a supply contract with a national supermarket chain. This had a significant impact on Pete's Cabbages DAC's finances. As a result, the finance director of Pete's Cabbages DAC (Jonathan Kenny) telephoned Helen Duffy, the sole director of Irish Sprinklers Ltd, in a panic. On this call, Jonathan explained to Helen that Pete's Cabbages DAC could only pay an additional €10,000, rather than the balance of €30,000. Helen sighed and responded as follows: 'Fine, but in that case, I will cancel the network calibration.' Jonathan asked Helen not to be so rash, before putting down the phone. Over lunch, Jonathan calmed down. As the calibration was needed in order for the sprinkler system to work, Jonathan sent an email to Helen in which he offered a case of champagne to whoever completed the network calibration. Helen printed this email out and stuck it on the bulletin board in the staff room next to a poster about an upcoming charity run. She never replied to Jonathan's email and there was no further communication between Jonathan and Helen.

---

[36] Based on a moot problem question used in an internal moot at Maynooth University.

The following Thursday, the network calibration was completed (as per the original schedule) by Gareth Sigg, who works for Irish Sprinklers Ltd. After this calibration, Gareth noticed a case of six bottles of champagne sitting at the reception desk of Pete's Cabbages DAC with a note saying 'thank you for the network calibration'. Gareth took the case of champagne home with him.

A week later, Irish Sprinklers Ltd's accounting department noticed a bank transfer from Pete's Cabbages DAC for the sum of €10,000 under the reference 'Final Payment'. Irish Sprinklers Ltd did not repay this amount and commenced proceedings against Pete's Cabbages DAC in the High Court to recover the balance of €20,000 due under the original contract. Twomey J in the High Court found in favour of Pete's Cabbages DAC, holding that Irish Sprinklers Ltd had accepted Pete's Cabbages DAC's part-payment of the debt. She noted that: 'while paying part of a debt is not valid consideration for giving up the balance of the claim, the receipt of a new benefit or concession is consideration for settlement of the sum originally owed. The terms agreed between the parties were varied accordingly.'

Irish Sprinklers Ltd appealed to the Court of Appeal (Civil Division) on the following grounds:

1. Twomey J erred in finding that Irish Sprinklers Ltd accepted Pete's Cabbages DAC's part-payment of the debt. No offer of part-payment was accepted by Irish Sprinklers Ltd, as a result, the terms of the original contract remain enforceable and Pete's Cabbages DAC's obligations have not yet been fully discharged; and

2. in the alternative, the case of champagne and the network calibration represent elements of a new contract between the parties. Pete's Cabbages DAC's obligations under the original contract were not varied and so remain unaltered.

Chapter 2

Relevant Aspects of the Irish Legal System

2.1 Introduction

Mooting tests not only your ability to argue a point before the moot judges, but also your ability to apply the law underpinning that point. It is a good idea to have an understanding of the Irish legal system (or the legal system of the jurisdiction where the moot court sits) before you begin your research. This knowledge will help you to select appropriate authorities to support your submissions and will make it easier for you to plan your research.

This chapter provides an overview of aspects of the Irish legal system that are relevant to a mooter, and it complements dedicated texts that consider the Irish legal system in detail. It focuses on the structure of the legal system, rather than on the legal issues raised by different areas of Irish law. While, in general, it is likely that substantive law will be the focus of your research and the basis of your submissions, this chapter provides you with a guide as to the sources of that substantive law and relevant hierarchies of sources and courts. This chapter should be read in conjunction with Chapter 3, which discusses how to find and select authorities from the sources of Irish law.

2.2 Sources of Irish law

Substantive law in Ireland is derived from a variety of sources. In a moot, you will use these sources as authority to demonstrate that your submissions have a sound legal basis (and are not just based on your own opinion). However, not all sources are equal in the eyes of the courts, and each source will be given different authoritative weight by judges. As this hierarchy of sources will have an impact on the extent to which a judge (including a moot judge) is persuaded by your submissions, you must be aware of: (1) what sources you are relying on to support your submissions; and (2) those sources' hierarchical relationship with other sources.

Set out below is a high-level overview of the sources of Irish law, together with the authoritative weight that the moot judges are likely to attribute to each of these sources.[1] In Ireland, legal principles originate in the primary sources, but other sources and secondary sources can influence a judge's decision when determining the applicable legal principle in a particular case.

In the context of a moot, the sources that are likely to be the focus of your research are Irish legislation and case law.

Nature of Source	Source	Authoritative Weight
Primary Sources	1. European Union law	Binding (other than recommendations and opinions) within areas of competence.
	2. Irish Constitution	Binding (European Union law exempt from having to comply with the Irish Constitution).
	3. Primary (Irish) Legislation	Binding (subject to European Union law and the Irish Constitution).
	4. Secondary (Irish) Legislation	Binding (subject to European Union law and the Irish Constitution).
	5. Irish case law	Binding if delivered by a court of superior jurisdiction. Not binding, but persuasive, if delivered by a court of equal or inferior jurisdiction. Subject in each case to European Union law, the Irish Constitution and Irish legislation.

---

[1] This book addresses European Union law before the Irish Constitution in the list of sources of Irish law. While the Irish Constitution is the supreme domestic law of the Irish State (and is usually addressed first in books dealing with the Irish legal system), European Union law will, in practice, take precedence in those areas in which the European Union has competence. As a result, when you are researching for a moot, the first source of Irish law that you should consider is European Union law.

Nature of Source	Source	Authoritative Weight
Other Sources	6. International law	Generally not binding, unless incorporated into Irish law.
	7. Case law from common law jurisdictions	Not binding, but persuasive (particularly decisions of the superior courts of England and Wales).
	8. Case law from civil law jurisdictions	Not binding, but persuasive (although not frequently cited).
Secondary Sources	9. Leading textbooks and articles	Not binding. Could be helpful to moot judges, but use with caution (and should not be used as an authority for a legal principle).

2.2.1 Primary sources of Irish law

A. European Union law

Within the hierarchy of sources of Irish law, European Union law ('EU law') is distinguishable from other sources of international law.[2] In Ireland (as in other member states of the European Union ('Member States')), EU law enjoys supremacy over conflicting national law, including any conflicting provision of the Irish Constitution, in those areas where the European Union has competence. This supremacy is acknowledged in the treaties establishing the European Union and its institutional framework (the 'Treaties') and has been confirmed in the case law of the Court of Justice of the European Union (the 'CJEU').[3] Under Irish law, EU law's supremacy derives from Article 29.4.6° of the Irish Constitution, which exempts EU law from having to comply with the Irish Constitution.[4] It has also been acknowledged in Irish case

---

[2] Allison Kenneally and John Tully, *The Irish Legal System* (Clarus Press 2013) 150.

[3] Most notably, Case C-26/62 *Van Gend en Loos v Nederlandse Administratie der Belastingen* [1963] ECR 1 (acknowledging the 'direct effect' within Member States of the provisions of the Treaty of Rome); Case C-6/64 *Costa v ENEL* [1964] ECR 585 (acknowledging the supremacy of EU law over national law of Member States); and Case C-11/70 *Internationale Handelsgesellschaft mbH v Einfuhr- und Vorratsstelle für Getreide und Futtermittel* [1970] ECR 1125 (acknowledging that EU law could not be challenged on the grounds of conflict with national law).

[4] Art 29.4.6° of the Constitution provides that no provision of the Constitution

law.[5] As a result of the European Communities Act 1972, laws made by the institutions of the European Union may automatically become part of Irish law.

In a moot problem question, EU law may be relevant to establish (or confirm) certain rights or obligations of a party. There are, however, areas of Irish law that remain largely unaffected by EU law, such as criminal law, family law and some aspects of company law. For a moot problem question dealing with these areas, EU law may not be relevant to your submissions.

Within EU law there is an internal hierarchy of sources:

(1) **The Treaties**: The Treaties have direct effect in Member States. As a result, the provisions of these Treaties confer certain rights on individuals in Member States.[6] These rights may be invoked before an Irish court, provided the Treaty provision in question is clear, precise, unconditional and does not call for additional discretionary national implementation measures.[7]

If a Treaty provision is relevant to your submissions, consider whether the particular Treaty provision meets the clear, precise, unconditional and unequivocal test before relying on it as authority in a moot. Remember, some Treaty provisions are more aspirational in nature than legally enforceable and so do not necessarily create specific rights that can be invoked before national courts.

(2) **Regulations**: Regulations are legally binding instruments enacted by the institutions of the European Union. From the date of their entry into force, Regulations have immediate and direct effect in Member States. This means that they become law in those Member States and can be invoked before national courts without the need for national implementation mechanisms.[8]

Because of this direct applicability, if a provision of a

---

will invalidate laws enacted, acts done or measures adopted by the Irish State that are necessitated by Ireland's obligations of membership of the European Union (and the European Atomic Energy Community). Allison Kenneally and John Tully, *The Irish Legal System* (Clarus Press 2013) 151.

5   *Meagher v Minister for Agriculture* [1994] 1 IR 329 (SC).

6   In Ireland, the Constitution is amended to provide for the direct effect of each new Treaty (Art 29.4.6° of the Constitution).

7   Case C-26/62 *Van Gend en Loos v Nederlandse Administratie der Belastingen* [1963] ECR 1, see generally, Damian Chalmers, Gareth Davies and Giorgio Monti, *European Union Law* (3rd edn, Cambridge University Press 2014) 293–308.

8   Consolidated version of the Treaty on the Functioning of the European Union [2012] OJ C326/13 ('Treaty on the Functioning of the European Union'), Art 288.

Regulation is relevant to your submissions, there may be no corresponding Irish law implementing that Regulation. In such circumstances, your authority in a moot will be the Regulation itself.[9]

(3) **Directives**: Like Regulations, Directives are legally binding instruments enacted by the institutions of the European Union. Unlike Regulations, however, Directives are only binding as to their ultimate result, rather than the mechanism for achieving that result in individual Member States.[10] Because of this, Directives do not have immediate direct effect in Member States and instead require implementation by Member States within national law.[11] This implementation typically requires the enactment of new national law and/or the amendment of existing national law.

If a provision of a Directive is relevant to your submissions, there will generally be a corresponding domestic instrument that you will use as authority in a moot.[12] In Ireland, implementation can be by way of an Act of the Oireachtas (parliament), but is more typically achieved through secondary legislation (discussed in more detail below).[13]

Practical Tip:

Do not get confused between a 'Regulation' in an EU law context and a ministerial 'regulation' in a domestic Irish law context. An Irish law ministerial regulation is a form of secondary legislation made under the authority of an Act of the Oireachtas. As a result, an EU law Directive can be implemented into Irish law by means of an Irish law ministerial regulation.

---

(4) **European Union Decisions**: European Union Decisions ('Decisions') are legal acts taken jointly or individually by European Union institutions. Like Regulations, they are

---

[9] Raymond Byrne and others, *Byrne and McCutcheon on the Irish Legal System* (6th edn, Bloomsbury Professional 2014) 842.

[10] Treaty on the Functioning of the European Union, Art 288.

[11] Damian Chalmers, Gareth Davies and Giorgio Monti, *European Union Law* (3rd edn, Cambridge University Press 2014) 310.

[12] If a Member State fails to implement a Directive by the deadline specified for this implementation, individuals may, in certain circumstances, still assert their rights under that Directive against the Member State before national courts (although those right cannot be invoked directly against other individuals), Case C-41/74 *Van Duyn v Home Office* [1974] ECR 1337, Joined Cases C-6/90 and C-9/90 *Francovich and Danila Bonifaci v Italian Republic* [1991] ECR I–5357.

[13] *Meagher v Minister for Agriculture* [1994] 1 IR 329 (SC). See Section 2.2.1(C) for a discussion of secondary legislation in Ireland.

binding in their entirety.[14] While some Decisions have no specific addressee,[15] a Decision may be addressed to one or more specific individuals, companies or Member States. Where a Decision specifies its addressees, it will only be binding on those addressees.[16] This means that if a Decision is addressed to specified individuals or companies, the rights and obligations created by the Decision can be invoked by those addressees before national courts. If the addressee of a Decision is one or more specified Member States, individuals within those Member States may invoke rights or obligations created by the Decision before national courts, but only against the Member State, rather than against other individuals.[17]

If a Decision is relevant to your submissions, consider whether that Decision is binding on the parties to the moot before you rely on it as authority.

(5) **Recommendations and Opinions**: Recommendations or opinions of European Union institutions are not binding on Member States.[18] As a result, they do not create rights or obligations that can be invoked before national courts, and should not be used as authority for any such rights or obligations in a moot. Nevertheless, relevant recommendations or opinions may still be helpful as part of your research.

(6) **Court of Justice of the European Union**: Decisions of the CJEU (made up of the Court of Justice, the General Court and certain specialised courts) bind the referring national court.[19] Decisions on the interpretation of EU law also bind the courts of all Member States.[20] An Irish court may (and, in the case of the Supreme Court must) refer a point of EU law to the CJEU where the interpretation of that law is necessary in order to reach a conclusion.[21] This falls away if the answer is obvious, or if it has already been dealt with in a previous decision of

---

14 Treaty on the Functioning of the European Union, Art 288.

15 These typically impose obligations on the European Union as an entity generally, rather than specifically imposing obligations on any specific private party.

16 Damian Chalmers, Gareth Davies and Giorgio Monti, *European Union Law* (3rd edn, Cambridge University Press 2014) 112.

17 EUR-Lex, 'European Union decisions' <https://eur-lex.europa.eu/legal-content/EN/TXT/?uri=LEGISSUM:ai0036> accessed 1 December 2018.

18 Treaty on the Functioning of the European Union, Art 288.

19 Case C-52/76 *Benedetti v Munari* [1977] ECR 163.

20 Case C-453/00 *Kühne and Heitz NV v Productschap voor Pluimvee en Eieren* [2004] ERC I–837.

21 Treaty on the Functioning of the European Union, Art 267. Case 75/63 *Mrs M.K.H. Hoekstra v Bestuur der Bedrijfsvereniging voor Detailhandel en Ambachten* [1964] ECLI:EU:C:1964:19; Case 20/64 *Albatros v Société des pétroles et des*

the CJEU. In practice, this reference is unlikely to be relevant in the context of a moot, where the moot judges will typically give a judgment on the law.

B. The Irish Constitution

Bunreacht na hÉireann (the 'Constitution') is the supreme domestic law of the Irish State and takes precedence over inferior sources of Irish law.[23] The Supreme Court, Court of Appeal and High Court are all conferred with the power to determine whether a law is valid having regard to the Constitution.[24] Subject to a small number of exceptions,[25] all Irish law must be consistent with the Constitution.[26]

(1) Relevance: Constitutional law may be relevant in a moot either with respect to the administration of the institutions of the Irish State, or with respect to the fundamental rights of persons. In such circumstances, you may decide to call upon the moot judges to declare a law (or parts thereof) invalid as

---

combustibles liquides [1965] ECLI:EU:C:1965:8; Joined Cases C-338/04, C-359/04 and C-360/04 *Placanica* [2007] ECLI:EU:C:2007:133.

[22] Council of Europe, 'Do not get confused' <www.coe.int/en/web/about-us/do-not-get-confused> accessed 1 December 2018.

[23] As discussed above, this supremacy is subject to Art 29.4.6° of the Constitution, which exempts EU law from having to comply with the Constitution.

[24] Arts 34.3.2° (High Court), 34.4.2° (Court of Appeal) and 34.5.5° (Supreme Court) of the Constitution.

[25] These exceptions are: (1) EU law and acts done or measures adopted by the Irish State that are necessitated by the obligations of membership of the European Union or the European Atomic Energy Community; (2) acts done or measures adopted by the Irish State that are necessitated by Ireland's obligations under the Treaty on Stability, Coordination and Governance in the Economic and Monetary Union (Art 29.4.10° of the Constitution); and (3) measures adopted pursuant to the emergency provisions in Art 28.3.3° of the Constitution.

[26] Art 15.4.1° of the Constitution.

being in conflict with the Constitution.[27] Before challenging the constitutionality of a law, remember:

- your client needs to have sufficient standing (locus standi) to challenge the constitutionality of the law;[28]
- post-1937 legislation enjoys a presumption of constitutionality and so the burden of proving unconstitutionality rests with the party making this claim;[29] and
- if a legislative provision is found to be in conflict with provisions of the Constitution, and the relevant unconstitutional text can be severed, the courts will look to declare invalid the smallest amount of text of the legislation as possible.[30]

Avoid making sweeping statements in your submissions challenging the constitutionality of a law without first having considered these elements carefully.

(2) Constitutional interpretation: There are various approaches that judges take when interpreting the Constitution. If an article of the Constitution is relevant to your submissions, consider how the moot judges may interpret that article.

(a) *Literal approach*: The literal approach construes articles of the Constitution according to the words used and gives those words their plain, ordinary meaning.[31] This approach is most relevant for articles whose meaning is unambiguous.

(b) *Harmonious approach*: The harmonious approach avoids interpreting articles of the Constitution in isolation from the rest of the document. Instead, these articles are interpreted in the context of the Constitution as a whole.[32]

(c) *Purposive approach*: The purposive approach tries to find the 'purpose' behind an article of the Constitution, rather than rigidly adhering to a literal interpretation.[33] Once the purpose has been determined, the true meaning of the words used can be established. If you use the purposive approach in your submissions, be careful not to speculate as to the purpose of an article of the Constitution.

---

[27] See, for example, *Dillon v DPP* [2007] IEHC 480, [2008] 1 IR 383.

[28] *Cahill v Sutton* [1980] IR 269 (SC). See generally, Oran Doyle, *Constitutional Law: Text, Cases and Materials* (Clarus Press 2008), 431–436.

[29] *Pigs Marketing Board v Donnelly (Dublin) Ltd* [1939] IR 413 (HC) 421–422 (Hanna J).

[30] *Desmond v Glackin (No 2)* [1993] 3 IR 67 (SC).

[31] *IRM v Minister for Justice and Equality* [2018] IESC 14 [11.5]–[11.7] (Clarke CJ) quoting from *People (DPP) v O'Shea* [1982] IR 384 (SC).

[32] *Twomey v Ireland* [1985] IR 289 (SC).

[33] *Attorney General v Paperlink Ltd* [1984] ILRM 373 (HC) 385 (Costello P).

(d) *Historical approach*: The historical approach uses the history behind the Constitution as an aid to its interpretation, and considers the legal, political and social situation at the time the Constitution (or any amendment thereto) was enacted.[34]

(e) *Natural law approach*: The natural law approach asserts that there are certain rights that exist independently of the Constitution.[35] Be cautious about asking moot judges to find a right in natural law where that right has not previously been acknowledged by the Irish courts.

> **Practical Tip:**
>
> As there are a variety of approaches to constitutional interpretation open to moot judges, you have some scope for adopting an approach that works best for your submissions. Work out whether, and if so how, the courts have interpreted the relevant article of the Constitution in previous cases. Avoid asking the moot judges to interpret the article in a manner that does not logically flow from one of the established interpretive approaches discussed above, and be prepared to make submissions on why a particular approach is the—or, at least, an—appropriate one in the circumstances. Present authorities to justify this interpretative approach, particularly if you adopt approaches (c), (d) or (e) above.

C. Irish legislation

While EU law and the Constitution are important sources of Irish law, in the context of a moot, Irish legislation and case law are likely to be the key sources of authority that you will use to support your submissions. Legislation takes precedence over case law in the hierarchy of sources of Irish law. When using legislation and case law as authority, therefore, cite applicable legislation first before citing cases.[36]

(1) **Types of legislation**: In Ireland, there are two types of legislation: primary legislation and secondary legislation.

(a) *Primary legislation*: Primary legislation comprises Acts of the Oireachtas (also known as statutes). Among other things, a statute can be passed by the Oireachtas to amend, or legislate for, a common law rule previously

---

[34] *Sinnott v Minister for Education* [2001] 2 IR 545 (SC) 680 (Murray J). See also, *Roche v Roche* [2006] IEHC 359, [2010] 2 IR 321.

[35] *Murphy v PMPA Insurance Company* [1978] ILRM 25 (HC).

[36] Unless those cases relate to the interpretation of an article of the Constitution or a provision of EU law, in which case, it follows that such cases should be cited first.

set out in case law.[37] If you are relying on cases in your submissions, confirm that any legal principle set out in those cases has not subsequently been addressed in statute.

(b) *Secondary legislation*: Secondary or delegated legislation comprises measures enacted by bodies or persons to whom the Oireachtas has delegated certain law-making powers. This delegation comes through primary legislation. The preamble to secondary legislation will generally confirm how any law-making powers have been delegated. For example, the preamble to the European Union (Payment Services) Regulations 2018[38] provides as follows:

> I, Paschal Donohoe, Minister for Finance [*this is the body/person to whom law-making power has been delegated*], in exercise of the powers conferred on me by section 3 of the European Communities Act 1972 (No. 27 of 1972) [*this is the primary legislation delegating law-making power*] … hereby make the following Regulations …

Secondary legislation includes statutory instruments, ministerial rules, regulations and orders, schemes and bye-laws. It often provides rules that fill in the details of more general principles and policies set out in primary legislation.[39]

---

[37] For example, the fiduciary duties of company directors were originally confirmed only in case law, but have now been codified by Companies Act 2014, s 228(1).

[38] European Union (Payment Services) Regulations 2018, SI 2018/6.

[39] Raymond Byrne and others, *Byrne and McCutcheon on the Irish Legal System* (6th edn, Bloomsbury Professional 2014) 563.

> **Practical Tip:**
>
> Be cautious about asking the moot judges to declare a piece of legislation to be invalid or inapplicable. Legislation is subject to the Constitution and to EU law and so, as a general rule, can only be declared invalid or inapplicable if contrary to the Constitution or EU law, respectively.[40] Secondary legislation may also be declared invalid if it was passed outside of the powers conferred in primary legislation (for example, the power exceeded that conferred, it was unreasonable or the power was exercised in bad faith).[41]

(2) **Interpretation of legislation**: If legislation is relevant to your submissions in a moot, you will need to read and understand the relevant legislative instrument as part of your research. You should also consider how the moot judges are likely to interpret the legislation in question. Your goal is to persuade the moot judges that they should interpret the legislation in a manner that is most favourable to your submissions.

The interpretation of legislation (both primary and secondary) in Ireland is governed by the Interpretation Act 2005 and various common law rules. The Interpretation Act 2005 sets out general rules on the construction of legislative provisions,[42] such as: '[a] word importing the singular shall be read as also importing the plural, and a word importing the plural shall be read as also importing the singular'.[43] It also defines words and phrases that are frequently used in Irish legislation.[44]

Where specific guidance is not provided in the Interpretation Act 2005, the approach to interpreting legislation is a matter for the courts. The two modern interpretative approaches used by the courts are the literal approach and the schematic/teleological approach.[45]

---

[40] *Re J.D. Brian Ltd (in Liquidation) T/A East Coast Print and Publicity* [2015] IESC 62 [80] (Laffoy J) where the Supreme Court acknowledged an issue with the drafting of a provision of the Companies Act 2014, but noted that without this being amended by the Oireachtas, the Supreme Court had to apply the law as set out in the legislation. See also, *McDonagh v Chief Appeals Officer* [2018] IEHC 407 [36] (Coffey J), where the High Court noted that '[w]here there is doubt or ambiguity it is the role of the court to discern the purpose and intention of the legislature. It is not within the interpretative entitlement of the court to usurp the function of the legislature or to engage in judicial legislation.' See also, *Agha v Minister for Social Protection* [2018] IECA 155 [65]–[68] (Hogan J).

[41] Raymond Byrne and others, *Byrne and McCutcheon on the Irish Legal System* (6th edn, Bloomsbury Professional 2014) 617–624.

[42] Interpretation Act 2005, pt 4.

[43] Interpretation Act 2005, s 18(a).

[44] Interpretation Act 2005, schedule.

[45] Raymond Byrne and others, *Byrne and McCutcheon on the Irish Legal System* (6th

(a) *Literal approach*: The literal approach requires a court to give the words of a legislative provision their plain, ordinary meaning.[46]

If a word is simple and has a widespread and unambiguous meaning, the judge should interpret it by drawing on his or her own experience of using it. On the other hand, if the legislative provision is aimed at a particular class of people who use a word in a particular way, or if the word in question has a specialised meaning within a particular field, then the technical meaning should be given to that word.[47]

(b) *Schematic/teleological approach*: If the literal approach would lead to absurdity, or a meaning that does not make sense in the context of the legislation more generally, the schematic or teleological approach can be adopted. This approach allows the court to look to the objective or purpose of the legislation in order to determine the meaning of its provisions.[48]

EU law and domestic measures implementing EU law are interpreted by the Irish courts using a schematic/ teleological approach.[49]

With both of these approaches to legislative interpretation, the primary source of guidance as to the meaning of a legislative provision will be the text of the legislation itself. If you are reviewing legislation as part of your research, make sure you review the substantive provisions of that legislation, not just its long title,[50] marginal notes,[51] or explanatory guidelines.

---

edn, Bloomsbury Professional 2014) 640–641. See *OCS One Complete Solution Ltd v Dublin Airport Authority Plc* [2014] IEHC 306 [14]–[25] (Barrett J) for a discussion of the different interpretative approaches.

[46] *Inspector of Taxes v Kiernan* [1981] IR 117 (SC) 121–122 (Henchy J).

[47] ibid.

[48] *Nestor v Murphy* [1979] IR 326 (SC). See also, Interpretation Act 2005, s 5(1) and (2).

[49] *Lawlor v Minister for Agriculture* [1990] 1 IR 356 (HC) 374–376 (Murphy J).

[50] While the courts have frequently consulted the long title of legislation for guidance when interpreting that legislation, the long title 'cannot be used to modify or limit the interpretation of plain and unambiguous language' in the legislation: see *People (DPP) v Quilligan* [1986] IR 495 (SC) 519 (Griffin J). See *Bederev v Ireland* [2015] IECA 38 [49]–[55], [2015] 1 ILRM 301 [49]–[55], for an extensive discussion by Hogan J of the use of long titles in legislative interpretation.

[51] The Interpretation Act 2005 specifically notes that marginal notes do not form part of the legislation (Interpretation Act 2005, s 18(g)). These notes should not be relied on as authority in a moot.

While Irish courts have traditionally been reluctant to look beyond the text of legislation in order to determine the meaning of its provisions, there are examples of cases where the courts have consulted dictionaries,[52] and international treaties and related preparatory materials[53] when interpreting legislation. Other than references to dictionaries (which is now relatively common), reference to external materials by courts as an aid to legislative interpretation remains the exception and should be approached with caution in a moot.[54]

Practical Tip:

Like constitutional interpretation, there are a variety of approaches to legislative interpretation. While this does allow some freedom with respect to the interpretation of legislation that you present to the moot judges, you cannot expect the moot judges to automatically follow the approach you propose.[55] Work out whether, and if so how, the courts have interpreted the legislative provision in previous cases. Make sure that any interpretation that you present respects the doctrine of precedent and logically flows from one of the established interpretative approaches. As with constitutional interpretation, be prepared to make submissions on why a particular approach is the—or, at least, an—appropriate one in the circumstances.

(3) **Aids to legislative interpretation and canons of construction**: Supplementing the approaches to legislative interpretation set out above, a number of aids to interpretation and canons of construction can be used when determining the meaning of a legislative provision. In a moot, you may decide to refer to one or more of these maxims and presumptions when explaining the basis for a particular interpretation of a

---

[52] *Rahill v Brady* [1971] IR 69 (SC).

[53] *Bourke v Attorney General* [1972] IR 36 (SC).

[54] *Howard v Commissioner of Public Works* [1993] ILRM 665 (SC) 689 (Egan J) where the Supreme Court confirmed that the 'dominant purpose in construing a statute is to ascertain the intention of the legislature as expressed in the statute, considering it as a whole and in its context'. While there have been occasions when the Irish courts have referred to a statute's legislative history (*People (DPP) v McDonagh* [1996] 1 IR 565 (SC), where the court traced a provision's history through previous legislative instruments) and related parliamentary debates (*Wavin Pipes Ltd v Hepworth Iron Co Ltd* [1982] 8 FSR 32 (HC)), the validity of such references has been largely rejected by the Irish courts.

[55] *Shannon Regional Fisheries Board v An Bord Pleanála* [1994] 3 IR 449 (HC) 456 (Barr J) noting that '[s]tatutory interpretation is solely a matter for the courts and no other body has authority to usurp the power of the court in performing that function'.

legislative provision. You must remember, however, that these are simply interpretative aids, rather than binding rules.

Maxims:

(a) *ejusdem generis*: Where a general word follows specific words of the same nature, the general word will take its meaning from the specific words and will be interpreted as including items of the same nature as the specific words.[56] For example, in a legislative provision that lists 'lions, elephants and other animals', the general reference to 'other animals' could be limited only to wild animals by the preceding reference to lions and elephants;

(b) *noscitur a sociis*: A word can derive its meaning by reference to the words or phrases that surround it.[57] For example, a reference in a legislative provision to 'public order' has been interpreted by the courts as meaning a serious threat to fundamental interests of the Irish State due to its proximity in the legislative provision to the words 'national security';[58]

(c) *expressio unius est exclusio alterius*: The express reference to one thing implies that another thing is excluded. For example, a legislative provision providing for two specific situations where a modification of a proposal is permitted has been interpreted by the courts as meaning that other situations not listed cannot be classified as modifications;[59] and

(d) *generalia specialibus non derogant*: A legislative provision dealing with general subject matter cannot affect or override an earlier provision dealing with a specific topic.[60]

Presumptions:

(a) *presumption of constitutionality*: It is presumed that post-1937 legislation enacted by the Oireachtas is constitutional;

(b) *presumption of compatibility with EU law*: Where relevant, Irish legislation should be interpreted in a manner that is consistent with EU law;[61]

(c) *presumption of compatibility with international law*: The

---

[56] *Cronin (Inspector of Taxes) v Lunham Brothers Ltd* [1986] ILRM 415 (HC) 417 (Carroll J), *Dunnes Stores v Taculla Ltd* [2018] IEHC 346.

[57] *Dillon v Minister for Posts and Telegraphs* (SC, 3 June 1981) (Henchy J).

[58] *Li v Governor of Cloverhill Prison* [2012] IEHC 493 [18]–[28], [2012] 2 IR 400 [18]–[28] (Hogan J).

[59] *Re Enright (a debtor)* [2018] IEHC 314 [39]–[43] (Baker J).

[60] *People (DPP) v Grey* [1986] IR 317 (SC).

[61] *OCS One Complete Solution Ltd v Dublin Airport Authority Plc* [2014] IEHC 306.

courts should, as far as possible, interpret legislation in such a way as to give effect to Ireland's international legal obligations;[62]

(d) *presumption against redundancy*: It is presumed that the Oireachtas intended for all words in a legislative provision to be relevant to its meaning;

(e) *presumption against unclear changes in the law*: When a legislative provision is unclear, it is presumed that the courts will not interpret that provision in a manner that changes existing law;

(f) *presumption that penal statues (those creating penal liability) and revenue statutes (those creating tax liability) will be interpreted strictly*: Penal and taxation legislation should be interpreted strictly and the meaning of any provision should not extend beyond what is set out in the text;[63]

(g) *presumption against retrospective effect*: It is presumed that legislation is only intended to apply going forwards, unless it provides otherwise; and

(h) *presumption against extra-territorial effect*: It is presumed that the effect of legislation will be confined to the territory of the Irish State, unless it provides otherwise.

(4) Foreign legislation: While EU law is a primary source of Irish law, and in certain circumstances provisions of international agreements may have legal force in Ireland,[64] be cautious about citing other foreign legislation in your submissions. This legislation does not have authority in Ireland.

Reference to foreign legislation in your submissions may be helpful, however, in the context of discussing the interpretation of Irish legislation. If an Irish legislative provision is unclear, or has not previously been considered by the Irish courts, an analysis of how a similar provision has been interpreted by foreign courts may help the moot judges.[65]

---

[62] *O'Domhnaill v Merrick* [1984] IR 151 (SC) 159 (Henchy J).

[63] *Inspector of Taxes v Kiernan* [1981] IR 117 (SC) 121–122 (Henchy J). *Montemuino v Minister for Communications Marine and Natural Resources* [2013] IESC 40 [19]–[24], [2013] 4 IR 120 [18]–[22] (Hardiman J) for a discussion of the interpretation of penal statutes.

[64] See Section 2.2.2(A) for a discussion of international law within Irish law.

[65] See for example, in *Re J.D. Brian Ltd (in Liquidation) T/A East Coast Print and Publicity* [2015] IESC 62 [81] et seq, [2016] 1 IR 131 [81] et seq (Laffoy J) in the context of interpreting a provision of the Companies Act 2014, the Supreme Court considered how the English and Australian courts had interpreted a similar provision of the United Kingdom and Australian companies acts, respectively.

D. Irish case law

Case law may not sit at the top of the hierarchy of sources of Irish law, but in the context of a moot, it is likely to be one of your principal sources of authority for your submissions. This is because most moot problem questions focus on topics where the law is unclear or incomplete. In such situations, you will need to rely on case law in your submissions to establish or support relevant legal principles.

Case law is, of course, a vast sea of judgments handed down in individual cases. Your role is to find cases whose statement of the law is authoritative enough to persuade the moot judges as to the correctness of your submissions and/or to challenge the correctness of your opponents' submissions. The extent to which the moot judges will be persuaded by these cases hinges on the doctrine of precedent.

(1) The doctrine of precedent

Practical Tip:

A common mistake amongst mooters is to present a case as authority in their submissions without considering the identity of the court that delivered the judgment in the case and where that court sits in the hierarchy of Irish courts. Avoid presenting a case as an authority that binds the moot judges in circumstances where the moot court is not actually obliged to follow the judgment in that case.

The doctrine of precedent (stare decisis) is central to the Irish legal system and dictates that a court of inferior jurisdiction is bound by earlier decisions of a court of superior jurisdiction. Irish courts are also generally expected to follow earlier decisions of courts of equal (or 'coordinate') jurisdiction, although this is not a rigid rule. The hierarchy of Irish courts is discussed in Section 2.4.[66]

The doctrine of precedent provides a degree of consistency and predictability when it comes to determining the law on a particular subject in Ireland, as two cases that raise the same legal issues should be dealt with in the same way by the courts. Because the moot court assumes the role of a court within the hierarchy of Irish courts, the doctrine of precedent will determine what cases you use as authority in your submissions and how these are presented to

---

[66] See Section 2.4 for a discussion of the hierarchy of courts in Ireland (and a number of other common law countries).

the moot judges. As you progress through your research, therefore, keep in mind where the moot court sits within the hierarchy of Irish courts and, as a result, the authoritative weight the moot judges will attach to each of the cases that you rely on.

(a) *Decisions of courts of superior jurisdiction*: The principle that a court of inferior jurisdiction will follow the decisions of a court of superior jurisdiction has rarely been called into question. As a result, the Court of Appeal is bound by previous decisions of the Supreme Court, and the High Court is bound by previous decisions of the Court of Appeal and the Supreme Court.

(b) *Decisions of courts of equal jurisdiction*: The Irish courts have accepted some flexibility to depart from decisions of a court of equal jurisdiction, but only in certain circumstances.

(i) The **Supreme Court** has adopted a moderately flexible approach to following its own decisions and, while it will usually follow these decisions, it can depart from them where there are compelling reasons for doing so (most notably, where the previous decision was 'clearly wrong'[67] and justice requires that it should be overruled or not followed).[68] It is not enough that the later Supreme Court judges would simply have reached a different conclusion.[69]

(ii) As the **Court of Appeal** has only existed in its current form in Ireland since 2014, there is limited judicial comment on whether the court is bound by its own decisions. Nevertheless, in 2017, Hogan J noted that absent any 'special circumstances',[70] a judge of the Court of Appeal should normally follow the majority view of previous decisions of the Court of Appeal, which are clearly on point.[71]

(iii) A **High Court** judge is usually bound by earlier High Court decisions. Only where there is something in the nature of 'a fundamental and

---

[67] *Attorney General and Minister for Defence v Ryan's Car Hire Ltd* [1965] IR 642 (SC) 667 (Kingsmill Moore J).

[68] ibid, *Finucane v McMahon* [1990] 1 IR 165 (SC), *K v The Minister for Justice & Equality* [2018] IESC 18 [12] (O'Donnell J).

[69] *K v The Minister for Justice & Equality* [2018] IESC 18 [12] (O'Donnell J).

[70] *ACC Loan Management Ltd v Connolly* [2017] IECA 119 [25], [2017] 3 IR 629 [81] (Hogan J).

[71] ibid.

obvious error'[72] involved in the earlier decision that, had it been avoided, 'it is likely that a different conclusion would have been reached'[73] (such as a failure to consider a relevant statutory provision) may such decisions be departed from. If your submissions call on the moot judges to depart from a previous decision of a court of equal jurisdiction, make sure that you explain why this is appropriate.

(c) *Decisions of courts of inferior jurisdiction*: Irish courts are not bound to follow the decisions of courts of inferior jurisdiction. Such decisions are, however, of persuasive authority in superior courts. If you refer to a decision of a court of inferior jurisdiction in your submissions, note the hierarchical position of that court so that there is no confusion as to the authoritative weight of the case. You should also be prepared to explain why the moot judges should be persuaded by the decision—for example, the facts of the case may be almost identical to those of the moot, or the decision of a court of inferior jurisdiction may have been reached taking into account relevant superior court cases.

Set out below is a table outlining the extent to which the superior courts of Ireland are bound by previous decisions of courts of superior, equal and inferior jurisdiction.

		Decisions by:		
		Supreme Court	**Court of Appeal**	**High Court**
Status in:	**Supreme Court**	Limited discretion to depart	Persuasive	Persuasive
	Court of Appeal	Binding	Limited discretion to depart	Persuasive
	High Court	Binding	Binding	Limited discretion to depart

(2) Ratio decidendi and obiter dicta

Not all parts of a case are binding on courts of inferior or (subject to

---

[72] *McCaffery v Central Bank of Ireland* [2017] IEHC 546 [97] (Noonan J).
[73] ibid.

the discussion above) equal jurisdiction. Only the ratio decidendi or 'central reasoning leading to the particular decision'[74] is binding on future courts. Obiter dicta (singular: obiter dictum) are statements of a judge that are 'ancillary observations made in the course of a judgment.'[75] Statements that are obiter dicta are not binding on future courts, but are still of persuasive authority. As part of your research, consider which parts of any relevant cases are binding on the moot court and which are not. The ratio decidendi of a case will be significantly more influential on the moot judges than a statement that was made obiter.

> **Practical Tip:**
>
> It is common for moot judges to ask mooters whether the moot court is bound by a particular authority. To answer this question, one thing that you will need to have considered is whether statements being relied on are the ratio decidendi or obiter dicta of a case (other things to consider are the court that delivered the judgment and the treatment of the case in subsequent cases).

Unfortunately, the distinction between the two types of judicial statements is not entirely clear-cut and judges typically do not flag in their written judgment when their statements are ratio decidendi and when they are made obiter—you will need to make this determination. While this lack of demarcation between the elements of a judgment does not give you the freedom to unilaterally declare what is or what is not the ratio decidendi of a case simply to suit your submissions, it does give you some scope for arguing that a particular part of a decision is or is not binding on the moot judges.

(a) *Ratio decidendi*: To determine the ratio decidendi of a case, work out the legal principle treated by a judge as the basis for his or her decision in light of the material facts of the case.[76] It is not the final decision itself, but rather the legal reasons without which the judge would not have been able to reach that decision. Where there is more than one majority written judgment delivered in a case, determine the legal reasons for each judge's decision and then select as the ratio decidendi the legal reasons supported by all or the majority of those judges[77]—do

---

[74] *IRM v Minister for Justice and Equality* [2018] IESC 14 [10.25] (Clarke CJ).

[75] ibid.

[76] ibid. There remains a debate as to the exact nature of ratio decidendi. For an extensive discussion of this debate, see Neil Duxbury, *The Nature and Authority of Precedent* (Cambridge University Press 2008), ch 3.

[77] Raymond Byrne and others, *Byrne and McCutcheon on the Irish Legal System* (6th

not forget to include any judges that concurred with the written judgment of another judge or dissenting judges that agreed in part with the majority.[78]

(b) *Obiter dictum*: Statements in a case that were not essential to the court's decision are obiter dicta.[79] Statements could, for example, be obiter: (1) where they are made in passing by a judge and are not the basis for the judge's decision; or (2) where they are the basis for the judge's decision, but they were made by a dissenting judge with respect to a legal issue on which the dissenting judge disagreed with the majority decision.

Practical Tip:

While only the ratio decidendi of a case is binding on future courts, do not discount obiter dicta.[80] The Supreme Court has recently noted that '[obiter] statements have been accepted subsequently as anticipating developments in the law and expressing principles of value.'[81] Obiter dicta may be helpful in a moot if, for example, the ratio decidendi of a case is not relevant to the legal principles raised by the moot problem question, but a judicial comment is still relevant to your submissions. Make sure that you acknowledge the persuasive nature of a statement made obiter and are able to explain why it is still relevant to your submissions.

2.2.2 Other Sources

In your submissions try, as far as possible, to support each of your submissions with authority that represents a primary source of Irish law. Sources other than primary sources may, however, be helpful in your submissions if there is no, or no adequate, higher authority available. When you refer to these sources in your submissions, consider the authoritative weight (if any) the moot judges are likely to give to the relevant source.

---

edn, Bloomsbury Professional 2014) 527. For a detailed discussion on situations where there are multiple written judgments delivered, all of which agree on the decision, but each of which gives a different basis for doing so, see Rupert Cross, 'The Ratio Decidendi and a Plurality of Speeches in the House of Lords' (1977) 93 LQR 378.

[78] ibid, 69.

[79] Raymond Byrne and others, *Byrne and McCutcheon on the Irish Legal System* (6th edn, Bloomsbury Professional 2014) 532.

[80] *IRM v Minister for Justice and Equality* [2018] IESC 14 [10.25] (Clarke CJ).

[81] ibid. See, for example, the English case of *Hedley Byrne & Co Ltd v Heller & Partners Ltd* [1964] AC 465 (HoL) where the House of Lords' statements on the existence of a legal duty of care for negligent misstatements were technically obiter dicta, but have been used as authority in subsequent cases.

A. *International law*

Public international law is the body of rules that governs the relationship between states and/or international organisations.[82] Article 29.6 of the Constitution provides that international law becomes part of Irish law only if the Oireachtas takes the steps necessary to bring this about.[83] As a result, an international agreement (such as a treaty or convention) does not become part of Irish law upon Ireland's ratification of that agreement.[84] Instead, it must first be incorporated into Irish law.

Once an international agreement is incorporated into Irish law, the provisions that have been given legal effect can be invoked before an Irish court.[85] In a moot, make sure that you understand how a relevant international agreement has been incorporated into Irish law, as this will influence how you present that agreement in your submissions. If the text of the agreement (or part of the text) has been given the force of law directly through Irish legislation, then you refer to the relevant provisions of the international agreement as authority in your submissions. If the substance of the international agreement has been reflected in Irish legislation, but the text of the international agreement itself has not been given the force of law, then you refer to the Irish legislation as authority in your submissions.[86] Although there is a presumption that Irish law will be interpreted in a manner that is consistent with Ireland's international obligations,[87] avoid presenting an international agreement as a source of enforceable rights in Ireland if that international agreement has not been incorporated in some way into Irish law.

B. *Foreign case law*

An Irish court is, as a general rule, not bound to follow the decision of a foreign court. If you refer to a decision of a foreign court in your submissions, make sure that you are aware of what country that court sits in and the likely authoritative weight the moot judges will attach to the decision.

---

[82] Raymond Byrne and others, *Byrne and McCutcheon on the Irish Legal System* (6th edn, Bloomsbury Professional 2014) 853.

[83] David Fennelly, *International Law in the Irish Legal System* (Round Hall 2014) 39.

[84] *Re Ó Laighléis* [1960] IR 93 (SC) 125 (Maguire CJ).

[85] David Fennelly, *International Law in the Irish Legal System* (Round Hall 2014) 62.

[86] ibid, 68–82.

[87] See Section 2.2.1(C) for a discussion of the various principles and presumptions that can be used to aid the interpretation of legislation.

(1) Jurisprudence of courts in common law countries: The decisions of courts from other common law countries are of persuasive authority in an Irish court. As a result, an Irish court may choose to follow such a decision, if appropriate.[88] The persuasiveness of these decisions on Irish courts is particularly evident with respect to decisions of the courts of England and Wales, which Irish courts have frequently followed.[89] Decisions of the courts of other common law countries (such as the United States of America and Australia) have also increasingly been followed by Irish courts.[90]

In a moot, decisions of the courts of common law countries could be an important source of guidance for you and the moot judges, particularly when there is little, or no, relevant Irish authority. If you refer to these cases in your submissions, make sure that you:

- acknowledge the country where the relevant court sits;
- are able to explain why you are making the reference; and
- try to limit references to decisions of the superior courts of a country (since these are at least binding on courts of inferior jurisdiction within that court's own country).[91]

(2) Jurisprudence of courts in civil law countries: Decisions from the courts of civil law countries have been referred to

---

[88] Raymond Byrne and others, *Byrne and McCutcheon on the Irish Legal System* (6th edn, Bloomsbury Professional 2014) 511. See *MMcM v J McC* [1994] 1 IR 293 (HC) 303 (Costello J): 'I think I have liberty to give effect to this opinion even though it is contrary to the decisions of the English courts on this subject. These decisions are of persuasive weight and should not lightly be ignored. But the Irish courts are not bound by them and I think I am not required to follow decisions which I think misconstrued the effect of an earlier decision of the House of Lords which I would be prepared to follow.'

[89] *Tromso Sparebank v Beirne (No 2)* [1989] ILRM 257 (HC) 261 (Costello J), noting that 'the High Court should be slow to refuse to follow a principle established in English law since 1883'.

[90] See, for example, *Camden Street Investments Limited v Vanguard Property Finance Limited* [2013] IEHC 478 [32] (Cross J) accepting as 'a correct statement of the law' the decision in *Bank of Baroda v Panesar* [1986] All ER 751 and the decision of the High Court of Australia in *Bunbury Foods Pty Limited v National Bank of Australasia* [1984] 51 ALR 609.' See also, *NN v The Minister for Justice and Equality* [2017] IEHC 99 [37] (Keane J) noting that the reasoning of the High Court of Australia is persuasive, but not the law in Ireland.

[91] *Constante Trading Ltd v The owners and all persons claiming an interest in the MV Kapitan Labunets* [1995] 1 IR 164 (SC) 168 (Barr J), citing with approval Diplock LJ in the English House of Lords in *Fothergill v Monarch Airlines Ltd* [1981] AC 251, 284 noting that: 'the persuasive value of a particular court's decision must depend upon its reputation and its status, the extent to which its decisions are binding upon courts of co-ordinate and inferior jurisdiction in its own country and the coverage of the national law reporting system'.

more infrequently by Irish courts.[92] If you refer to these cases in your submissions, make sure that:

- there is no more persuasive authority from a common law country available to support your submissions; and
- you are able to explain why you are making the reference.

(3) **Jurisprudence of international courts:**

- *decisions of the CJEU*: As an exception to the principle that the decisions of foreign courts are only of persuasive authority in an Irish court, judgments of the CJEU are binding on an Irish court that has referred a matter of EU law to the CJEU and are binding on Irish courts as to matters of interpretation of EU law;[93] and
- *judgments of the ECtHR*: Ireland undertakes to abide by final decisions of the ECtHR in cases to which Ireland is a party.[94] Irish courts will also take judicial notice of judgments, advisory opinions and decisions of the ECtHR, and due account of the principles they lay down when interpreting and applying provisions of the ECHR.[95]

2.2.3 Secondary sources

Secondary sources, such as books, journal articles or Law Reform Commission reports, can be an invaluable resource to help you to understand the legal principles that are relevant to a moot. However, such sources are not binding on an Irish court. While you should certainly consult secondary sources as part of your research, never present the text of these sources as representing the law in Ireland or as an authority for a principle of Irish law. The law in Ireland comes from the primary sources of law.

This does not mean that you cannot refer to secondary sources in your submissions, it just means that you should do so cautiously. A well-placed quotation from a pre-eminent academic or the Law Reform Commission on an area of Irish law that is unclear or where there is no binding or persuasive authority could be a welcome aid for the moot judges. In such circumstances, ensure that there is no more authoritative statement of law available and that you have acknowledged in your submissions the non-binding nature of the

---

[92] Raymond Byrne and others, *Byrne and McCutcheon on the Irish Legal System* (6th edn, Bloomsbury Professional 2014) 516.
[93] See Section 2.2.1(A) for a discussion of decisions of the CJEU.
[94] European Convention on Human Rights, Art 46.
[95] European Convention on Human Rights Act 2003, s 4.

secondary source. You should also be able to provide reasons why, notwithstanding the non-binding nature of a source, the moot court should still be persuaded by the relevant submission.

When referring to a secondary source in your submissions, choose that source carefully. With respect to books, try to refer to the (or at least a) leading practitioner text on the subject, rather than student textbooks or study guides. You should also make sure that you refer to the most recent edition of the text. Though not a complete list, examples of practitioner texts that have been cited in the Irish courts include:

Subject	Title[96]
Civil procedure	Hilary Biehler, Declan McGrath and Emily Egan McGrath, *Delany and McGrath on Civil Procedure* (4th edn, Round Hall 2018)
Child law	Geoffrey Shannon, *Children and Family Relationships Law in Ireland: Practice and Procedure* (Clarus Press 2015)
Company law	Thomas B Courtney, *The Law of Companies* (4th edn, Bloomsbury Professional 2016)
Conflicts of law	William Binchy, *Irish Conflicts of Law* (Butterworths 1988)
Constitutional law	Gerard Hogan and others, *JM Kelly: The Irish Constitution* (5th edn, Bloomsbury Professional 2018)
Contract law	Paul A McDermott and James McDermott, *Contract Law* (2nd edn, Bloomsbury Professional 2017)
Criminal law	Liz Campbell, Shane Kilcommins and Catherine O'Sullivan, *Criminal Law in Ireland; Cases and Commentary* (Clarus Press 2010)
Employment law	Neville Cox, Val Corbett and Des Ryan, *Employment Law in Ireland* (Clarus Press 2009)
Evidence	Declan McGrath, *Evidence* (2nd edn, Round Hall 2014)
Tort law	Bryan McMahon and William Binchy, *Law of Torts* (4th edn, Bloomsbury Professional 2013)

---

[96] The editions of the texts that are cited above are the most recently published editions (rather than the editions that were cited in case law).

Land law	JCW Wylie, *Irish Land Law* (5th edn, Bloomsbury Professional 2013)

With respect to academic articles, try to limit your references to the writings of judges or leading academics (such as those who wrote the practitioner text on the subject) printed in peer-reviewed journals. Only cite websites in your submissions as a last resort.

2.3 Arguments based on public policy or arguments to change the law

As you conduct your research, you may come to the conclusion that an argument based on public policy or an argument to change the law could be relevant. Be cautious about proposing either of these types of arguments and only consider them where there is no contradictory binding authority.

In 2017, the Supreme Court confirmed that 'public policy is primarily a matter for the Oireachtas, not least because it is better placed than the courts to weigh up and balance the relevant competing considerations.'[97] Nevertheless, public policy arguments have been raised before the Irish courts. This usually occurs where there is a dispute that has a foreign law element and the Irish courts have been called upon to refuse to apply that law on the basis that it conflicts with Irish public policy,[98] or where legislation specifically provides for 'public policy' to be considered in a particular circumstance.[99] The Irish courts have also considered public policy arguments with respect to the concept of fair procedures[100] and to avoid an abuse of process.[101] Use public policy arguments sparingly in a moot and try to avoid asking the moot court to depart from a previous decision of a court of equal jurisdiction simply on the grounds of public policy.

Subject to Article 29.4 of the Constitution,[102] the sole and

---

[97] *HAH v SAA* [2017] IESC 40 [22], [2017] 1 IR 372 [90] (O'Malley J).

[98] *Mayo-Perrott v Mayo-Perrott* [1958] IR 336 (SC); see *HAH v SAA* [2017] IESC 40, [2017] 1 IR 372 for an extensive discussion on public policy in the context of conflicts of laws before the Irish courts.

[99] *Meadows v Minister for Justice, Equality and Law Reform* [2010] IESC 3, [2010] 2 IR 701 where the Immigration Act 1999, s 3 allowed for public policy to be considered in a decision.

[100] *Re Eurofood IFSC Ltd* [2005] 1 ILRM 161 (SC) 171 (Fennelly J).

[101] *Re Vantive Holdings and the Companies Acts* [2010] 2 IR 118 (SC) [85] (Murray CJ).

[102] Discussed in Section 2.2 in the context of the supremacy of EU law over national law in areas in which the European Union has competence.

exclusive power of making laws for the Irish State is vested in the Oireachtas.[103] As discussed in Section 2.2.1(C), you should be cautious about asking moot judges to declare a piece of legislation to be invalid or inapplicable. Outside of legislation, the extent to which the courts can change and develop an existing common law position is not clear-cut.[104] The Irish courts have confirmed that judges cannot usurp the legislative function,[105] but they have also acknowledged that judges have a part to play in the 'evolution' of the common law 'to meet new circumstances and conditions'.[106] The courts have also confirmed that law can change 'by means of constitutionally mandated changes resulting from the role of the courts as interpreters of the Constitution.'[107]

If you argue that the moot court should alter the existing common law position, be prepared to explain why it is appropriate for the judiciary, and not the Oireachtas, to assume this power. In doing so, you may want to consider the following arguments:

(a) the common law is not immutable[108] and should evolve with social and economic conditions to avoid injustice;

(b) once a change is reflected in legislation, it may become more difficult to apply to developing circumstances until it is amended by subsequent legislation. A change implemented by judges can more easily be adapted to fit new circumstances;[109] and

(c) the parties have asked the court to address the issue before it and, if the court deems it appropriate to do so, it should not leave it for the Oireachtas to deal with at a later date. This argument is particularly relevant where the court is being asked to rule in circumstances where there is no authority that the court can rely on.

Of course, if your opponents argue that the moot judges should alter the existing common law position, you may want to raise counter-arguments during your rebuttal against such an assumption of power. The following arguments could be considered:

---

[103] Art 15.2.1° of the Constitution.

[104] Raymond Byrne and others, *Byrne and McCutcheon on the Irish Legal System* (6th edn, Bloomsbury Professional 2014) 541.

[105] *Maher v Attorney General* [1973] IR 140 (SC) 148 (Fitzgerald CJ).

[106] *R v An tArd Chláraitheoir* [2014] IESC 60 [2.4], [2014] 3 IR 533 [407] (Clarke J).

[107] ibid.

[108] ibid.

[109] ibid, [2.7], [410] (Clarke J).

(a) judges are not elected and law that they develop lacks democratic legitimacy;

(b) changes to the law implemented through legislation may be more detailed or consider an issue in a broad context. In contrast, developments in the law implemented by judges originate in light of the facts of a specific case. The applicability of those rules to different circumstances may not, therefore, be easily determined. This could lead to unfairness and the inconsistent application of a legal principle;

(c) the exact time a legislative change comes into effect is easily determined and, unless the legislation specifically provides otherwise, that change will not have retrospective effect. The extent to which law developed by judges applies retrospectively in Ireland is unclear. If such a change did apply retrospectively, it would involve applying an interpretation of the law to facts that occurred before the relevant interpretation had been expressed. This is something that the Supreme Court has noted creates a 'risk of unfairness'[110] and could have unanticipated consequences;

(d) to allow judges to freely develop the law risks undermining the consistency and predictability that are facilitated by the doctrine of precedent; and

(e) for matters of public importance, or where there are issues of public policy, judges should avoid developing the law in a specific case. These types of changes should be developed centrally through the Oireachtas.

2.4 Hierarchy of courts

Being comfortable with the hierarchy of Irish courts is an important element of participating in a moot. Understanding this hierarchy is most clearly relevant when it comes to the doctrine of precedent, as the authoritative weight that the moot judges will give to an Irish case will be influenced by: (1) the hierarchical position of the court that delivered the judgment; and (2) the hierarchical position of the moot court itself. It is also important that you consider the route through the Irish courts that the case has taken before arriving at the moot court (to the extent that this information is provided). Being aware of this procedural history will give you a more solid

---

[110] ibid, [10.3], [511]. The situation with respect to the retrospective nature of judicially developed changes to the common law is unsettled in Ireland.

understanding of the moot problem question and will reflect the detail that you would expect to know in a real appeals case.

Though the hierarchy of courts is slightly less relevant in the context of decisions of foreign courts (since such decisions are only of persuasive authority in an Irish moot court), the position of a foreign court within its own domestic hierarchy of courts is still something to consider. A decision of the highest court of a country is likely to be more influential on an Irish moot court than one delivered by a court of first instance in that country.

2.4.1 Ireland

Within the Irish State, the Supreme Court sits at the top of the hierarchy of courts and is the court of final appeal.[111] Sitting below the Supreme Court, the Court of Appeal was established in 2014[112] and is an appellate court that has both civil and criminal divisions. The Court of Appeal will hear appeals in civil proceedings from the High Court[113] (unless the appeal proceeds directly to the Supreme Court because it involves a matter of general public importance and/or it is in the interests of justice)[114] and criminal appeals that would previously have been heard by the Court of Criminal Appeal.[115] As the third superior court in Ireland, the High Court can be a court of first instance and an appellate court in civil matters and in certain family law matters from the Circuit Court.[116] Below the superior courts, the Circuit Court and District Court are courts of first instance with limited appellate jurisdiction.

Set out below is a simplified diagram showing the hierarchy of Irish courts, together with routes of appeal. A moot is likely to be set in one of the courts within the grey box.

---

[111] Art 34.5.1° of the Constitution.
[112] Court of Appeals Act 2014.
[113] Art 34.4.1° of the Constitution.
[114] Art 34.5.4° of the Constitution.
[115] Court of Appeal Act 2014, s 8.
[116] Art 34.3.1° of the Constitution.

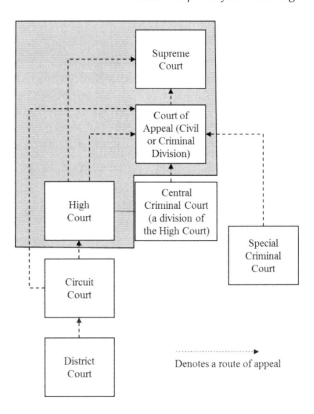

2.4.2 England and Wales

Within the English legal system, the Supreme Court is the final court of appeal for all United Kingdom civil cases and all criminal cases from England, Wales and Northern Ireland.[117] In 2009,[118] the Constitutional Reform Act 2005 transferred the judicial function of the House of Lords to the Supreme Court.[119] Decisions of the Supreme Court and pre-transfer decisions of the House of Lords bind courts of inferior jurisdiction in England and Wales. Below the Supreme Court sit the Court of Appeal, the High Court, crown courts, county courts and magistrates' courts. Each court is bound by decisions of all superior courts (although decisions of crown courts, county courts and magistrates' courts do not create binding precedents).[120]

---

[117] Constitutional Reform Act 2005, s 40.
[118] Constitutional Reform Act 2005 (Commencement No 11) Order 2009, SI 2009/1604.
[119] Constitutional Reform Act 2005, sch 9.
[120] For a more detailed discussion of the court system of England and Wales, see Gary Slapper and David Kelly, *The English Legal System* (18th edn, Routledge 2017), chs 6, 8 and 9.

The Judicial Committee of the Privy Council is a slightly different court to the others in the hierarchy of courts in England and Wales. The Judicial Committee of the Privy Council is the court of final appeal for UK overseas territories, Crown dependencies and for certain Commonwealth countries. Subject to limited exceptions, the courts of England and Wales are expected, but are not bound, to follow a decision of the Judicial Committee of the Privy Council, unless there is inconsistent binding precedent from a superior court.[121]

Decisions of the courts of England and Wales, as well as decisions of the Judicial Committee of the Privy Council, have frequently been cited and followed by Irish courts.

2.4.3 United States of America

The United States of America operates a federal system. As a result, there exist both state level and federal level hierarchies of courts. Certain classes of cases can only be heard by federal courts, while others can only be heard by state courts (some matters may be heard in both systems). At federal level, the Supreme Court of the United States is the highest court on federal matters and its decisions are binding on all inferior federal courts and all state courts with respect to matters of federal law. Below the Supreme Court of the United States sit multiple intermediate federal Courts of Appeal, organised by geographical territory, and federal trial or district courts. There are also a number of specialised federal courts, such as the United States Court of International Trade.

At state level, each state has established its own hierarchy of courts. Every state has a supreme court and trial courts. Most (but not all) states also have one or more intermediate courts of appeal. The decisions of a state's supreme court regarding that state's law are binding on inferior state courts within that state and, in certain circumstances, on courts in other states and on federal courts that are interpreting that state's law.[122]

Decisions of the courts within the United States of America, particularly decisions of the Supreme Court of the United States, have been referred to relatively frequently in Irish cases.

---

[121] *Willers v Joyce (No. 1)* [2016] UKSC 43, [2017] 2 All ER 327.

[122] For more information on courts in the United States of America, see United States Courts, 'Court Role and Structure' <www.uscourts.gov/about-federal-courts/court-role-and-structure> accessed 1 December 2018 and Federal Judicial Center, 'About the U.S. Courts: General Information' <www.fjc.gov/content/about-us-courts-%E2%80%94-general-information> accessed 1 December 2018.

2.4.4 Australia

Like the United States of America, Australia operates a federal system, with both state and federal courts. The High Court of Australia sits at the top of the hierarchy of courts in Australia and its decisions are binding on all Australian courts.[123]

At federal level, the Federal Court of Australia has jurisdiction to hear matters arising under Australian federal law and appeals from the Federal Circuit Court. Appeals from the Federal Court are heard by the Full Federal Court. At state level, the Supreme Court of each state represents the highest court within that state and operates as the Court of Appeal in appeals cases. The Supreme Court sits above the district courts and local courts within the state hierarchy of courts. Decisions of each state Court of Appeal and the Full Federal Court are binding on each single judge sitting in the Supreme Court and Federal Court, and on district and local courts.[124]

Reference has been made to decisions of the High Court and Federal Court of Australia, as well as those of state Supreme Courts, in a number of Irish cases.

2.5 Chapter summary

1. In order to construct persuasive submissions and to answer questions from moot judges, you should understand the structure of the Irish legal system (or the legal system of the jurisdiction where the moot is taking place).

2. In Ireland, there are a number of sources of law:
    *   primary sources (EU law, the Constitution, Irish legislation and case law from Irish courts);
    *   other sources (international law — when incorporated into Irish law — and case law from foreign courts); and
    *   secondary sources (books, articles and reports).

3. Irish law is found in primary sources, but other and secondary sources can influence and inform the decision of judges (including moot judges).

---

[123] When reading cases from Australian courts, pay close attention to the court that delivered the decision. The High Court of Australia sits *above* the various Supreme Courts.

[124] For more information on Australian courts, see Australian Government, Attorney-General's Department, 'The courts' <www.ag.gov.au/LegalSystem/Courts/Pages/default.aspx> accessed 1 December 2018.

4.   The doctrine of precedent is of central importance when presenting cases to moot judges and you should understand and respect the doctrine of precedent when making your submissions—remember, moot judges are not bound by every earlier decision of the Irish courts, nor are they bound by every part of an earlier decision.

5.   In addition to considering the hierarchy of sources of Irish law, bear in mind the hierarchy of Irish courts, as only decisions of a court of superior jurisdiction will be binding on the moot judges.

Chapter 3

Legal Research for a Moot

3.1 Introduction

Between receiving the moot problem question and presenting your oral submissions, you will: (1) research relevant legal issues; and (2) draft your written submissions.[1] This chapter considers how to conduct your legal research and how you can find sources to use as authority for your submissions.

It is important not to underestimate the amount of research and work that go into mooting successfully. Too often, mooters do not spend enough time before a moot researching the legal issues, or they submit written submissions that have been hastily put together. Your talent in oral submissions should be backed up by solid research skills and articulate written submissions.

3.2 Legal research

Developing legal research skills should help you to more accurately and efficiently find the material needed to solve legal problems.[2] In the context of a moot, the legal problems to be solved are the various legal issues raised by each ground of appeal.

3.2.1 Researching a moot problem question

There is no specific formula for successful legal research—as you research, you will develop a research style that works for you. Nevertheless, there are a number of steps to consider when researching for a moot:

---

[1]   The rules of the moot may provide that you do not need to exchange a full memorial with your opponents. However, in practice, you may still find it helpful to prepare a form of memorial and you will almost certainly have to prepare a list of authorities.

[2]   For an in-depth discussion about research techniques, see Laura Cahillane and Jennifer Schweppe (eds), *Legal Research Methods: Principles and Practicalities* (Clarus Press 2016).

Step 1: Read the moot problem question
Step 2: Analyse the issues
Step 3: Conduct your legal research
Step 4: Build your submissions and list of authorities
Step 5: Prepare for your opponents' submissions
Step 6: Update your research

3.2.2 Step 1: Read the moot problem question

It goes without saying that your first task when you receive a moot problem question is to read it carefully with your teammate. Analyse each sentence. Ensure that you are both in agreement on the factual and procedural matrix underpinning the question.

You may find it helpful at this stage to make a note of certain core details as you read the moot problem question, including:

(a) *The identity of the moot court*: Determine the court that the moot is being heard in and its position in the hierarchy of Irish courts.

(b) *The identity of the parties*: Note the full names of all parties and determine which party is the Appellant and which party is the Respondent. The Appellant is always the party that is bringing the appeal, regardless of the respective role of the parties in the original trial.

(c) *The background facts and procedural history of the case*: The facts of the moot are not in dispute—you must accept these as stated. Nevertheless, make sure that you understand these facts and the sequence of events leading up to the moot.

(d) *The relevant areas of law and legal topics*: Note the broad areas of law (such as contract law) and legal topics (such as offer and acceptance or part-payment of a debt) raised by the moot problem question.

During your research, refer back to the moot problem question. Facts or words that you initially thought were irrelevant may become significant once you have conducted further research.

Example:

- **Moot court**: Court of Appeal (Civil Division) (bound by Supreme Court decisions)

- **Parties**: Irish Sprinklers Ltd (Appellant); Pete's Cabbages DAC (Respondent)

- **Background facts and procedural history**
  - o Contract agreed: €100,000 to install sprinkler system and network calibration.
  - o €70,000 paid upfront and sprinkler system installed.
  - o Balance due one week after the network calibration. Payment not contingent on completion.
  - o J Kenny (finance director Respondent) called H Duffy (sole director Appellant): only €10,000 more could be paid.
  - o H Duffy: fine, but no network calibration. J Kenny: do not be rash.
  - o Email from J Kenny to H Duffy: case of champagne to whoever calibrates network. Posted on bulletin board in staff room of Appellant, but no further communication between J Kenny and H Duffy.
  - o G Sigg (works for Appellant) calibrated network as per original schedule. Took case of champagne.
  - o Respondent paid €10,000 by bank transfer.
  - o Appellant sued for balance in High Court.
  - o High Court found in favour of Respondent.

- **Relevant area(s) of law and legal topics**
  - o Contract law
    - — Offer and acceptance.
    - — Contract formation and variation.
    - — Part-payment of a debt.
    - — Estoppel.

3.2.3 Step 2: Analyse the issues

Once you and your teammate are in agreement about the core details of the moot problem question, determine what outcome your client wants and what needs to be addressed in your research so that you can prepare persuasive submissions. In doing so, there are a number of points to consider.

(a) *Who you represent*: This will determine whether you need to persuade the moot judges that the appeal should be allowed (if you represent the Appellant) or dismissed (if you represent the Respondent). The rules of the moot may require that you prepare separate submissions for both parties.

(b) *The findings of the trial judge*: These explain why the trial judge reached the decision he or she did and will tie into the grounds of appeal.

(c) *The grounds of appeal*: These set out why the Appellant is appealing the decision of the trial judge. The Appellant's counsel must demonstrate why these grounds have a basis in law and why the trial judge was incorrect. The Respondent's counsel must demonstrate why the grounds do not have a basis in law and why the trial judge was correct. If the moot problem question specifically sets out the grounds of appeal, you should use these and not create your own. You will present these grounds of appeal from your client's perspective in your submissions. If the moot problem question does not explicitly set out the grounds of appeal, you must determine the overarching reasons why, based on the trial judge's findings, the appeal should be allowed (if you represent the Appellant) or dismissed (if you represent the Respondent). In such circumstances, the moot problem question will generally be structured so that there will be two broad grounds of appeal for each mooter.

Having confirmed who you represent, the findings of the trial judge and the reasons for the appeal, consider the legal issues that you will need to address as part of your research—ask yourself: for each ground of appeal, what needs to be proven in order to persuade the moot judges to find in favour of my client?

Example:

- **Findings of the trial judge**: Twomey J: Irish Sprinklers Ltd accepted Pete's Cabbages DAC's part-payment of the debt (new benefit was valid consideration) and terms varied accordingly—not entitled to the remaining balance due.

- **Grounds of Appeal**
  - o   Twomey J erred—no offer of part-payment was accepted by the Appellant, the terms of original contract remain enforceable and the Respondent's obligations have not yet been fully discharged.
  - o   In the alternative, the case of champagne and network calibration represent element of a new contract—obligations under the original contract were not varied and so remain unaltered.

- **Legal issues**
  - o Ground of Appeal 1: whether the Appellant accepted the offer of part-payment.
    - — What are the elements of a valid offer and acceptance of that offer?
    - — Can acceptance come through conduct?
    - — Was there a counter-offer?
    - — Can an offer of part-payment of a debt be accepted (was there valid consideration)?
  - o Ground of Appeal 2: whether champagne and network calibration constituted a new contract or a variation of the original contract.
    - — Was there a new contract or was the original contract varied? What elements are needed for these?
    - — Could the Appellant be estopped from claiming the original sum?

3.2.4 Step 3: Conduct your legal research

Once you have considered the legal issues raised by each ground of appeal, you will then conduct research in order to confirm the applicable legal principles. Try to adopt a layered approach to your research. Start by building up your general understanding of the relevant areas of law and legal topics, before moving on to more detailed, targeted research of specific legal issues.

To make the most of the resources that you have access to, you may find it helpful to make a list of key search terms that are relevant to the areas of law raised by the moot problem question. Try to think about the underpinning legal concepts raised by the question, rather than focusing on fact-specific search terms. You can then use these key search terms to direct your research when looking at a book's index or when using online legal databases.

A. Allocating research

Before you conduct your general and detailed research, agree with your teammate how you are going to apportion the research required for each ground of appeal. There is no right or wrong way to do this, and the best approach for your team will depend on each team member's particular strengths. However, one of three broad approaches to apportioning research could be considered:

- all team members share the research on all grounds of appeal and collate ideas;
- each team member researches specific grounds of appeal for a period of time and then swaps grounds of

appeal with the other team member so that everyone ultimately researches all grounds of appeal; or

- each team member takes specific grounds of appeal and only researches these.

The first and second approaches are collaborative in nature and could facilitate the contribution of ideas, arguments or authorities by one team member that another team member would not otherwise have considered. These approaches also help each team member to better understand all of the team's submissions and so could make it easier for these submissions to be presented as a coherent whole. On the other hand, the third approach is more efficient and may encourage each team member to thoroughly research the specific grounds of appeal they have been assigned. This facilitates a more in-depth understanding of the legal issues raised than may be possible using the first or second approaches.

B. Research the issues generally

Start your research with a resource that gives you a general overview of the law governing the legal issues raised by each ground of appeal. Textbooks or practitioners' texts on relevant areas of law are the best place to start.

> **Example:**
>
> For a ground of appeal dealing with offer and acceptance, contract formation and part-payment of a debt, you could begin by looking at Paul A McDermott and James McDermott, *Contract Law* (2nd edn, Bloomsbury Professional 2017) chapters 2 to 5 and Robert Clark, *Contract Law in Ireland* (8th edn, Round Hall 2016) chapters 1 to 4.

As you read these books, keep a running list of potentially relevant authorities (such as cases and legislative provisions) referred to in the text or footnotes. Highlight any of these authorities that appear multiple times, or seem particularly useful or important. You will use this list to conduct your detailed research of primary sources.

As discussed in Chapter 2, textbooks and practitioners' texts are not primary sources of law and are not authority for principles of Irish law. If one of these secondary sources discusses a legal principle, always review the primary source from which that legal principle has been derived.

C. Conduct detailed research

Once you have confirmed your understanding of the applicable legal principles, move on to your detailed research. This involves reading more targeted secondary sources (such as academic articles or topic-specific books) which specifically address legal issues raised by each ground of appeal. Continue to note any potentially relevant authorities referred to in the targeted secondary sources.

> **Example:**
>
> For detailed research on part-payment of a debt, you could review articles such as: Gearóid Carey, 'Can part-payment constitute full satisfaction?' (2006) 13(1) Commercial Law Practitioner Journal 3.

With the information gathered from your general and targeted review of secondary sources, you will then move on to locate, read and evaluate the relevance of primary sources as authorities for your submissions. Your objective is to find the authorities that most convincingly support your submissions on each legal issue.

Depending on the number of primary sources on your list, you may find it helpful to develop a system of prioritising your review of this material:

- review any authorities that you have highlighted as appearing multiple times in other sources, as being particularly relevant to your submissions or as being important to the legal issue you are researching;
- read the most recent authorities first and for cases, start with the judgment from the highest court that heard the case. This should reduce the risk that you read something that has subsequently been repealed or overturned; and
- divide material by ground of appeal to help focus your research.

As you review primary sources, continue to note any further potential authorities referred to in those sources.

D. Keep a research trail

Make accurate and detailed notes of everything you read as part of your research. You do not want to start drafting your written submissions only to realise that you have forgotten the name of a case that is authority for a particular submission. As you read relevant material, you should ideally make a note of:

- its full citation;
- the page or paragraph number of any quotations or important passages within the material; and
- in the case of a primary source, any relevant statements of law it is authority for and whether, and if so why, it supports your submissions.

3.2.5 Step 4: Build your submissions and select your authorities

As you progress through your research, consider potential arguments that you could make on your client's behalf (these will form your 'positive case' in your written and oral submissions).[3] Make a note of these as you go along and then add references to any on-point authorities as you read them. Be open to the possibility that additional, or even more persuasive, arguments may come to light with further research.

Example:	
Potential argument (Appellant)	**Relevant authority**
1. No valid acceptance by the Appellant of the Respondent's offer of part-payment	• *Tansey v College of Occupational Therapists Ltd* [1995] 2 ILRM 601 (HC) 615 (Murphy J): Quotation describing elements of a valid agreement. • *Mespil Limited v Capaldi* [1986] ILRM 373 (SC) 376 (Henchy J): Referred to a 'meeting of the minds' being 'essential for an enforceable contract'.
2. There was a counter-offer, but this was not accepted	• *O'Mahony v Promontoria (Gem) DAC* [2018] IEHC 63: Notes that a clear counter-offer cannot be acceptance but rather is a rejection. • *Tansey v College of Occupational Therapists Ltd* [1995] 2 ILRM 601 (HC) 616 (Murphy J): 'it is difficult to conceive of an acceptance which would itself prescribe conditions.'

---

[3] See Chapter 5 (Section 5.3.2) for more discussion about making your positive and negative cases in submissions.

Once you have finished your research, you can begin piecing together the various authorities that you have gathered in order to build your final submissions within each ground of appeal. You may find that you have a large number of authorities from different sources. At this stage, you will need to select the authorities that are most likely to persuade the moot judges that your submissions are correct. Section 3.5 discusses how to make this selection.

As you build your submissions, make sure that the arguments that you make as a team complement, rather than undermine, each other. This is where working together and communicating with your teammate are vital.

3.2.6 Step 5: Preparing for your opponents' submissions

As there is typically simultaneous exchange of written submissions between teams in a moot, your written submissions should not specifically address your opponents' submissions (as you will not know what these are at the time you exchange written submissions).

However, you will need to challenge your opponents' submissions as part of your oral submissions (this will form your 'negative case' in your oral submissions).[4] As you conduct your research and build your own submissions, consider what arguments your opponents are likely to make and what authorities they are likely to rely on. Keep a list of these, together with a note of any inadequacies that you think exist in these arguments and authorities.[5] By doing this, you can make sure that your own submissions are sufficiently robust, and you can begin preparing for the task of analysing your opponents' written submissions following exchange. Chapter 5 discusses arguments that you may consider making in oral submissions to rebut your opponents' submissions.[6]

3.2.7 Step 6: Update your research

Before exchanging written submissions with your opponents and, if the rules of the moot give you sufficient time for this, before your oral submissions, check whether there have been any very recent developments in the law that you are referring to in your submissions. These developments could be a new piece of

---

[4] See Chapter 5 (Section 5.3.2) for more discussion about making your positive and negative cases in submissions.

[5] In mooting competitions where each team is required to prepare written submissions for both the Appellant and Respondent, teams will already be considering submissions from both clients' perspective.

[6] See Chapter 5 (Section 5.4) for a discussion of rebuttal and surrebuttal.

legislation or EU law, but are more likely to be a newly decided case. To perform this updating check, do a final search for your key search terms in online legal databases, particularly the databases of the Courts Service of Ireland (www.courts.ie), the British and Irish Legal Information Institute ('BAILII') (www.bailii.org) and the Irish Legal Information Initiative ('IRLII') (www.irlii.org) (each of which is discussed in more detail in Section 3.3.2).

3.3 Finding authorities

3.3.1 Printed sources

With an increasing volume of material now available in electronic format, it can be tempting to do all of your research online and to avoid visiting your university or institution's library.

While a number of English law-specific textbooks and some practitioners' texts on matters of English law have been digitised (and so you may be able to access these through your library's online catalogue), few Irish law-specific books have been made available in full online. Particularly when conducting your general research, therefore, your library will be an invaluable source of material.

> **Practical Tip:**
>
> Remember, books should not be quoted in your submissions as sources of law. You may, however, want to refer the moot judges to a helpful quotation or discussion in a book. If you do refer to a book, try to refer to one written by a leading academic or used as a practitioners' text. Refer back to the list of practitioners' texts in Chapter 2 for a list of books that have been cited in Irish cases.[7]

Your library is also likely to have printed copies of law reports from Ireland (and possibly from other jurisdictions) containing printed versions of written judgments delivered in cases.[8] While judgments delivered in more recent Irish cases are generally also available online, you may still have to refer to printed law reports for older judgments.

3.3.2 Electronic sources

There is a wealth of information available online. However, the

---

[7] See Chapter 2 (Section 2.2.3).
[8] Jennifer Schweppe, Rónán Kennedy and Lawrence Donnelly, *How to Think, Write and Cite: Key Skills for Irish Law Students* (2nd edn, Round Hall 2016) 149.

quality and accuracy of this information varies considerably between websites. Search engines (like Google) and online-only encyclopaedias (like Wikipedia) may be useful for giving you an initial overview of an area of law or for directing you towards more targeted sources of information, but you should avoid using these to conduct substantive legal research. As far as possible, limit your substantive online legal research to legal databases that bring together individual or multiple primary and secondary sources into searchable collections. Most (but not all) of these databases require payment of a subscription fee, although you may be able to access them for free through your library's online catalogue.

To make the most of legal databases, think not only about *what* you search for, but *how* you search. Simply typing in a list of words into the search box of a legal database could produce a large number of search results, many of which are only marginally relevant to the legal issue you are researching. Instead, consider using some of the following techniques to make your searches more relevant and useful.

Search Technique[9]	Explanation	Example
Connectors	Connectors (also referred to as Boolean operators) define the relationship between your search terms. These connectors are **AND, OR** and **NOT**.	
	• Linking two words with **AND** will retrieve material containing both words.	• offer AND acceptance
	• Linking two words with **OR** will retrieve material containing either word (use this connector when searching for synonyms).	• contract OR agreement
	• Linking two words with **NOT** will retrieve material containing the first, but not the second, word.	• payment NOT services

---

[9] There will be slight differences between how these search techniques are used for each database. The 'help' (or equivalent) section of each database will usually confirm how each of these searches can be conducted on that database.

Field searching	The advanced search function of most legal databases allows you to search specific fields (such as author, date, title). If you use these fields to search for specific words, then only material containing the words in the specified context will be retrieved.	Westlaw IE allows you to narrow your searches for cases to the following fields: Free Text; Party Names; Citation; Subject/ Keyword.
Phrase searching	If you search for a phrase within a legal database, the material retrieved will typically include all of your search terms, but not necessarily in the same sentence or phrase. To limit your search to an exact phrase, surround the phrase with quotation marks (whether these are single or double depends on the database— check the 'help' section of the database to confirm).	"part-payment of a debt"
Truncation/ word expansion	A truncated word is one where the root of the word is included in the search, followed by a symbol (this is usually !, but it varies between databases—check the 'help' section of the database to confirm). A search using a truncated word will retrieve material containing words with the same root as the search term, but with various different word endings.	A search for **negligen!** on Westlaw IE retrieves material containing the following words: negligen**t**, negligen**ce**, negligen**tly**.
Wild card/ universal characters	Including a universal character (this is usually *, but it varies between databases— check the 'help' section of the database to confirm) in the middle of a word will retrieve material containing words with the same characters as the search term, but where the universal character acts as a placeholder and can be substituted for any other letter.	A search for **wom*n** on Westlaw IE retrieves material containing the following words: wom**a**n, wom**e**n.

Nearby words	If you want to search for material in which certain words are connected, but do not necessarily appear in a particular order, you can narrow your search results to those where two words appear within a particular number of words of each other. The character used for this varies between databases (check the 'help' section of the database to confirm) but is **/n** (where n is the number of words) on Westlaw IE.	A search for **part /3 payment** on Westlaw IE retrieves material where 'part' and 'payment' appear within three words of each other.
Searching within results	Once your search results are displayed, you can further narrow these down by searching for more specific search terms within the results—this will search only within the original results.	A search for "valid contract" on Westlaw IE can be further narrowed by searching for "acceptance" within the search results.

A. Subscription-based legal databases

Your university or institution's library may have access to one or a number of subscription-based legal databases. Depending on the areas of law raised by a moot problem question, you may need to search several of these databases to find relevant authorities.

(1)   **Westlaw IE (www.westlaw.ie)**: Westlaw IE is the primary subscription-based legal database for Irish law-related research. Its coverage includes the Irish Law Reports Monthly from 1976, the Irish Law Times Reports from 1871 and unreported Irish judgments from 2000. It also contains some consolidated Irish legislation (which reflects subsequent amendments and repeals of the text of the legislation) and primary legislation in its original (unamended) form, but with accompanying commentary. The database includes a wide selection of Irish academic and practitioner journals.

(2)   **Westlaw UK (www.westlaw.co.uk)**: For cases, consolidated legislation, journal articles and some books from the United Kingdom and the European Union, Westlaw UK is a comprehensive legal database. It also contains full-text Irish Jurist articles from 2000.

The 'Case Analysis' link under each case is particularly helpful. This provides an abstract of the case (although you should always read the full written judgment), together with a list of cases cited in the judgment, a list of cases that subsequently cite the case, any legislation cited and related journal articles.

(3) **LexisLibrary (www.lexisnexis.com)**: Like Westlaw UK, LexisLibrary is a useful database for cases, consolidated legislation, journal articles and books from the United Kingdom. It also contains international legislation and a comprehensive list of full-text international journals. LexisLibrary's coverage includes the Irish Reports from 1919 and unreported Irish judgments from 1967.

(4) **JustisOne (app.justis.com)**: JustisOne, which replaced Justis (www.justis.com), JustCite (www.justcite.com) during the course of 2018, is a user-friendly database that gives you an overview of the status of cases from the United Kingdom, the European Union and Ireland. For cases included on JustisOne, the 'Overview' link above each case sets out the main categories of legal research that are relevant to the case, together with extracts of those passages from the case that have been most frequently cited in other cases. The remaining links above each case provide details of cases cited in the judgment, legislation that was substantively relied on in the judgment and the treatment of the case in subsequent cases — for example, it may note that the case has been overturned or reversed, distinguished, applied or considered in a subsequent case. This is an excellent way of determining whether a case remains good law.

In terms of Irish cases, JustisOne includes full-text judgments published in the Irish Reports from 1832 (in pdf format taken directly from the law reports),[10] and unreported judgments continuously from 1998. Be aware that if you are using the unreported Irish judgments from JustisOne in your submissions, these are given a JustisOne-specific citation, 'JIC', unless they also have a neutral citation. If you cite an unreported case in your submissions, use the standard citation method for unreported judgments (discussed below), rather than the 'JIC' citation.[11]

---

[10] JustisOne contains a small number of older Irish cases published within a variety of different law reports.

[11] See Chapter 4 (Section 4.6.1) for a discussion of how to cite material in your written submissions.

JustisOne's coverage also includes legislation from the United Kingdom from 1235, EU law from 1952 and Irish legislation from 1925.

(5) **Others**: There are a number of other subscription-based legal databases that you may find helpful, such as HeinOnline (www.heinonline.org) and JSTOR (www.jstor.org). Both of these databases are North American law-centric and focus primarily on journal articles.

B. Free legal databases

In addition to subscription-based legal databases, there are a number of free legal databases that can be useful when researching for a moot.

(1) **Courts Service of Ireland (www.courts.ie)**: The Courts Service of Ireland website is a very useful resource for finding recent Irish cases. Within the 'Judgments & Determinations' link, you can search for Irish cases from 2001 by court, year or judge— this will retrieve cases that are so recent, they have not yet been included in books, articles or law reports. For cases where multiple written judgments were delivered, there are links below the case details that will take you to each individual written judgment. Using the website's 'Search' function allows you to search the entire database for key search terms.

(2) **Law Reform Commission (www.lawreform.ie)**: The Law Reform Commission's website contains a large number of reports on areas of Irish law. While these reports are not sources of Irish law, they contain information about areas of law that are unsettled or in need of reform and so may be helpful in your research. The Law Reform Commission's website also includes a database of consolidated legislation under the 'Revised Acts' link. Almost every Act of the Oireachtas since 2006 that has subsequently been amended is included in consolidated form on the database, together with approximately 135 frequently used pre-2006 Acts.[12]

(3) **Electronic Irish Statute Book (www.irishstatutebook.ie)**: The electronic Irish Statute Book ('eISB') is a database of Irish legislation. It also includes an updated version of the Constitution, reflecting amendments.

While the eISB database is helpful for searching for legislation

---

[12] Law Reform Commission, 'Revised Acts–Introduction' <http://revisedacts.lawreform.ie/revacts/intro> accessed 1 December 2018.

that includes key search terms, the legislative instruments included in this database are generally in the form they were when originally enacted and do not reflect subsequent amendments or repeals. As a result, when searching for legislation on the eISB database, always check for subsequent amending legislation. This resource is best used in conjunction with Westlaw IE or the Law Reform Commission website, each of which contains some consolidated legislation reflecting amendments and repeals.

(4) **BAILII (www.bailii.org), IRLII (www.irlii.org) and the World Legal Information Institute ('WorldLII') (www.worldlii. org)**: BAILII contains British and Irish cases, legislation and materials such as papers and reports from the Law Reform Commission. It also includes cases from the European Union and decisions of the ECtHR. IRLII includes Supreme Court, High Court and Court of Criminal Appeal cases, as well as links to Irish legislation.[13] If you are researching jurisdictions beyond the United Kingdom and Ireland, WorldLII includes legal information relating to international organisations and 123 jurisdictions.

(5) **EUROPA (www.europa.eu) and EUR-Lex (eur-lex.europa. eu)**: EUROPA, the official website of the European Union, contains useful information on the European Union, including EU law and European Union publications. EUR-Lex, EUROPA's companion website, provides access to Treaties, EU law documents (including Regulations, Directives, Decisions and opinions), preparatory documents, related national law and case law, certain international agreements and European Free Trade Association documents.

(6) **HUDOC (www.hudoc.echr.coe.int)**: HUDOC is a database of cases from the ECtHR and includes judgments, decisions, advisory opinions and reports.

C. Other electronic sources: a word of caution

The above is not a definitive list of online sources of legal information, but it does include legal databases that you are likely to find helpful when conducting research for a moot. For other online resources, be cautious before using these as part of your research. As noted above, general search engines and online-only encyclopaedias should not be used as authorities, and should not be

---

[13] Please note, however, that IRLII does not yet contain new Court of Appeal decisions.

cited or quoted in your submissions. Similarly, blog posts, opinion pieces and newspaper articles may be informative, but they may also be one-sided or lacking in rigorous legal analysis. They should, therefore, be cited as a last resort. Finally, avoid consulting online essay writing websites as part of your research and never cite these in your submissions.

3.4 Reading authorities

3.4.1 Reading legislation for a moot

Although books are a helpful place to start your research, relying on descriptions of Irish legislation in textbooks or practitioners' texts alone will not be sufficient to construct persuasive submissions in a moot. If you think a legislative provision is relevant to one of your submissions, ensure that you find a full-text version of the legislation using one or more of the resources discussed above. As you read this legislation, consider the following points:

1. Type of legislation	Determine whether the legislation is primary or secondary legislation.
2. Short title and citation	The short title of legislation is its name and its year. In the case of statutory instruments, also make a note of the statutory instrument number.
3. Is it in force?	The date of promulgation of an Act of the Oireachtas is the day it was signed into law by the President. Unless the text of the statute provides otherwise, it will enter into force immediately.[14] However, it is common that the entry into force of some, or all, provisions of a statute is delayed. In such circumstances, the commencement section of the statute will confirm which provisions come into force at a later date. These provisions will then only become law in Ireland on a specified date, or following a commencement order by way of statutory instrument made by the relevant government minister.

---

[14] Art 25.4.1° of the Constitution.

	Before you cite a legislative provision in your submissions, check that the provision is in force (and so is actually law in Ireland). This can be done by checking the commencement section of the statute. If commencement is delayed, confirm whether a relevant provision is in force: • by searching for the name of the statute in the eISB database and reviewing connected statutory instruments whose title includes the word 'commencement'; or • for a statute that has been consolidated on Westlaw IE or by the Law Reform Commission, by searching for the section or sub-section of the statute and checking whether it is marked as in force or not (it is prudent to then double-check this on eISB).
4. Has it subsequently been amended?	Legislation is frequently amended or repealed. For the purposes of your submissions, you should refer to the most up-to-date version of legislation, reflecting all amendments and repeals. Legislation available in hard copy or on eISB is generally not consolidated and so does not reflect subsequent changes. Before you cite a legislative provision in your submissions, ensure that it reflects all amendments. This can be done: • by searching for the name of the statute in the eISB database and then searching within the results for the specific section or sub-section number that you are relying on. Review any results to determine their relevance to your submissions and whether they are themselves in force; or • for a statute that has been consolidated on Westlaw IE or by the Law Reform Commission, by searching for the specific section or sub-section of the statute and checking whether it has been amended or repealed (it is prudent to then double-check this on eISB).

5. Follow up on all defined terms	When reading a legislative provision, check the definition of any capitalised (or 'defined') terms used in that provision. These terms should be defined in the interpretation section of the statute or in the Interpretation Act 2005. Defined terms in statutory instruments have the same meaning as is given to them in the main statute delegating law-making powers.[15]
6. What legal principle(s) is the legislative provision authority for?	Consider the legal principle or principles for which the legislative provision is authority. In doing so, consider the interpretative approach the court may give to the provision and whether one approach may be more helpful to your submissions than the other.[16] Make a note of any relevant provisions.
7. Are there any exceptions?	If you find a legislative provision that is relevant to your submissions, read the provision and any related provisions thoroughly to ensure that you have not missed any exceptions to the legal principle established by the legislation.
8. Related cases	Cases in which the courts have considered specific provisions of legislation could be helpful in forming your submissions. Searching for legislation on Westlaw IE and JustisOne will retrieve a list of cases in which that legislation has been discussed.

3.4.2 Reading a case for a moot

Being able to read a case and to apply legal principles confirmed in that case to the facts of a moot problem question are important elements of mooting. Your role is to persuade the moot judges that every case that you rely on is good authority for a particular submission. In order to do this, you need to be able to explain why a case is being relied on as authority. Equally, be prepared to explain why cases relied on by your opponents are not good authority for your opponents' submissions. Relying on summaries of cases in books will not be sufficient for this. These summaries may not go into detail about the facts of the case, the reasoning of the judges or comments of dissenting judges. Without this additional information, it could be difficult for you to convincingly argue

---

[15] Interpretation Act 2005, s 19.
[16] These interpretative methods are discussed in Chapter 2 (Section 2.2.1(C)).

that a case is, or is not, authority for a particular submission or to answer questions from the moot judges.

Once you have identified a case that is potentially relevant, check JustisOne to ensure that the case remains good law. You should then read any judgment delivered in the case, in full. If you do not do this, you risk missing a quotation or judicial statement that is critical to your submissions. You may also misunderstand the reasoning of the judges and incorrectly discount or rely on a case as authority.

Cases published in law reports or on legal databases will often be accompanied by a headnote and a list of catchwords. Headnotes summarise the facts of a case, the decision of the court and the reasoning for that decision. They may also summarise the arguments of counsel and dissenting judgments.[17] Catchwords pick out words, phrases, concepts or legislative provisions that are relevant to the case. Because of the nature of the information provided in a case's headnote and catchwords, it can be tempting to refer only to these during your research. However, while they can be a useful place to start when reading a case, you should avoid relying exclusively on headnotes and catchwords in your research for a number of reasons: (1) they do not form part of the written judgment in a case and so cannot be relied on as authority in your submissions; (2) they do not give you precise references to sections of the written judgment and so are not sufficiently detailed for the purposes of citations; and (3) they are summaries prepared by a barrister whose reading of the case you may not agree with.[18]

When reading the written judgment of cases, consider the following points:

1. Country of court that delivered the decision	Determine whether an Irish or a foreign court delivered the decision. If it was a foreign court, confirm the country (or international body) of which it is a court.

---

[17] Jennifer Schweppe, Rónán Kennedy and Lawrence Donnelly, *How to Think, Write and Cite: Key Skills for Irish Law Students* (2nd edn, Round Hall 2016) 23.
[18] ibid.

2. Court in which the case was decided	Determine where the court that delivered the decision sits in its jurisdiction's hierarchy of courts. Where the court is an Irish court, note whether it is of superior, equal or inferior jurisdiction to the moot court. If it is an appeals case, note why it was appealed and whether it was an appeal on a point of law, by way of case stated or a full re-hearing.
3. Complete citation of the case	Make a complete and accurate note of the full name and citation of the case, the full name of all judges who heard the case and whether those judges were in the majority or were dissenting. Also note whether dissenting judges dissented with all, or only part, of the majority's decision. Note which judges delivered written judgments.
4. Material facts of the case	The facts of every case will be different. Do not be concerned if you cannot find a case whose facts match exactly with those of the moot problem question—a case can be strong precedent for a submission in a subsequent case, even where some of the facts of the two cases are different. When reading a case, consider the material facts of the case and, in light of those facts, what the parties wanted the court to decide. Make a note of similarities, or clear differences, between these material facts and those of the moot problem question.
5. Legal issue that the judges are trying to decide	Establish the legal issue or issues that the judges needed to determine in order to reach a decision in the case. Make a note of any similarity with legal issues raised by the moot problem question. It can be helpful to read the arguments that were made by counsel in the case (if these are provided in the written judgment) as these may highlight what legal issues are in dispute. They can also be helpful in providing you with ideas that can be adapted for your submissions.

6. The applicable legal principle and the legal reasoning used to get there	Determine what the court decided the law was on each legal issue and the court's reasons for reaching this decision. Make a note of any statements of law that are relevant to the legal issues raised by the moot problem question and carefully record page or paragraph numbers of important passages that you may want to refer to in your submissions. Where legal reasoning was essential to the court reaching its final decision on the legal issue, it will be the ratio decidendi of the case and binding on future judges. Judicial comment that is not essential to the court's final decision is obiter dictum. It is still persuasive and so should not be ignored when you are reading a case. The doctrine of precedent is discussed in more detail in Chapter 2.[19]
7. Dissenting judgments, if any	Do not stop reading a case after the majority written judgments.[20] Dissenting judgments may include discussion that is helpful to your submissions, particularly in circumstances where the majority decision is not specifically relevant or you are arguing that it should not be followed. Dissenting judgments may also not disagree with the majority decision on all points and so some elements of a dissenting judgment could, in fact, be included in the ratio decidendi of the case. Make sure you do not forget to note when a judgment is dissenting, to avoid the risk of incorrectly presenting dissenting statements as binding on the moot judges.
8. Subsequent consideration of the case	Use online legal databases to determine whether a case was subsequently considered by the courts. In particular, make a note of any cases where the decision was affirmed, overruled or not followed (you should avoid relying on cases that have subsequently been overruled). This information will heavily influence the precedential value of the case.

---

[19] See Chapter 2 (Section 2.2.1(D)) for a discussion of the doctrine of precedent.
[20] Jennifer Schweppe, Rónán Kennedy and Lawrence Donnelly, How to Think, Write and Cite: Key *Skills for Irish Law Students* (2nd edn, Round Hall 2016) 31.

3.5 Choosing which authorities to rely on

As your research progresses, you will build up a collection of relevant authorities. These authorities should be the strongest authorities that you can find to support the legal principles that you argue are applicable in the moot. It is unlikely, however, that you will find one single authority that indisputably confirms the law in your client's favour. Instead, you may have a range of different authorities from which you have drawn legal principles that support elements of your submissions.

As you fine-tune your submissions ahead of a moot, you will need to decide which authorities you are going to rely on. When selecting your authorities check whether the rules of the moot impose any limit on the number of authorities that each team can rely on. If they do, check whether this limit relates only to some types of authorities (for example, cases) and ensure that you remain within any limit imposed. Even if there is no limit placed on the number of authorities that can be relied on, you may not need to rely on every authority that you have found. This is because you simply will not have the space in your written submissions, or the time in your oral submissions, to refer to a large number of authorities. In addition to this, the moot judges want you to demonstrate the legal principles underpinning your submissions. Once you have been able to do this convincingly with one or more strong authorities, referring to multiple other authorities that all support a submission in the same or similar manner will not make that submission any more persuasive, and may actually make your submissions harder to follow.

You therefore need to select authorities that are likely to be given the greatest authoritative weight by the moot judges. In doing so, the key things that you need to consider are:
- the hierarchy of sources of Irish law; and
- the hierarchy of courts within Ireland.

An authority that is closer to the top of the hierarchy of sources of Irish law will be given more authoritative weight (even if it is not binding on the moot court) than one nearer the bottom. Equally, a decision delivered by a court of superior jurisdiction to the moot court will be more influential than one delivered by a court of inferior jurisdiction. Chapter 2 discusses the sources of Irish law and the hierarchy of Irish courts.[21]

---

[21] See Chapter 2 (Section 2.2 and Section 2.4).

If you have multiple authorities that support a submission, all of which are likely to be given the same authoritative weight by the moot judges, select the most recent authority, as this is the most up-to-date statement of the law.

A. Binding authority

> (a) Ideally, you will be able to cite a provision of EU law, the Constitution, Irish legislation or binding case law to support each of your submissions.
>
> (b) If any of these binding authorities is available, cite them in your submissions in the order of their hierarchy as a source of Irish law (with provisions of EU law and the Constitution (in each case, if relevant) cited first).

B. Persuasive authority

> (a) There may be limited, or no, binding authority that clearly favours one side's arguments over the other. Make sure that in the absence of binding authority, you do cite appropriate persuasive authority in your submissions.
>
> (b) Your role is to persuade the moot judges that, notwithstanding the lack of binding authority, there is still authority that they should be persuaded by. This is something that you will elaborate on in your oral submissions.
>
> (c) When citing non-binding authority, be mindful of what authoritative weight the moot judges are likely to place on that authority, and be prepared to explain why the moot judges should be persuaded by such authority. Chapter 2 discusses the authoritative weight of non-binding authorities.
>
> (d) Avoid citing an overruled case or legislation that has subsequently been repealed.

C. No authority

> (a) If you are struggling to find authority that supports one or more of your submissions, review the sources of Irish law again. There may be authorities that you had initially discounted, but from which an analogy can be drawn with the facts of, or legal principles relevant to, the moot.
>
> (b) If this does not work, consider with your teammate whether the relevant submissions that you are making

are logical and coherent. There may be a reason why you cannot find supportive authority.

(c) If, having considered this, you still think that the submissions are worth making, determine whether you can make any public policy arguments to support your submissions or whether you can argue that the law should be changed by the moot court. These types of arguments should be made with caution.[22]

3.6 Chapter summary

1. While you will adopt your own approach to research, consider the following steps when researching for a moot:
    -   step 1: Read the moot problem question;
    -   step 2: Analyse the issues;
    -   step 3: Conduct your legal research;
    -   step 4: Build your submissions and list of authorities;
    -   step 5: Prepare for your opponents' submissions; and
    -   step 6: Update your research.

2. Consider the full range of printed and online resources that you may be able to use during your research. Online resources, in particular, should be carefully selected—as far as possible, limit your substantive online legal research to legal databases.

3. When reading a case or legislation during your research, read the source in full, consider how it addresses relevant legal issues and make useful notes.

4. Select the strongest authorities that you can find to support your submissions.

---

[22] See Chapter 2 (Section 2.3) for a discussion of arguments asking the moot judges to consider issues of public policy or to change the law.

Chapter 4

Written Submissions

4.1 Introduction

4.1.1 What are written submissions?

In a moot, written submissions will typically consist of: (1) a memorial (or similar document); and/or (2) a list of authorities. Moots often require teams to prepare written submissions on behalf of one or both parties in advance of oral submissions.

Your written submissions will be exchanged simultaneously with those of your opponents (with a copy also given to the moot judges), although the length of time allocated for teams to read the exchanged written submissions will vary between moots (it could be several days or merely minutes). Exchanging written submissions in advance provides each team with an opportunity to consider (and prepare responses to) submissions that may be made, and the authorities that will be relied on, by their opponents in oral submissions. This also gives moot judges an opportunity to read and reflect on each team's submissions and to consider the authorities being relied on.

Preparing written submissions is not unique to moots. In the context of an appeals case before an Irish court, written submissions are filed with the relevant court and served on the other parties to the appeal, in each case prior to the hearing.[1] The Practice Directions for the Court of Appeal (civil division), for example, set out prescriptive rules for written submissions, including their required format and the process to be followed when agreeing and submitting a list of authorities.[2] Preparing written submissions for a moot will give you some experience of this process and help you to develop the skills required to effectively present your submissions in written format.

4.1.2 Written submissions: initial points to consider

When participating in a moot, you and your teammate should be

---

[1] Practice Directions SC13: Appeals and cases stated and SC15: Written submissions. Practice Directions CA06: Submissions, books of appeal and authorities in civil appeals.

[2] Practice Directions CA06: Submissions, books of appeal and authorities in civil appeals [1]–[5], [10].

aware of any requirements for written submissions that are set out in the rules of the moot, including:

(1) The maximum word count or page limit of written submissions
- Does this maximum word count or page limit relate only to the memorial, or does it also include the list of authorities?
- Will footnotes be counted in the maximum word count?

(2) Whether a particular method of citation has been specified
- If it has, make sure you follow this.
- If it has not, choose a widely accepted method of citation (such as OSCOLA Ireland[3]) and use it consistently.

(3) The deadline and method for exchanging written submissions
- Make a note of any deadline for exchanging or submitting written submissions. Missing this deadline looks unprofessional and is unfair on your opponents and the moot judges.

4.2 Memorials

4.2.1 What should a memorial do?

A memorial[4] is a document in which your team presents the submissions that you are making on behalf of your client with respect to each ground of appeal.

Memorials should:[5]

(1) Be concise, but contain sufficient detail
- Make sure your memorial is to the point, factually correct and presents submissions in as persuasive a manner as possible.
- Avoid verbosity and emotive language—keep your written submissions clear, brief and professional.

---

[3] See Section 4.6.1 for details on the OSCOLA Ireland method of legal citation.

[4] Memorials may be referred to by a different title in the rules of the moot, such as a 'memorandum'. These documents may also be referred to as 'skeleton arguments', particularly in English moots. Skeleton arguments are typically shorter and less detailed than memorials, but perform the same function and are structurally and substantively similar to memorials.

[5] These characteristics are similar to what is required of written submissions in the real courts in Ireland, as set out in the Practice Directions for the superior courts (Practice Directions SC16: Conduct of proceedings in Supreme Court; Practice Directions CA06: Submissions, books of appeal and authorities in civil appeals; and Practice Directions HC68: Written submissions).

(2) Be well structured and logically laid out

- Number each paragraph in a memorial. This should make your memorial easier to follow and will allow you to direct the moot judges to particular paragraphs of your memorial during oral submissions.

(3) Be self-contained

- The reader should be able to determine what your submissions are for each ground of appeal by reading your memorial and without having to refer to external material.

(4) Not include long quotations

- Use of long quotations should be limited. They eat into your memorial's word count or page limit and also risk being ignored by the reader.
- Any quotations that you do include should be put into context to make it clear why you are citing them — try to avoid quoting a passage and then expecting the reader to understand why it is relevant to a particular submission.

(5) Refer to any authorities in a clear and useful manner

- Cite authorities, such as legislation or cases, correctly and consistently.
- When you refer to an authority, explain the legal principle that the authority establishes or confirms, and why it is relevant to your submissions.

(6) Include all your team's submissions

- In oral submissions, you will typically not be able to make submissions where the foundations of these submissions have not already been laid down in your memorial.

(7) Be formatted correctly

- Follow any guidance provided in the rules of the moot.
- In the absence of such guidance, a suggested presentation format for your memorial is as follows:
  - A4-size paper;
  - printed single-sided, with numbered paragraphs and pages;
  - font size 12, Times New Roman (or similar);
  - justified alignment;
  - 1.5 line spacing; and
  - standard margins.

As your memorial should be clearly structured and address, at least in outline, the submissions that your team will be making in oral submissions, you may want to consider completing your legal research before you begin drafting your written submissions. Depending on the amount of time between exchange of written submissions and the beginning of oral submissions, you may also need to do additional research following exchange of your written submissions. This research may relate to authorities that your opponents are relying on, or last minute updates in areas of law that are relevant to your submissions.

4.2.2 Structure of a memorial

A memorial should contain four distinct parts:

- cover page;
- introduction;
- main submissions (on each ground of appeal); and
- conclusion outlining what your client wants.

A. Cover page

The cover page of a memorial will provide basic details of the case that is the subject of the moot. Unless the rules of the moot have specific requirements for the cover page, the contents of this page are typically formulaic and broadly in line with the following structure:

(1) **The moot court**: The full name of the court (including, in the case of the Court of Appeal, the relevant division) where the appeal is being heard should be identified at the top of the cover page. It should be centred on the page, written in bold uppercase letters and underlined. It is important here to identify the court where the appeal *will* be heard, not the trial court.

(2) **The parties and their roles**: Immediately below the identity of the court, include the word 'between'. This should be aligned to the left-hand side of the page, written in bold uppercase letters and followed by a colon.

The names of all of the parties to the moot (not just the party that you represent) should then be set out in full, with the Appellant's name appearing first. If one or more of the parties is a natural person, include his or her full name, but do not include any prefix (such as Mr, Ms or Dr). If one or more of the parties is a company, include the full name of that company (including the type of company, if this appears in its name).

The names of the parties should appear in the centre of the cover page on separate lines, in bold uppercase letters and should be separated by the word '-and-', which is written in bold lowercase letters.

Immediately below each party's name, indicate whether that party is the Appellant or the Respondent. Each party's role should be aligned to the right-hand side of the page, underlined and written in bold lowercase letters.

(3) **On whose behalf the memorial is being served**: Identify whether the memorial is being served on behalf of the Appellant or the Respondent. This information should be set out in the centre of the cover page between two parallel lines and should be written in bold uppercase letters.[6]

(4) **Your team number and group number (if applicable)**: Identify your team and group number, if these have been assigned to you. In the context of an intervarsity mooting competition, you may be asked not to identify which university you represent.

Set out below is a template cover page. Information to be amended is included in square brackets.

[NAME OF THE COURT WHERE THE APPEAL IS BEING HEARD]
BETWEEN:
<div align="center">**[NAME OF APPELLANT]**</div><div align="right">**Appellant**</div>
<div align="center">**-and-**</div>
<div align="center">**[NAME OF RESPONDENT]**</div><div align="right">**Respondent**</div>
MEMORIAL ON BEHALF OF THE [APPELLANT]/[RESPONDENT]
<div align="center">**Team [X], Group [Y]**</div>

B. Introduction

A memorial should include an introduction where you briefly introduce the appeal, state your client's position with respect to that appeal and outline the basis for this position. The introduction

---

[6] The reference to 'memorial' on your cover page should be amended to reflect the title of the document used in the rules of the moot.

should begin on a new page after the cover page and should include a heading. Each paragraph within the introduction should be numbered.

While the introduction can be a useful place to start building your submissions, its length will depend on the maximum word count or page limit of your written submissions. If the rules of the moot impose a very restrictive word count or page limit, adjust the length of your introduction accordingly and focus on the grounds of appeal rather than on a discussion of the facts. It is always a good idea to draft the introduction to your memorial last, once the rest of your written submissions have been prepared. This way you will know how much space you have left and how you are planning to frame your submissions.

Set out below are elements to include in the introduction to a memorial.

(1) The introduction should begin by introducing the parties and briefly noting the trial judge's decision

> **Example:**
>
> **'A. Introduction**
>
> 1. This is an appeal by the Appellant (Irish Sprinklers Ltd) against the decision of Twomey J in the High Court finding in favour of the Respondent (Pete's Cabbages DAC).'

(2) The introduction should then give a summary of the facts: This should not be a lengthy verbatim repetition of the facts as set out in the moot problem question, but should act as a helpful summary of the salient facts for someone who has not read the moot problem question. Effectively, the introduction should answer the question: why is the appeal happening?

Never misrepresent the facts, even if they do not appear to be favourable for your client.[7] You should also never assume facts that have not been set out in the moot problem question. Inaccuracies or assumptions in your introduction will be picked up by your opponents and the moot judges. This will not only be embarrassing, but could undermine your credibility in the eyes of the moot judges.

You can, however, use the introduction to subtly present the facts in a way that portrays your client in the best possible light,

---

[7] Andrew Goodman, *Effective Written Advocacy: A Guide for Practitioners* (2nd ed, Wildy, Simmonds & Hill Publishing 2012) 56.

while always remaining truthful. In doing so, you can cause the moot court to focus on and remember facts that are most helpful to your submissions, while reframing or explaining away facts that are least helpful to your submissions. You can also distance your client from unhelpful facts by using passive, neutral language when presenting those facts.

Example:

The facts as presented by the Appellant:

'2.   The Appellant is a small family-run business. It has traditionally contracted only with small farmers, but as part of an expansion programme, it entered into a contract with the Respondent, a large vegetable company. Under the terms of this contract, the Respondent agreed to pay €100,000 for a new sprinkler system to be installed on its Co. Kildare farm and for a follow-up network calibration. €70,000 was paid by the Respondent when the contract was signed and the sprinkler system was installed. The balance of €30,000 was due one week after the network calibration although its payment was stated not to be contingent on completion of the network calibration. After installation of the sprinkler system, Mr Kenny, the finance director of the Respondent, telephoned Ms Duffy, the sole director of the Appellant, stating that the Respondent could only pay an additional €10,000, rather than the full amount due. No other offer was made by the Respondent. Ms Duffy noted that if this was the case, the network calibration would be cancelled. In response to this, Mr Kenny asked Ms Duffy not to be so rash. Mr Kenny subsequently sent an email to Ms Duffy offering a case of champagne to whoever calibrated the network. Ms Duffy did not reply to this email. The network was calibrated a week later by the Appellant, as per the original schedule. After finishing this calibration, Mr Sigg (who works for the Appellant) saw a case of champagne sitting at the Respondent's reception desk with a note saying 'thank you for the network calibration' and took it. One week later, €10,000 was transferred by the Respondent to the Appellant's bank account. The balance remaining under the contract was not paid.'

In this introduction, the Appellant:

- emphasises its weaker position (as a small family-run business trying to expand) as compared to the larger corporate Respondent. This tries to build the reader's sympathy with the Appellant;
- notes that the Appellant completed the installation

as per the agreed schedule. This suggests that the Appellant was willing to uphold its part of the contract;

- refers to Mr Kenny offering €10,000 and nothing more. This suggests unreasonableness on Mr Kenny's behalf;
- notes that the second part of the contract was also completed by the Appellant as per the original schedule; and
- distances the Appellant from any suggestion that it accepted Mr Kenny's offer of part-payment.

Example:

The facts as presented by the Respondent:

'2. The Respondent operates a vegetable company with 300 employees. In order to improve its water consumption, it entered into a contract with the Appellant for the installation of a sprinkler system on the Respondent's Co. Kildare farm, together with a follow-up network calibration, for a total of €100,000. The Respondent paid €70,000 when the contract was signed and the Appellant installed the sprinkler system. However, due to the loss of a supply contract with a national supermarket chain, the Respondent could only afford to pay €10,000 of the balance due to the Appellant. Mr Kenny, finance director of the Respondent, telephoned Ms Duffy, the sole director of the Appellant, to make her aware of this issue. Ms Duffy replied stating that this was 'fine', but that it would mean the network calibration would be cancelled. As calibration of the network was needed for the sprinkler system to work, Mr Kenny asked Ms Duffy not to be so rash. He also emailed Ms Duffy offering a case of champagne to whoever calibrated the network. While no one replied to this gesture, a week later the network was calibrated and the case of champagne, left at the Respondent's reception, was taken. The Respondent transferred €10,000 to the Appellant's bank account.'

In this introduction, the Respondent:

- highlights the Respondent's attempt to conserve water and the large number of people it employs. This tries to soften the reader's impression of the Respondent;
- emphasises the difficulty that the Respondent has been placed in if the network is not calibrated; and
- suggests that Mr Kenny was led to believe that the offer of part-payment was accepted and that by paying €10,000, the Respondent was fulfilling the varied terms of the contract. This makes the Appellant's request for full repayment seem unreasonable.

(3) The introduction should go on to explain the trial judge's decision in more detail

> **Example:**
>
> '3. In the High Court, Twomey J held that the Appellant accepted the Respondent's part-payment of the debt and was not entitled to the remaining balance due under the original contract as, "while paying part of a debt is not valid consideration for giving up the balance of the claim, the receipt of a new benefit or concession is consideration for settlement of the sum originally owed. The terms agreed between the parties were varied accordingly".'

(4) The introduction should give details of the grounds of appeal from your client's perspective: These should be framed to reflect your client's case. If you represent the Appellant, you will submit that the trial judge erred by outlining each ground of appeal. If you represent the Respondent, you will submit that the trial judge was correct as each ground of appeal is without basis.

> **Example:**
>
> For the Appellant's case:
>
> '4. The Appellant appeals on the following grounds:
>   4.1 Twomey J erred in finding that the Appellant accepted the Respondent's part-payment of the debt. No offer of part-payment was accepted by the Appellant, the terms of the original contract remain enforceable and the Respondent's obligations have not yet been fully discharged; and
>   4.2 in the alternative, the case of champagne and the network calibration represent elements of a new contract between the parties. The Respondent's obligations under the original contract were not varied and so remain unaltered.'
>
> For the Respondent's case:
>
> '4. The Appellant's grounds of appeal are without basis for the following reasons:
>   4.1 the Appellant accepted the Respondent's offer of part-payment through conduct; and
>   4.2 in the alternative, the terms of the original contract were varied and the Appellant is estopped from claiming that the original debt remains due.'

(5) Conclude the introduction by setting out what your client wants the moot court to do

> **Example:**
>
> For the Appellant's case:
>
> '5. The Appellant respectfully asks the Court to allow the appeal.'
>
> For the Respondent's case:
>
> '5. The Respondent respectfully asks the Court to dismiss the appeal.'

C. Submissions on each ground of appeal

Once you have introduced the facts of the case, you will present submissions on each ground of appeal. These submissions are your client's legal arguments and they form the most important section of your written submissions.

(1) Structure of your submissions on each ground of appeal: The grounds of appeal set out what is in dispute between the parties. Each ground of appeal is likely to raise a number of legal issues. These legal issues are the points of law that you need to address in order to persuade the moot judges as to the correctness of your submissions on that particular ground of appeal. Each legal issue individually may not seem very substantial, but cumulatively, your submissions on these legal issues should lead the moot judges to determine that there is only one conclusion to be reached on each ground of appeal: the one your client wants.

How you and your teammate choose to structure your submissions on each ground of appeal is something that you should agree in advance. Ultimately, there is no single correct way of presenting submissions, so long as you do so in a way that is logical, based on sound legal reasoning and authority, and internally consistent. Each ground of appeal should, however, start with a heading, each submission on a legal issue should start with a sub-heading and each paragraph should be numbered.

One method of presentation that you may choose to adopt is a modified version of the ILAC method. Using this approach, for each ground of appeal:

(a) *Begin by stating your client's position with respect to a ground of appeal*: Make this position clear, rather than requiring the reader to guess. If you represent the Appellant, you will be establishing the ground of appeal, if you represent the Respondent, you will be responding to the ground of appeal. If you have space, also consider summarising each of the submissions that you will be making with respect to that ground of appeal.

(b) *Present submissions on each legal issue raised by the ground of appeal*:

    (i) *Establish the legal Issue raised and your submission with respect to it:*
- what is the legal issue in dispute that you need to address in order to persuade the moot judges to find in favour of your client and what is your submission with respect to it?

    (ii) *Outline the applicable Law:*
- what is the legal principle established by the authorities that you have selected?

    (iii) *Apply this law to the facts of the moot:*
- do not simply state the law—draw on the legal principle established by your authorities to explain how it applies to the specific facts of the moot; and
- to explain the connection between the law and the facts of the moot you will engage in legal reasoning, such as deductive reasoning or inductive reasoning. Deductive and inductive reasoning are discussed in more detail in Chapter 1.[8]

    (iv) *Reach a Conclusion on the legal issue:*
- how does the application of the law to the facts of the moot affirm your submission on the legal issue?

(c) *Tie all of the legal issues together to reach a conclusion on the ground of appeal.*

The level of detail included for each legal issue will depend on what you agree as a team and the available word count or page limit set by the rules of the moot.

---

[8] See Chapter 1 (Section 1.2) for a discussion of deductive and inductive reasoning in a moot.

Practical Tip:

It is vital that you apply the law to the facts of the moot. Without this connection, you are simply stating general legal principles, without demonstrating why these are relevant—always make sure that you connect a legal principle established by your authorities to the facts of the moot before you reach any conclusion on a legal issue.

Set out below is an abridged example (drafted from the Appellant's perspective) of how the modified ILAC method could be used to present your submissions on a ground of appeal.

Example:

State your client's position on the ground of appeal

'B. The offer of part-payment of the debt was never accepted by the Appellant

6. No offer of part-payment was accepted by the Appellant and the terms of the original contract remain enforceable.'

For the first legal issue	
	'7. *No valid acceptance by the Appellant*
Issue	7.1 There was no valid acceptance by the Appellant of the Respondent's offer of part-payment.
Law	7.2 In *Tansey v College of Occupational Therapists Ltd*,[9] Murphy J described an agreement as being "an offer by one party to perform the action on certain terms and the acceptance of that offer by the other."[10] In order to be valid, therefore, an offer must be communicated to the person for whom it is intended. Acceptance of that offer must be communicated back to the offeror.[11] There must be a clear offer made and an unconditional and understood acceptance of that offer

---

9   *Tansey v College of Occupational Therapists Ltd* [1995] 2 ILRM 601 (HC).
10 ibid, 615 (Murphy J).
11 ibid.

	such that there was a "meeting of the minds"[12] of the parties.
Application	7.3 In the instant appeal, the Appellant never clearly communicated a reply to the Respondent's offer of part-payment.
Conclusion	7.4 There was, therefore, no meeting of the minds of the parties and so there could be no valid acceptance by the Appellant of the Respondent's offer of part-payment.'
For further legal issues	Repeat the ILAC method as above.

Conclude the ground of appeal

'8. In order for an agreement to be binding, there must be a valid offer and acceptance of that offer. The Appellant never accepted the Respondent's offer of part-payment and instead made a counter-offer to the Respondent, thereby rejecting the offer of part-payment. Even if the offer of part-payment had been accepted, part-payment of a debt is not valid consideration for waiving the balance of that debt. There was, therefore, no concluded agreement between the parties with respect to part-payment of the amount due.'

(2) **Order of submissions**: Present your submissions in a logical order. Where the moot problem question specifically provides you with the grounds of appeal, deal with each ground of appeal in the order that it appears in the moot problem question (unless you have a good reason for not doing so). If the moot problem question does not specifically provide you with the grounds of appeal, consider dealing with each ground of appeal in the order of the trial judge's findings.

The order in which you present each legal issue within each ground of appeal is more flexible and is something that you should agree as a team. You may find that your submissions are best presented in a particular sequence (this approach is most effective when later submissions build on earlier ones). Alternatively, you may choose to present your strongest submission first, followed by weaker submissions (this approach is most effective when submissions are alternatives to each other).

---

[12] *Mespil Limited v Capaldi* [1986] ILRM 373 (SC) 376 (Henchy J).

(3) Complementing (not competing) submissions and grounds of appeal: Your submissions should complement, rather than compete with, each other. Make sure that you carefully read your memorial in full to check that it presents as a coherent whole.

Including linking phrases between connected submissions is appropriate if you want the reader to consider two submissions together, or if you want to clarify the relationship between them. These linking phrases are helpful where one submission builds on a previous submission to reach your conclusion on a ground of appeal.

> **Example:**
>
> 'In addition ...' or
> 'Further to the above ...'.

If you are presenting submissions that are alternatives to each other, also ensure that this is made clear in your memorial. Alternative submissions present the reader with different routes that can be taken, each of which should lead to the same conclusion on a ground of appeal. This way, even if the reader does not agree with your first submission, this will not necessarily prevent him or her from agreeing with your second submission and so still agreeing with your conclusion on the ground of appeal.

> **Example:**
>
> 'In the alternative ...' or
> 'Alternatively ...'.

The grounds of appeal in a moot are themselves often argued as alternatives. In such circumstances, even if the reader disagrees with your submissions on the first ground of appeal, he or she is still able to consider your submissions on the second ground of appeal in determining whether the appeal should be allowed or dismissed.

D. Conclusion outlining what your client wants

End your memorial with an overall conclusion where you state clearly what your client wants the moot court to do. This conclusion should include a heading and numbered paragraphs. If you represent the Appellant, you will ask the moot court to allow the appeal.

> **Example:**
>
> **'C. Conclusion**
>
> 9.   For the reasons set out above, the Appellant respectfully submits that the Appellant's appeal be allowed.'

If you represent the Respondent, you will ask the moot court to dismiss the appeal.

> **Example:**
>
> **'C. Conclusion**
>
> 9.   For the reasons set out above, the Respondent respectfully submits that the Appellant's appeal be dismissed.'

Include the name of each member of your team at the end of the memorial. These names should be aligned to the right-hand side of the page, written in bold text and follow one below the other on separate lines.

> **Example:**
>
> **'Alex Brown**
> **Siobhan Smith'**

4.2.3 Additional considerations in a memorial

A. Use of headings

Include headings and sub-headings in your memorial as signposts to help guide the reader along the path that you have laid in your written submissions. This path begins with your introduction. It moves through the grounds of appeal and your submissions on each of those grounds. It culminates in your conclusion, as the statement of what your client wants the moot court to do. By including clear and relevant headings and sub-headings, you will make it easier for the reader to navigate your written submissions and to understand why you have reached your conclusion.

Rather than simply including neutral headings and sub-headings, consider using argumentative headings and sub-headings where you emphasise the argument that you will be making in the paragraphs that follow. These will highlight your client's position on the particular ground of appeal or the legal issue to be discussed.[13] In this way, you are using your headings and sub-headings to reinforce your submissions.

> **Example:**
>
> Rather than the heading for a ground of appeal being neutral, such as '**Part-payment of a debt**', clearly state your client's proposition on that ground of appeal, such as '**The offer of part-payment of the debt was never accepted by the Appellant**'.

B. Use of authority

(1) **The importance of authority**: Support each of your submissions with relevant authority.[14] Remember, it is not part of a mooter's function to opine on the law as the moot court is neither bound by, nor likely to be persuaded by, your opinion. Instead, you need to present relevant legal principles and demonstrate the correctness of these principles with reference to binding or persuasive authority.

When you refer to authority in your memorial, explain the legal principle that the authority establishes or confirms and why this authority is being relied on to support your submissions. It is no help to the reader if you simply refer to an authority out of context without explaining why it is relevant to your submissions.

Whenever you cite authority, make sure that you respect the hierarchy of sources of Irish law. Reflecting this, authority that your team refers to in your memorial should be the authority that is most likely to persuade the reader to agree with your submissions. Chapter 3 discusses how you can select authority to rely on.[15]

(2) **Unhelpful authority**: In the course of your research, you may come across authority that is unhelpful to one or more of your submissions. Before exchange of written submissions, you will not know whether your opponents have also found this authority. However, if a binding authority appears to directly contradict one of your submissions, then consider whether it should be addressed in your memorial—to ignore a glaringly obvious authority completely may mislead the moot court into

---

[13] Andrew Goodman, *Effective Written Advocacy: A Guide for Practitioners* (2nd ed, Wildy, Simmonds & Hill Publishing 2012) 60.

[14] See Chapter 2 for a discussion on the various sources of Irish law and Chapter 3 for a discussion on using those sources in your research.

[15] See Chapter 3 (Section 3.5).

believing that there is no authority against your submissions. Your role is to persuade the moot judges that notwithstanding this unhelpful authority, your submissions remain valid.

More typically, an unhelpful authority may be more marginally relevant to one of your submissions (rather than clearly contradicting them). In such circumstances, you do not necessarily have to deal with this authority in your memorial. However, do keep a note of it. You should then ensure that your submissions are sufficiently robust and supported by appropriate authority that any unhelpful authority will not undermine them, and that the omission of any such authority from your written submissions will not mislead the moot court. Be prepared to explain in your oral submissions why the moot judges should not follow an unhelpful authority.[16]

C. Use of footnotes and citations

The rules of the moot may specify whether citations should be included in footnotes or within the body of your written submissions. In the absence of such information, your team should decide which approach you will be taking and you should follow this approach consistently throughout your memorial.

Footnotes or in-text citations should never include substantive arguments.[17] They should be used only for citing authorities referred to in the text, or for cross-referencing to another part of your memorial. When citing authorities, ensure that footnotes and in-text citations are as precise and as complete as possible. This includes pinpointing the exact page or paragraph numbers of any identified sections, passages or quotations. It is, for example, unhelpful to the reader if you cite only the first page of a law report where a case is reported, without also identifying the page or paragraph number of a referenced passage. Section 4.6.1 provides more information about the format of citations.

4.2.4 What your memorial should not include

There are a number of things that you would not expect to see in a memorial:

---

[16] See Chapter 5 (Sections 5.3 and 5.4) for more information on how to deal with authority in the context of your oral submissions.

[17] Andrew Goodman, *Effective Written Advocacy: A Guide for Practitioners* (2nd ed, Wildy, Simmonds & Hill Publishing 2012) 53.

(1) Rebuttal of your opponents' submissions

- As there is typically simultaneous exchange of written submissions between parties, you will not have seen your opponents' written submissions before you finalise your own. As a result, you cannot know what submissions your opponents will be making. Do not try to second-guess your opponents' submissions by speculatively addressing these in your memorial.
- Instead, try to make your own submissions as persuasive as possible.

(2) Citation of multiple similar authorities on the same submissions

- A memorial should persuade the reader as to the correctness of your submissions. The best way to do this is to rely on authorities that support these submissions. However, rather than citing multiple authorities that all equally support a submission, cite the authority or authorities that most clearly and convincingly support that submission.
- Prioritise quality of authorities, not quantity.

(3) Excessive discussion of the facts of the moot

- While a memorial's introduction should provide necessary information on the facts of the moot, do not waste your word count or page limit by going into excessive and unnecessary detail about those facts.

(4) Waffle

- A memorial should demonstrate that you can take large amounts of information and distil it into clear and logical submissions. You will not have the word count or page limit to include rambling, unfocused discussions. When drafting your memorial, always consider what each sentence is contributing to your client's overall argument.

4.3 List of authorities

The second element of your written submissions is a list of authorities. This is where you set out the authorities that your team is relying on to support your submissions, together with the full citation for those authorities. The rules of the moot may require, or your team may think that it is helpful, to include this list in your written submissions.

Do not be tempted to include decoy authorities or to purposely exclude key authorities to try to throw your opponents off. Your list of authorities should include all of the authorities that you intend to rely on in your oral submissions. If, following exchange of your written submissions, you decide that you will no longer be relying on an authority in your list of authorities or that you want to rely on a new authority that was published following exchange, it is good mooting practice to notify the moot's organiser (who can inform the moot judges and your opponents).

A list of authorities should start on a new page, after the conclusion of your memorial.[18] It should include a heading that is centred on the page and written in bold uppercase letters. Within the list of authorities, include a sub-heading for each different type of authority (for example, one for any legislation and one for any cases). List the authorities under each sub-heading in a logical order (for example, chronologically or alphabetically). Each authority should follow the same citation method as was used in your memorial.

Depending on any specific requirements set out in the rules of the moot, you may also want to consider dividing legislation and cases by jurisdiction, with Irish authorities listed first under each sub-heading, then any English authorities, and finally authorities from other jurisdictions. While not necessary, including the name or initials of the courts that decided any cases that you have included should demonstrate to the moot judges that you are aware of the hierarchy of courts.

Set out below is an abridged example of a list of authorities.

Example:

LIST OF AUTHORITIES ON BEHALF OF THE APPELLANT

Legislation:
1. European Communities (General Food Law) Regulations 2007, SI 2007/747.

Cases:
Ireland
1. *O'Mahony v Promontoria (Gem) DAC* [2018] IEHC 63 (HC).
2. *Harrahill v Swaine* [2015] IECA 36 (CoA).
3. *Barge Inn Ltd v Quinn Hospitality Irl Operations 3 Ltd* [2013] IEHC 387 (HC).

---

[18] If you are only required to submit a list of authorities and not a memorial, the format for that list of authorities would be the same (subject to the rules of the moot).

4. *Tansey v the College of Occupational Therapists Ltd* [1995]
    2 ILRM 601 (HC).
5. *Mespil Limited v Capaldi* [1986] ILRM 373 (SC).
6. *Billings v Arnott* (1945) 80 ILTR 50 (HC).

England and Wales
1. *Beechwood House Publishing v Guardian Products Ltd* [2010]
    EWPCC 12 (Patents County Court of England and Wales).
2. *Jones v Padvatton* [1969] 2 All ER 616 (CoA).
3. *Brogden v Metropolitan Railway Co* (1877) 2 AC 666 (HoL).

Canada
1. *Saint John Tug Boat Co v Irving Refinery Ltd* [1964] SCR 614
    (SC).

Unless a maximum number of authorities is set by the rules of the moot (in which case you must adhere to this cap), there is no strict limit on how many authorities each team can rely on in a moot. A total of between six and twelve good quality authorities should usually be sufficient, although this number will vary depending on the complexity of the moot problem question and the number of grounds of appeal.

4.4 Following exchange of written submissions

4.4.1 Dealing with your opponents' written submissions

After exchange of written submissions, the amount of time that you are given to read your opponents' written submissions will be dictated by the rules of the moot. In mooting competitions, you may be given only a few minutes to read your opponents' written submissions, whereas in a mooting module, you may be given several days. What you do following exchange of written submissions will depend on the amount of time that you are given to read these submissions.

If you receive your opponents' written submissions one or more days in advance of oral submissions:

    (a) read their memorial thoroughly and note each of their submissions. Make a note of the strengths and weaknesses of these submissions. Consider how you will respond to each submission in oral submissions.[19] If possible, support each of your responses with appropriate authority; and

---

[19] See Chapter 5 (Section 5.4) for more information on how to deal with your opponent's authorities in the context of your oral submissions.

(b) make a note of every authority that they are relying on. If there are any authorities that you have not read, read these and consider the impact of these authorities on your submissions (determine whether there is anything in these authorities that helps or undermines your submissions). Consider how you will address each of these authorities in oral submissions.[20]

If you receive your opponents' written submissions on the day of oral submissions:

(a) you may not have a chance to conduct further research. As such, you will need to be particularly focused on trying to determine in advance the submissions that your opponents are likely to make and the authorities that they are likely to rely on. Consider how you would respond to each possible submission and how you will address each potential authority in oral submissions; and

(b) once you receive your opponents' memorial, read it and note their submissions and authorities. Note the strengths and weaknesses of these and the extent to which you have already anticipated the submissions that they have made. Consider how you will respond to any additional submissions in oral submissions.

4.4.2 Dealing with an error in your written submissions

Once you have exchanged written submissions with your opponents, you may realise that your written submissions contain an error. This could take the form of a typographical error in your drafting or a more fundamental error in one of your submissions.

(1) **Minor errors**: Where the error is typographical, such as a spelling or grammatical mistake, there is little that you can do following exchange, and there is generally no need for you to highlight the mistake in oral submissions. If a moot judge passes comment, provide a brief apology for the mistake and move on. If an error is typographical, but could lead to confusion (for example, an incorrect citation of an authority), correct this mistake during your oral submissions, provide a brief apology and move on. These types of errors are not fundamental, but they reflect the importance of proofreading your written submissions.

(2) **More serious errors**: A more serious error in a moot is if you realise that one of your submissions is unarguable in

---

[20] ibid.

oral submissions. You may realise this after reading your opponents' written submissions, or if you come across an authority that you had missed or misunderstood. In such circumstances, remain calm and discuss your submissions with your teammate. You may decide that a submission is still valid or that it can at least be presented in oral submissions in a way that avoids or reframes the part of the argument that you are concerned about. If, however, you decide that a submission cannot be argued, graciously acknowledge this in oral submissions and move on. When doing so, simply note to the moot judges that you will not be pursuing the relevant submission.

Another serious error that you must try to avoid is missing a deadline for exchanging or submitting your written submissions. If this does happen, contact the moot's organiser as soon as possible so that he or she can let your opponents and the moot judges know. Missing a deadline may affect the mark that your team receives for the moot.

4.5 Template: written submissions

Set out below is a template for a moot's written submissions including a cover page, memorial and list of authorities. Information to be completed is included in square brackets and guidance notes are included in italics.

[NAME OF THE COURT WHERE THE APPEAL IS BEING HEARD]

BETWEEN:

[NAME OF APPELLANT]

Appellant

-and-

[NAME OF RESPONDENT]

Respondent

MEMORIAL ON BEHALF OF THE [APPELLANT]/[RESPONDENT]

Team [X], Group [Y]

—- page break —-

A. **Introduction**[21]

1. This is an appeal by the Appellant, [*insert full name*] against the decision

---

[21] Length to be adjusted to reflect permitted word count or page limit.

of [*insert name of trial judge*] in the [*trial court*] finding [*brief description of what the trial judge held*].

2. The facts of the case are summarised as follows [*brief summary of facts, consider how you can make these persuasive*].

3. In the [*trial court*], [*insert name of trial judge*] held that [*details of what the trial judge concluded and why he or she reached this decision*].

4. The [Appellant]/[Respondent] submits that:/The Appellant appeals on the following grounds:/The Appellant's grounds of appeal are without basis for the following reasons:

    4.1 [*Details of the first ground of appeal from your client's perspective*].

    4.2 [*Details of the second ground of appeal from your client's perspective*].

5. The [Appellant]/[Respondent] respectfully asks the Court to [allow]/[dismiss] the appeal.

B. [Insert argumentative heading for the first ground of appeal]

6. [*State your client's perspective on the first ground of appeal*].[*If you have space, consider summarising each of your submissions*].

7. [*Insert argumentative sub-heading for your submission on the first legal issue to be addressed under this ground of appeal*].

    7.1 [*Issue*] [*Outline first legal issue*].

    7.2 [*Law*] [*Go through the applicable law and authorities being relied on*].

    7.3 [*Application*] [*Apply the law to the facts of the moot*].

    7.4 [*Conclusion*] [*Tie the law and the facts to the legal issue raised*].

8. [*Insert argumentative sub-heading for your submission on the second legal issue to be addressed under this ground of appeal*].

    8.1 [*Issue*] [*Outline second legal issue*].

    8.2 [*Law*] [*Go through the applicable law and authorities being relied on*].

    8.3 [*Application*] [*Apply the law to the facts of the moot*].

    8.4 [*Conclusion*] [*Tie the law and the facts to the legal issue raised*].

[*Repeat for any more legal issues raised by the first ground of appeal*].

9. [*Conclude the first ground of appeal*].

C. [Insert argumentative heading for the second ground of appeal]

10. [*State your client's perspective on the second ground of appeal*]. [*If you have space, consider summarising each of your submissions*].

11. [*Follow same process as for the first ground of appeal (ie repeat discussion of legal issues as set out in paragraphs 7 to 9 above, but for the legal issues raised by the second ground of appeal)*].

D. Conclusion

12. For the reasons set out above, the [Appellant]/[Respondent] respectfully submits that the Appellant's appeal be [allowed]/[dismissed].

[first mooter's name]
[second mooter's name]

—- page break —-

**LIST OF AUTHORITIES ON BEHALF OF THE [APPELLANT]/
[RESPONDENT]**

EU Law:
[insert any EU law relied on]

Constitution:
[insert any provisions of the Constitution relied on]

Legislation:
[insert any legislation relied on]

Cases:
Ireland
[insert any Irish cases relied on]

England and Wales
[insert any English and Welsh cases relied on]

[insert cases from any other jurisdictions relied on]

[insert other authorities]

4.6 Legal writing skills for mooting

Attention to detail and presenting your work in an appropriate written format are central skills of a lawyer and, therefore, of a mooter. This book does not give an exhaustive overview of legal writing skills, but it highlights some areas of legal writing that are particularly relevant to a mooter.

4.6.1 Citing authorities in written submissions

Correctly cite your authorities. These citations should provide enough detail to allow the reader to find the relevant authority and to pinpoint any specific quotations that you include, or passages that you paraphrase, in your written submissions. Making a note of complete citations of authorities as you conduct your research will make this part of the mooting process easier.

> **Practical Tip:**
>
> So often, mooters include a general citation for an authority, but do not then also pinpoint the specific page, paragraph or section number that they are relying on. Any time you quote from, or paraphrase the text of, an authority you should: (1) cite that authority; and (2) try to pinpoint the place in the authority to which your citation is referring.

There are different methods for citing material referred to in your written submissions. The first thing you must do when preparing your written submissions is to check whether the rules of the moot require mooters to follow a particular method of citation. If these rules do not specify a method of citation to use, choose a method of citation that is widely accepted. For the purposes of this book, the OSCOLA Ireland method of citation is followed. The citations below are an example of how you would cite certain types of material in your written submissions using OSCOLA Ireland. These examples do not cover all materials that you may need to cite. Because of this, you should obtain the full citation guide for OSCOLA Ireland[22] and follow it as you draft your written submissions.

A. EU law[23]

> Treaties:
> **Legislation title | [year] | OJ | series type | issue | / | first page, | pinpoint [if relevant].**
>
> Example: Consolidated Version of the Treaty on European Union [2012] OJ C326/13, Art 5.
>
> Other EU law legislation (such as Regulations):
> **Legislation type | number | title | [year] | OJ L | issue | / | first page, | pinpoint [if relevant].**
>
> Example: Council Regulation (EU) 1215/2012 of 12 December 2012 on jurisdiction and the recognition and enforcement of judgments in civil and commercial matters (recast) [2012] OJ L351/1, Art 45.

---

[22] OSCOLA Ireland (2nd edn 2016) ('OSCOLA Ireland') and the related quick reference citation guide can be downloaded for free at: <http://legalcitation.ie/> accessed 1 December 2018.

[23] OSCOLA Ireland, section 2.5.

B. Irish Constitution[24]

> **Article OR Art | article number. | section number. | sub-section number°.**
>
> Example: Art 15.2.1°.

- If it is not obvious from the text, consider including reference to 'of the Constitution' in the citation.
- Capitalise the 'A' when you are referring to one or more specific Articles within the Constitution.

C. Primary legislation[25]

> **Short title | year, | s/sch/pt [space] | pinpoint [if relevant].**
>
> Example: Companies Act 2014, s 228(1)(f).

- Cite primary legislation by its short title and year.

D. Secondary legislation[26]

> **Name | year, | SI [year/serial number], | reg/r/art [space] | pinpoint [if relevant].**
>
> Example: Companies (Accounting) Act 2017 (Commencement) Order 2017, SI 2017/246, art 4.

- Cite secondary legislation by its name, year and (after a comma), its statutory instrument number.

E. Irish case law[27]

> For cases with both a neutral citation and law report citation:
> *Name of case in italics* **(if not given in text) | [year] | court | case number | pinpoint [if relevant and available], | [year] OR (year) | volume | law report (abbreviation) | page number of first page of case(,) | pinpoint (surname of judge CJ/J/P)[if relevant].**
>
> Example: *Bederev v Ireland* [2015] IECA 38 [3], [2015] 1 ILRM 301 [3] (Hogan J).

---

[24] OSCOLA Ireland, section 2.1.
[25] OSCOLA Ireland, section 2.3.
[26] OSCOLA Ireland, section 2.4.
[27] OSCOLA Ireland, section 2.2.

For older cases with no neutral citation:
> *Name of case in italics* **(if not given in text) | [year] OR (year) | volume | law report (abbreviation) | page number of first page of case | (court) | pinpoint (surname of judge CJ/J/P) [if relevant].**

> Example: *Tansey v College of Occupational Therapists Ltd* [1995] 2 ILRM 601 (HC) 615 (Murphy J).

For cases with only a neutral citation:
> *Name of case in italics* **(if not given in text) | [year] | court | case number | pinpoint (surname of judge CJ/J/P) [if relevant and available].**

> Example: *O'Mahony v Promontoria (Gem) DAC* [2018] IEHC 63.

For unreported cases (without a neutral citation):
> *Name of case in italics* **(if not given in text) | (initials of court, date) | pinpoint (surname of judge CJ/J/P) [if relevant and available].**

> Example: *Flynn v District Judge Kirby* (HC, 19 December 2000).

- Neutral citations identify the year of the judgment, the court where the case was heard and the case number.
- Older cases may not have a neutral citation and instead are unreported or reported in one of the law reports (such as the Irish Reports or the Irish Law Reports Monthly). Newer cases may only have a neutral citation. Some cases have both types of citation (in which case, you should cite both).
- There are no official law reports in Ireland (although the Irish Reports and the Irish Law Reports Monthly are regarded as the most authoritative reports).
- If a judgment has numbered paragraphs, your pinpoint should refer to a specific paragraph in square brackets (with no comma before the pinpoint). If a judgment has no paragraph numbers, but does have page numbers, your pinpoint should refer to a specific page (only include a comma if the pinpoint follows directly after another number). If a judgment has no paragraph or page numbers, do not include a pinpoint.
- If you are quoting from a judgment, identify the judge who delivered the judgment as follows: 'pinpoint (surname of judge CJ/J/P)'.

F. Foreign cases[28]

Cite a foreign case in the same way that it is cited in its home jurisdiction. For English cases, you may find it helpful to refer to the OSCOLA method of citation.[29] Judgments from English courts may be published in multiple law reports—the Law Reports series is regarded as the most authoritative and should be the law report cited, if available. If a case has not been reported in the Law Reports, the Weekly Law Reports or the All England Law Reports version can be cited.

G. Secondary sources[30]

Books:
> **Name of Author, | *Title of book in italics* | (edition, | publisher | year of publication) | pinpoint [if relevant].**

> Example: Paul A McDermott and James McDermott, *Contract Law* (2nd edn, Bloomsbury Professional 2017) 57.

Articles:
If the journal does not have volume numbers:
> **Name of Author, | 'title' | [year] | journal name or abbreviation | first page of article, | pinpoint [if relevant].**

> Example: William P Marshall, 'Bad Statutes Make Bad Law: Burwell v Hobby Lobby' [2014] Supreme Court Review 71, 73.

If the journal has volume numbers:
> **Name of Author, | 'title' | (year) | volume | journal name or abbreviation | first page of article, | pinpoint [if relevant].**

> Example: Robert Noonan, 'Stare decisis, Overruling, and Judicial Law-Making: the Paradox of the JC Case' (2017) 57 The Irish Jurist 119, 120.

---

[28] OSCOLA Ireland, section 1.4.

[29] The OSCOLA method of citation (on which OSCOLA Ireland is based) can be downloaded for free at: <www.law.ox.ac.uk/sites/files/oxlaw/oscola_4th_edn_hart_2012.pdf> accessed 1 December 2018. More information about OSCOLA can be found on the University of Oxford, Faculty of Law, 'OSCOLA' website: <www.law.ox.ac.uk/research-subject-groups/publications/oscola> accessed 1 December 2018.

[30] OSCOLA Ireland, section 3.

4.6.2 Legal writing in written submissions

A. *Refer to judges correctly*

In legal writing, judges are referred to by their surname followed by 'J', 'CJ' or 'P', as appropriate.

> **Example:**
>
> Mr Justice Frank Clarke, Chief Justice, is written as Clark CJ
> Mr Justice Peter Kelly, President of the High Court, is written as Kelly P
> Ms Justice Úna Ní Raifeartaigh is written as Ní Raifeartaigh J

B. *Keep your tone professional and unemotional*

Avoid using emotional or inflammatory language in legal writing, including in your written submissions.[31] This does not mean that you should not argue your client's case strongly and logically, but in doing so you must come across as calm, professional and in control of your emotions. As a result, avoid using words such as 'appalling' or 'outrageous'.

Legal writing should also avoid using clichés (such as 'the Respondent pulled the wool over the Appellant's eyes'), slang or other colloquial language. This type of casual language could detract from the strength of your submissions. While jargon (expressions used by a particular profession or group of people) has a place in legal writing, avoid using it in your written submissions unless the context of the moot suggests that such jargon would be appropriate. If you are in any doubt about the use of a particularly technical word or expression in your written submissions, consider providing an explanation of that word or expression the first time you use it.

C. *Do not write in the first person or present personal opinions*

In a moot you are advancing arguments on behalf of your client, not in your personal capacity. As a result, your written submissions should not express personal opinions and should avoid using first person pronouns such as 'I think ...', 'I believe ...' or 'I want

---

[31] In *Doherty v Government of Ireland* [2010] IEHC 369 [25], [2011] 2 IR 222 [25], Kearns P noted, and then sought to ignore, the 'hyperbole associated with many of the submissions advanced on behalf of both the applicant and the respondents is dispensed with in this case, particularly those on behalf of the respondents which suggested that it would "tear asunder" the tripartite division of powers under the Constitution ...'.

...'. Instead, you advance your client's arguments to the court using phrases such as 'the Appellant submits that ...', 'it is the Respondent's submission that ...', 'the Appellant respectfully asks that ...' or 'it is the Respondent's case that ...', or by simply stating (politely) what it is that your client wants.

D. Keep sentences short and simple

Good legal writing is precise, clear and unambiguous. Keeping your sentences short and your language simple should make your written submissions easier to read.[32] To achieve this, include one main idea in each sentence, rather than dealing with multiple ideas at the same time. Also consider how punctuation can be used to break down long sentences into sentences that are more accessible to the reader—a long sentence could, for example, be broken down into two shorter sentences, or a subsidiary point could be included within parenthesis to bring the main idea to the reader's attention.

Unnecessarily complicated words or old-fashioned phrases should also be avoided, as both reduce the readability of your legal writing. There are situations where a longer word is appropriate, but if a short, simple word can be used to convey an idea, then use that in preference to the longer word. For example, rather than using 'hereinafter', use 'below'; rather than using 'henceforth', use 'from now on'; and rather than using 'hereinbefore', use 'above'.

4.6.3 Spelling, grammar and punctuation in written submissions

A. Spelling: common spelling mistakes in written submissions

With spell checking functions now available on all word processing software, you should try to avoid misspelling words in your written submissions. In particular, make sure that you correctly spell the names of the parties to the moot, the name of the trial judge and any other key words included in the moot problem question. In addition to avoiding obvious spelling mistakes, also be conscious about how you spell words that are frequently confused.

Affect/Effect	<ul><li>'Affect' (typically a verb) means to influence or make a difference to something.</li><li>'Effect' (typically a noun) means a result.</li></ul>

---

[32] Iain Morley, *The Devil's Advocate* (3rd edn, Sweet & Maxwell 2015) 101.

Judgment/ Judgement	• 'Judgment' means a pronouncement of a judge. • 'Judgement' means someone's opinion.
Its/It's	• 'Its' is the possessive of 'it' and is an exception to the apostrophe rule referred to below. • 'It's' is a contraction of 'it is' and should be avoided.
Practice/Practise	• 'Practice' (noun) is used in the context of a lawyer's practice, to describe the application of an idea, method or belief, or a way of doing something. • 'Practise' (verb) is used in the context of 'to practise something'.
Principal/Principle	• 'Principal' means main or most important. • 'Principle' means rule, idea or belief.
Advice/Advise	• 'Advice' (noun) means a recommendation or opinion. • 'Advise' (verb) means to offer a recommendation or opinion.
Council/Counsel	• 'Council' (noun) means a meeting or grouping. • 'Counsel' (verb) means to offer advice. • 'Counsel' (noun) means someone offering advice.
Their/There/They're	• 'Their' is the possessive of 'they'. • 'There' indicates direction or position. It is also used to introduce a noun or clause. • 'They're' is a contraction of 'they are' and should be avoided.

B. Grammar: common grammar mistakes in written submissions

(1) **Not ensuring subject-verb agreement and pronoun-antecedent agreement**: Make sure that within a sentence: (1) the verb agrees in number with the subject; and (2) the pronoun agrees in number and gender with the word that the pronoun refers back to (the antecedent).

• If the subject is singular, the verb must be singular; if the subject is plural, the verb must be plural.

• If the antecedent is singular and female, the pronoun

must be singular and female; if the antecedent is plural and male, the pronoun must be plural and male.

> **Example:**
>
> Subject-verb agreement
> • Incorrect: 'The **offer** of part-payment of a debt **were** never accepted.'
> • Correct: 'The **offer** of part-payment of a debt **was** never accepted.'
>
> Pronoun-antecedent agreement
> • Incorrect: 'The **Appellant** submits that **they** never accepted the offer ...'
> • Correct: 'The **Appellant** submits that **he/she/it** [delete as appropriate] never accepted the offer ...' as 'Appellant' is singular.

(2) **Using contractions**: Contractions (where two words are shortened to form a single word divided by an apostrophe, such as 'it's', 'you're', 'haven't') have no place in legal writing and should not be used in your written submissions.

C. Punctuation

You may consider the correct use of punctuation to be something that is so basic that it no longer requires active consideration in the context of your legal writing. It is precisely for that reason that you will be expected to use punctuation correctly in your written submissions. When proofreading your written submissions pay close attention to your use of punctuation.

(1) **Full Stops**: Use full stops to manage sentence length. If a long sentence can more easily be read as two shorter sentences, use a full stop to divide it in two. If you are including a footnote at the end of a sentence, the footnote mark should be included after the full stop. Each footnote should itself end with a full stop.

(2) **Commas**: Commas are useful tools for making your legal writing more readable. They can be used in a number of situations:
   • to separate text that could otherwise be included in parenthesis. If using commas for this purpose, include a comma immediately before and immediately after the text that you want to separate;

Using parenthesis: 'After finishing this set up Mr Sigg (who works for the Appellant) saw a case of champagne ...'

Using commas: 'After finishing this set up Mr Sigg, who works for the Appellant, saw a case of champagne ...'

- for clarity, where the meaning of the sentence would be unclear without the comma;
- before certain conjunctions ('and', 'but', 'for', 'or', 'so', 'nor', 'yet') to separate two independent clauses;
- to separate elements in a list of three or more items;
- to separate adjectives;
- before a quotation included within a sentence; or
- to separate introductory or contrasting elements in a sentence.

Separating introductory elements: 'While no one replied to this gesture, a week later the network was calibrated.'

Separating contrasting elements: 'The Appellant's business is small, but ambitious.'

(3) **Colons and semi-colons**: Colons introduce a pause between related information. In this way, colons can be used to introduce a list of items, a quotation or an explanation of an earlier statement.

'The Appellant appeals on the following grounds: (1) no offer of part-payment was accepted ...'

Like colons, semi-colons introduce a pause between related information. Semi-colons can be used to separate items in a list (but never to introduce a list), or in circumstances where the elements on either side of the semi-colon could be read as independent sentences.

'The Appellant never accepted the Respondent's offer of part-payment; instead, the Appellant made a counter-offer.'

(4) **Apostrophes**: In legal writing, apostrophes should only be used to indicate possession. If the subject is singular, the apostrophe is placed before the 's'.

> **Example:**
>
> 'The Appellant's agreement ...'

If the subject is plural, the apostrophe is placed after the 's'.

> **Example:**
>
> 'The parties' disagreement on the nature of the agreement ...'

Apostrophes should not be used to indicate that something is plural, nor should they be used to form a contraction.

(5) **Quotation marks**: Whenever you include a direct quotation of up to three lines in your written submissions (for example, a statement from a judgment in another case), surround that quotation by single (' ') or double (" ") quotation marks. Whichever type of quotation marks you choose, use them consistently throughout your written submissions. A quotation of more than three lines should be presented as an indented paragraph without quotation marks. Each direct quotation should, if possible, be followed with a citation pinpointing where in an authority the particular quotation has been taken from.

(6) **Other punctuation**: In legal writing, limit your use of more informal punctuation, such as exclamation marks. Questions expressed as interrogatives that end with a question mark are also generally not appropriate in legal writing (for example: 'Surely that cannot be right?').

(7) **Capitalisation**: Incorrect use of capital letters is a frequent error made by mooters in written submissions. Proper nouns (such as the name of a person, place, court or organisation) should generally be capitalised. When proofreading your written submissions, do a word search for any proper nouns used and ensure these are correctly and consistently capitalised.

Words that you have defined in your written submissions (for example, the 'Agreement') should also be consistently capitalised. If you capitalise a word that is not a proper noun, ensure that you have previously defined it in your written submissions.

4.6.4 Proofread your work

Although proofreading your work will be the last thing that you do before exchanging your written submissions, it is a vital stage in preparing for a moot. It is also a stage that is so often rushed, or missed completely, by mooters. Proofreading helps to prevent your hard work from being overshadowed by careless errors.

When you proofread your written submissions, look carefully for spelling or grammatical mistakes, inconsistent references to people, courts or concepts, formatting errors and inconsistent use of capitalisation. You should also check your citations to ensure these are both correct and consistently presented.

4.7 Chapter summary

1. The rules of a moot may provide that each team should prepare and exchange written submissions. While the exact format of these written submissions will vary between moots, they are often comprised of a memorial (or similar document) and/or a list of authorities.

2. A memorial sets out your client's arguments (known as submissions) on each ground of appeal. You will use this document to set out the submissions that your team will be making during oral submissions.

3. These submissions should be supported by appropriate authority that establishes or confirms the applicable legal principles.

4. A list of authorities sets out the authorities that your team is relying on in your submissions.

5. Your written submissions should be well presented and use appropriate language—do a final proofread of your written submissions before exchange to catch mistakes or inconsistencies.

Chapter 5

Oral Submissions: Preparation

5.1 Introduction

5.1.1 What are oral submissions?

Your output in a moot will usually take two forms: written submissions and oral submissions. Oral submissions take place after exchange of written submissions and they may be the part of the moot that you are the most worried about. Unlike written submissions, where one set of submissions is prepared per team, members of a team will speak individually during oral submissions.

Oral submissions are where you can really stand out in a moot. Use your oral submissions as an opportunity to demonstrate the quality of your research and legal reasoning, and to actively work to persuade the moot judges as to the superiority of your submissions. If you are concerned about your oral submissions, there are two things to be mindful of:

- your oral submissions are something that you have a degree of control over. You can prepare for, and practise, your oral submissions to help you to maintain control; and
- while some people are more comfortable with oral advocacy than others, behind gifted advocates there is often a great deal of work. Do not assume that this is something that you cannot do, just because you are nervous about it—with practice and preparation, you can succeed in this part of a moot.

This chapter guides you through the stages of a moot's oral submissions and provides you with information to help you to prepare these submissions. Chapter 6 discusses additional points and skills to consider so that you can demonstrate your abilities as an advocate when you are in the moot court.

5.1.2 Role of each party

As a general rule, two mooters will speak for each side in a moot. You will be representing the same client as you were when you prepared your written submissions.[1] Depending on the structure of the moot problem question, you should typically be able to divide the grounds of appeal evenly between mooters. It will then be for your team to determine which mooter addresses which ground or grounds of appeal in oral submissions. Unless each mooter has researched and prepared written submissions for all grounds of appeal equally, you are likely to feel most comfortable taking the grounds of appeal that you were primarily responsible for in the research and writing stages of the moot.

In oral submissions, counsel for the Appellant opens the moot. This is because the Appellant is the party bringing the appeal and so it is for counsel for the Appellant to explain why the moot is taking place. In an Irish moot, the mooters will then typically speak in the following order (this assumes there are one ground of appeal per mooter):

1. Counsel 1[2] for the Appellant takes the first ground of appeal;
2. Counsel 2 for the Appellant takes the second ground of appeal;
3. Counsel 1 for the Respondent takes the first ground of appeal;
4. Counsel 2 for the Respondent takes the second ground of appeal;
5. rebuttal by counsel for the Appellant; and
6. if permitted by the rules of the moot, surrebuttal by counsel for the Respondent to respond to points raised by counsel for the Appellant in rebuttal.

Once all parties have spoken, the moot judges will give their judgment.

---

[1] As noted previously, some mooting competitions require you to be able to represent either side in oral submissions, but in such circumstances, you will also generally have prepared written submissions for both sides.

[2] As noted in Chapter 1, the rules of the moot may refer to Counsel 1 as 'lead' or 'senior' counsel and Counsel 2 as 'junior' counsel.

> **Practical Tip:**
>
> While counsel for the Appellant opens the moot, the rules of the moot or the moot judges on the day of the moot may stipulate that all arguments with respect to each ground of appeal will be heard in one go—this means that Counsel 1 for the Appellant will present submissions on the first ground of appeal, followed by Counsel 1 for the Respondent. Counsel 2 for the Appellant will then present submissions on the second ground of appeal, followed by Counsel 2 for the Respondent. This should not affect how you prepare for your oral submissions.

5.1.3 Timing in oral submissions

The length of each mooter's oral submissions will be determined by the rules of the moot. This could be anywhere from as little as five minutes up to 25 minutes or more per mooter in some mooting competitions.[3] The rules of the moot should also confirm whether the timer will or will not be stopped for judicial interventions.[4]

You will usually receive a warning (either from a moot judge or the court clerk) when you have a specified number of minutes or seconds left to speak (for example, when you have one minute left) and again when you reach the end of your allotted speaking time. Pay close attention to these warnings. You may also want to place your own timer on the desk in front of you (this should not be your mobile phone).

Information on timing is important in a moot. Poor time management suggests a failure to prepare and may mean that you are not able to present all of your submissions.

---

[3] By way of example, both the National Moot Court Competition and the Silken Thomas National Moot Court Competition provide that each mooter will speak for seven minutes, while the Philip C Jessup International Moot Court Competition provides that each mooter will speak for between 20 and 25 minutes.

[4] Chapter 6 discusses how to approach judicial interventions in oral submissions. See Chapter 6 (Section 6.2).

> **Practical Tip:**
>
> Before you begin preparing for your oral submissions, confirm the following:
> - speaking time allotted for each mooter;
> - whether one mooter in each team will be allotted more time than the other;
> - whether the timer will be stopped for judicial interventions;
> - whether you will receive a warning before your time has elapsed (and if so, at what intervals); and
> - time allotted for rebuttal/surrebuttal.

(1) **If the timer is stopped for judicial interventions**: If the timer is stopped for judicial interventions, time taken for judicial comments and questions, and your responses to them, will not reduce the time that you have left to make your submissions. In such circumstances, give yourself a small timing margin to allow you to regain your composure if you stumble or lose your place in your submissions. If you structure your oral submissions so that you will be speaking for approximately 90 to 95 percent of the allotted time, then even if you do stumble or lose your place, you should have time to present your submissions without needing to rush.

(2) **If the timer is not stopped for judicial interventions**: It is common in moots for the timer not to be stopped for judicial interventions. In such circumstances, the timer will continue to run during judicial comments and questions, and your responses to them. Make sure that you have built in a reasonable timing margin to account for this.

Unfortunately, there is no way of determining in advance how many (or what type of) judicial interventions you will receive. If you structure your oral submissions so that you will be speaking for approximately 75 percent of the allotted time, this should give you enough time to adequately deal with judicial interventions, while still presenting your submissions as planned. Ultimately, it is important to be flexible and comfortable with your submissions as this should help you to adjust your presentation of these submissions in response to judicial interventions.

5.1.4 Aids for moot judges

Oral submissions that are clearly structured and easy for moot judges to follow will be more persuasive than ones that are equally correct about the law, but are rambling and confusing. There are a number of techniques that you can use to help moot judges during your oral submissions.

A. Road-mapping and signposting

An effective way of helping moot judges to follow your submissions is to present a roadmap of these submissions and then to signpost each element of that roadmap. This signposting should be done throughout your submissions. This will help the moot judges to understand the structure of your submissions as a whole and to follow your progression through these submissions.

> (a) At the beginning of your submissions, you will lay out the overall roadmap of your submissions by outlining what ground or grounds of appeal you will be addressing and what submissions you will be making.
> (b) As you begin and end each submission, you will signpost this to show the moot judges where you are in your roadmap. These submissions should, of course, mirror the submissions identified in your initial roadmap.
> (c) At the end of your submissions, you will signpost your conclusion and lead the moot judges to the end of your roadmap and the decision that your client wants (that is, to either allow or dismiss the appeal).

You may find this use of signposting repetitive, but it is an important element of oral submissions. It helps you to ensure that the moot judges are in no doubt about the structure of your submissions and where you are in these.

B. Linking and separating

Connected with the process of signposting is the manner in which you explain the relationship between two points or two submissions. Where you want to make it clear to the moot judges that two elements within your submissions are linked, make this clear by using linking phrases. These phrases demonstrate how the two elements are connected.

> **Example:**
>
> 'as a result'; 'in support of this submission'; 'in light of this authority'; or 'in addition'.

You may also want to highlight that two elements of your submissions are separate or are alternatives to each other. You do this by using separating phrases to indicate the end of one element and the start of another, or to show the moot judges that two elements are alternatives.

> **Example:**
>
> - **Separating elements**: '... that concludes my first submission ... If the court has no further questions, I shall proceed with my second submission'.
> - **Showing elements are alternatives**: 'in the alternative' or 'should the Court find that the authorities are against me with respect to my first submission, it is alternatively my second submission that ...'.

The relationship between elements of your submissions should be made obvious, rather than being left to the moot judges for them to make the relevant connections themselves.

C. Bundles

As you progress through your oral submissions, you will refer the moot judges to authorities that you are relying on. As discussed in Section 5.3.2, this reference may be to a specific section or passage in the text of the authority. A bundle is a file containing the text of the authorities that you will be referring to in your oral submissions and allows you to direct the moot judges to the relevant section or passage in question.

Bundles are generally not required for moots in Ireland, although they are commonly used in English moots, and they are required in real courts in Ireland.[5] Check the rules of the moot to determine whether bundles are required and, if so, who should receive a copy (this is usually the moot judges and your opponents). Even if a bundle is not required by the rules of the moot, your team may nevertheless decide to prepare one, so that you and the moot judges have a copy. If, however, your memorial already contains all of the quotations or passages that you will be referring to in your oral submissions, you may decide that a bundle is not needed.

(1) **Preparing a bundle**: If you do prepare a bundle, ensure that: (1) you prepare a sufficient number of copies; and (2) your bundle is well presented. Check the rules of the moot for instructions on how the bundle should be presented. In

---

[5] Bundles are referred to as 'books of authorities' in the Irish superior courts. See Practice Directions SC16: Conduct of proceedings in Supreme Court; Practice Directions CA06: Submissions, books of appeal and authorities in civil appeals; Practice Directions HC68: Written submissions.

the absence of these, the easiest way to neatly put together a bundle is to:

- print out (single-sided) the full text of each authority that you will be referring to (other than where this reference is to a passage from a book, in which case you should copy a sufficient number of pages on either side of the relevant passage to provide context);
- hole-punch each page;
- place each page in a ring-binder or lever arch file;
- separate documents with numbered tabs so that you can direct the moot judges to specific authorities by asking them to turn to a particular tab; and
- if you think it will help with navigating your bundle, number the bottom right of each page sequentially.

(2) **Including the correct authorities**: Authorities that you include in your bundle must be the same as those referred to in your written submissions—you should not generally add or remove authorities when preparing your bundle. For cases that you include in your bundle, copy the same version of the case as you referred to in your written submissions. For example, if an English case is reported in the All England Reports and the Weekly Law Reports, but you refer to the All England Reports version in your written submissions, then this is the version you should include in your bundle. For Irish cases with both a neutral citation and a law report citation, include only the law report version in your bundle.

(3) **Contents of your bundle**: Your bundle should, unless the rules of the moot provide otherwise, include the following documents:

(a) an index in which you set out the court in which the case is being heard, the name of the parties, the party on whose behalf the bundle is being served and the full citation of each authority included in the bundle. Set out below is a template bundle index;

[NAME OF THE COURT WHERE THE APPEAL IS BEING HEARD]

BETWEEN:

[NAME OF APPELLANT]

Appellant

-and-

[NAME OF RESPONDENT]

Respondent

**BUNDLE INDEX ON BEHALF OF THE
[APPELLANT]/[RESPONDENT]**

Contents	Tab Number	Page Number
Moot Problem Question	1	[...]
Memorial	2	[...]
[Citation of each authority]	3	[...]

    (b) an unmarked copy of the moot problem question;

    (c) your memorial; and

    (d) a copy of every authority that you intend on referring to in your oral submissions (this should align with the list of authorities that you exchanged with your opponents). Include authorities in your bundle in the order they appear in your memorial.[6]

5.2 Spoken conventions to be used throughout your oral submissions

In a moot, formality is key. Moots in Ireland are generally set in one of the superior courts and, like a barrister making submissions before a superior court, a mooter is expected to use specific words and phrases when addressing the moot court and those within it.

While specific expressions are used at each stage of your oral

---

[6] Please note that in the Irish superior courts, books of authorities should be arranged in the following order: (i) any relevant provisions from the Constitution; (ii) any relevant statutory provisions; (iii) Irish authorities set out in chronological order; (iv) any international authorities relied on, organised by jurisdiction, and within such jurisdictions, in chronological order; and (v) other materials, including extracts from text books and journals. Practice Directions SC16: Conduct of proceedings in Supreme Court [22]; Practice Directions HC68: Written submissions [5].

submissions, there are also expressions that you should use throughout your oral submissions. By using these expressions when mooting, you will demonstrate to the moot judges that you are taking the moot seriously and that you are treating those within the moot court with respect.

Situation	Expression to use	Discussion
When addressing a moot judge individually	• 'Judge'; or • 'A Bhreithimh'.[7] Example: 'Judge, I am grateful for your question ...'	Do not address moot judges by their first name. In an Irish moot, do not address a moot judge as 'your Honour', 'your Lordship' or 'your Excellency'.[8]
When addressing the moot court generally	• 'The Court'; or • 'An Chúirt'.[9] Example: 'If the Court has no further questions ...'	In an Irish moot, do not address the moot court generally as 'you', 'your Honours', 'your Lordships' or 'your Excellencies'.
When referring to the trial judge or a judge in an authority	• 'Judge [*surname*]'; or • (if the judge sits in one of the superior courts) 'Ms/Mr Justice [*surname*]'. Example: 'Judge O'Brien, sitting in the Cork Circuit Court held that ...' Example: 'Ms Justice O'Regan noted that ...'	Make sure that you also do not refer to a judge as '[*surname*] J'—this method of reference is *only* appropriate in written submissions. Avoid referring to judges as 'him' or 'her' or by their first name.

---

[7] The same mode of addressing individual judges is required in the superior courts: Rules of the Superior Courts Ord 119: Mode of address of judges; robes of bench and bar.

[8] The modes of address in English and other international moots differ from those in Irish moots. For more information on modes of address in English moot courts, see Eric Baskind, Mooting: The Definitive Guide (Routledge 2017) 176–181.

[9] The same mode of addressing the court generally is required in the superior courts: Rules of the Superior Courts, Ord 119: Mode of address of judges; robes of bench and bar.

Situation	Expression to use	Discussion
When referring to your teammate	• 'My co-counsel, Ms/Mr [*surname or full name*]'; or • 'Ms/Mr [*surname or full name*].'	Do not refer to your teammate by his or her first name. In Irish moots, practice is mixed when it comes to referring to your teammate as your 'learned' co-counsel. This terminology is not used in the Irish courts and so you may want to consider not using it in an Irish moot.
When referring to your opponents	• 'Counsel for the [Appellant] [Respondent], Ms/Mr [*surname or full name*]'; or • 'Ms/Mr [*surname or full name*]'; or • 'My friend, Ms/Mr [*surname or full name*].'	Do not refer to your opponents by their first names. As above, practice is mixed when it comes to referring to an opponent as your 'learned' friend. As this terminology is not used in Irish courts, you may want to consider not using it in an Irish moot.
When making a submission	• 'It is submitted that ...';[10] or • 'The [Appellant] [Respondent] submits/argues that ...'; or • 'It is my respectful submission that ...'; or • simply state what it is that you want to say.	Avoid expressing your personal opinions, such as 'I want'.
Whenever a moot judge provides you with assistance or confirms something	• 'Judge, I am obliged'; or • 'Judge, I am grateful'; or • 'Thank you, Judge.'	Always express gratitude to the moot judges if they provide you with assistance or guidance, or if they confirm something in response to your submissions.

---

[10] Use of the phrase 'it is submitted' is common in oral submissions, although you may find its excessive use makes your submissions appear a little passive.

5.3 Structure of your oral submissions

Each mooter's oral submissions will consist of:

- opening remarks;
- submissions on each of the grounds of appeal that the mooter is addressing; and
- a conclusion.

There are moderate, but important, differences between the expressions and content of oral submissions depending on which party you represent and whether you are Counsel 1 or Counsel 2. The following section will build your oral submissions, stage by stage. Section 5.5 provides a template summary of the expressions used by each mooter in oral submissions.

> **Practical Tip:**
>
> The expressions set out below are designed to be used as a guide, rather than a strict verbatim script to be read out in a moot court. Always read the rules of the moot to check whether the moot's organiser has provided any particular expressions for mooters to use.

5.3.1 Opening remarks

Your opening remarks are an opportunity for you to create a strong first impression on the moot judges. Though relatively formulaic in their structure, the length and content of your opening remarks will depend on the position that you occupy in the speaking order of mooters. Counsel 1 for the Appellant introduces the moot as a whole and, as a result, will have the longest opening remarks of all of the mooters.

A. Counsel 1 for the Appellant

(1) **Introduce the mooters and the parties**: If you are Counsel 1 for the Appellant, you will introduce all of the mooters appearing before the moot court. First, introduce yourself, unless the moot judges called you by name to give your submissions (in which case you do not need to re-introduce yourself). Then refer to each mooter by his or her surname or full name, in each case preceded by 'Mr' or 'Ms', as appropriate. Never introduce fellow mooters by their first name only. As you introduce each mooter, turn slightly towards him or her in acknowledgement. This shows respect and ensures that the moot judges know who each mooter is.

As Counsel 1 for the Appellant, you will also introduce the parties to the moot, identifying them as the Appellant and the Respondent. Include each party's full name (preceded by 'Ms' or 'Mr' if they are a person).

> **Example:**
>
> 'May it please the court, my name is Mr Alex Brown and, together with my co-counsel, Ms Siobhan Smith, I appear in this matter for the Appellant, Irish Sprinklers Limited. Ms Jade Byrne and Mr Robert Delany will appear in this matter for the Respondent, Pete's Cabbages DAC.'

(2) **Explain why the appeal is happening**: Introduce the moot and explain why the parties are before the moot judges. Here you will refer to the trial judge's decision, noting the title of the trial court and the name of the trial judge.

> **Example:**
>
> 'This is an appeal by the Appellant against the decision of Ms Justice Twomey sitting in the High Court, where it was held that the Appellant was not entitled to the balance due under a contract entered into between the parties.'

(3) **Provide a roadmap of the Appellant's submissions**: Counsel 1 for the Appellant will set out the overarching structure of the Appellant's submissions. This acts as the roadmap for the moot judges and signposts the grounds of appeal and the division of those grounds of appeal between the Appellant's counsel.

> **Example:**
>
> 'The Appellant appeals against the decision of the trial judge on two grounds. The first is that no offer of part-payment was accepted by the Appellant, as a result, the terms of the original contract remain enforceable and the Respondent's obligations have not yet been fully discharged. The second is that, in the alternative, the case of champagne and the network calibration represent elements of a new contract between the parties, leaving the Respondent's obligations under the original contract unaltered. I shall be addressing the Court on the first ground of appeal. My co-counsel, Ms Smith, will be addressing the Court on the second ground of appeal.'

(4) **Offer a summary of the facts**: The moot judges will almost certainly have read the moot problem question before the moot. Nevertheless, Counsel 1 for the Appellant should offer to provide the moot judges with a summary of the facts. Ask the moot judges if this summary would be helpful, rather than

launching into it automatically. The moot judges may say that they do or do not want this summary and you should adjust your submissions to reflect their preference.

When summarising the facts of the moot, avoid reading the moot problem question back to the moot judges. The moot judges want to see that you are able to accurately distil the facts that you were presented with into a short, helpful summary. Your summary should focus on facts that are key to the legal issues to be decided and provide a summary of the chronology of events leading up to the moot. As with the introduction to your memorial, you can use your opening remarks to subtly highlight facts that are most favourable to the Appellant's submissions. When you do so, make sure that you do not omit any critical facts or present the facts in a manner that is not truthful.

If the moot judges indicate at the start of the moot that they have read and are aware of the facts of the moot, then you do not need to offer to provide them with a summary.

Example:

'Would the Court find a brief summary of the facts of the case helpful?'
   [**Moot judge: 'Yes'**]
'Certainly Judge. The Appellant entered into a contract with the Respondent under which the Respondent agreed to pay €100,000 for the installation of a sprinkler system on the Respondent's farm and a follow-up network calibration. €70,000 of this amount was paid by the Respondent upfront and the sprinkler system was installed on schedule. The remaining €30,000 was due one week after the network calibration, although its payment was stated in the contract not to be contingent upon completion of the network calibration. In a telephone conversation prior to the network calibration, Mr Jonathan Kenny, finance director of the Respondent, indicated that the Respondent could only pay €10,000 of the balance remaining. In response to this, Ms Helen Duffy, the sole director of the Appellant, noted that in that case, the network calibration would be cancelled. Mr Kenny asked Ms Duffy not to be so rash before ending the call. Mr Kenny subsequently sent Ms Duffy an email, to which she did not reply, offering a case of champagne to whoever calibrated the network. The network was calibrated on schedule by a representative of the Appellant, who also took a case of champagne waiting at the reception desk of the Respondent. The Respondent transferred €10,000 to the Appellant's bank account, but failed to pay the balance remaining under the contract. The Appellant sued for the remaining balance, but at trial, Ms Justice Twomey held that

> the Appellant had accepted the Respondent's part-payment of the debt as, while paying part of a debt is not valid consideration for giving up the balance of a claim, the receipt of a new benefit or concession is consideration for settlement of the sum originally owed and the terms agreed between the parties were varied according.'
>
> OR
>> [**Moot judge: 'No, thank you'**]
>> 'Judge, I am obliged [*move on without providing a summary*]'

(5) **Confirm the moot judges have your written submissions/ bundle**: Before you begin your submissions on the first ground of appeal, check that the moot judges have received a copy of the Appellant's written submissions or, if applicable, bundle. If the moot judges confirm that they have, acknowledge this by thanking them for confirming. It is a good idea to bring extra copies of your written submissions and bundle with you to a moot so that you can hand these to the moot judges if they have not received them.

> **Example:**
>
> 'Before I move onto my submissions, may I confirm that the Court has received a copy of the Appellant's [written submissions] [bundle]?'
>> [**Moot judge: 'Yes'**]
>> 'Judge, I am obliged.'
>
> OR
>> [**Moot judge: 'No'**]
>> 'Thank you, Judge. If it would assist the Court, I have brought additional copies of these documents...'

B. Counsel 2 for the Appellant

Mooters other than Counsel 1 for the Appellant will have comparatively short opening remarks. There is no need to re-introduce the other mooters, the parties to the moot, the reason for the moot or its facts. If you are Counsel 2 for the Appellant, you will instead re-introduce yourself, acknowledge what your co-counsel has done before you and confirm the ground or grounds of appeal that you will be addressing.

> **Example:**
>
> 'May it please the court, my name is Ms Siobhan Smith. My co-counsel, Mr Brown, has addressed the Court on the first ground of appeal. I shall be addressing the court on the second ground of appeal that, in the alternative, the case of champagne and the network calibration represent elements of a new contract between the parties, leaving the Respondent's obligations under the original contract unaltered.'

C. Counsel 1 for the Respondent

Counsel 1 for the Respondent will re-introduce the members of the Respondent's team and set out the overarching structure for the Respondent's submissions. Counsel 1 for the Respondent should also check that the moot judges have received a copy of the Respondent's written submissions or, if applicable, bundle. If the moot judges confirm that they have, acknowledge this by thanking them for confirming. If they have not, provide them with the extra copies that you have brought with you.

> **Practical Tip:**
>
> When signposting the division of the grounds of appeal between the Respondent's counsel, Counsel 1 for the Respondent should try to present each ground of appeal in a manner that suggests it needs to be proven. You could do this by rephrasing the ground of appeal as an indirect question, beginning with the word 'whether'.

> **Example:**
>
> 'May it please the court, as has already been stated, my name is Ms Jade Byrne and, together with my co-counsel, Mr Robert Delany, I appear in this matter for the Respondent, Pete's Cabbages DAC. I shall be addressing the Court on the first ground of appeal; that is, whether the offer of part-payment was accepted by the Appellant. My co-counsel, Mr Delany, will be addressing the Court on the second ground of appeal; that is, whether the case of champagne and the network calibration represented elements of a new contract or were part of the original contract agreed between the parties. Before I move onto my submissions, may I confirm that the Court has received a copy of the Respondent's [written submissions] [bundle]?'
>   [**Moot judge: 'Yes'**]
> 'Judge, I am obliged.'
>
> OR
>   [**Moot judge: 'No'**]
> 'Thank you, Judge. If it would assist the Court, I have brought additional copies of these documents...'

D. Counsel 2 for the Respondent

If you are Counsel 2 for the Respondent, you will re-introduce yourself, acknowledge what your co-counsel has done before you and confirm the ground or grounds of appeal that you will be addressing.

> **Example:**
>
> 'May it please the court, my name is Mr Robert Delany. My co-counsel, Ms Byrne, has addressed the Court on the first ground of appeal. I shall be addressing the Court on the second ground of appeal; that is, whether the case of champagne and the network calibration represented elements of a new contract or were part of the original contract agreed between the parties.'

5.3.2 Submissions on each ground of appeal

The submissions on each ground of appeal are the most important section of your team's oral submissions. These submissions are your team's arguments on the legal issues raised by each ground of appeal and, reflecting the approach taken in your memorial, you will typically be making a number of submissions within each ground of appeal.[11] These submissions should work together to persuade the moot judges as to the legal correctness of your client's position on each ground of appeal. Unless permitted by the rules of the moot, you should avoid making submissions that were not addressed in your memorial. You can, however, develop or elaborate on submissions made in your memorial.

A. Structure of your submissions on each ground of appeal

Like your opening remarks, your submissions on each ground of appeal should generally follow a prescribed structure.

Begin by introducing your submissions on the first ground of appeal that you are addressing. This provides the moot judges with signposts along the roadmap of your submissions.

---

[11] This, of course, will depend on the disputed legal issues raised by the ground of appeal–there may be multiple legal issues that you need to address, or only one.

Example:

Counsel 1 for the Appellant:

'[If the court has no [further] questions on the facts of the case]*/ [If it pleases the court],** I shall proceed to my submissions with respect to the first ground of appeal. I shall be making two submissions: first, that there was no valid acceptance by the Appellant of the Respondent's offer of part-payment and second, in the alternative, even if the offer of part-payment had been accepted, part-payment of a debt is not valid consideration for waiving the balance of that debt.'

Counsel 2 for the Respondent:

'If it pleases the court, I shall proceed to my submissions with respect to the second ground of appeal. I shall be making two submissions: first, that in the course of the negotiations between the parties, there was a variation of the terms of the original contract, not the creation of a new contract and second, as a result of this variation, the Appellant is estopped from enforcing the original terms of the contract.'

* Include if the moot judges asked for a summary of the facts. If the moot judges asked you no questions during the summary of the facts, you can omit reference to 'further'.
** Include if no summary of the facts was required.

Once you have introduced your submissions on a ground of appeal, you will proceed to make each individual submission in turn. Signpost the beginning and end of each submission to remind the moot judges where you are in your roadmap.

Example:

'If it pleases the court, I shall begin with my first submission ... [*Go through submission in detail*]. That concludes my first submission .... If the court has no further questions, I shall proceed with my second submission ... [*Go through submission in detail*]. That concludes my second submission ....'

B. Content of your submissions on each ground of appeal

There is no single correct way of structuring submissions on each ground of appeal, and how you and your teammate structure these submissions is something that you should agree as a team. Ultimately, you want to persuade the moot judges to agree with your submissions, rather than those of your opponents.

As part of your oral submissions, you will present your positive case and your negative case. A 'positive case' is where you make arguments in your submissions that support your client's position with respect to a ground of appeal. A 'negative case' is where you rebut arguments made by your opponents in their submissions and challenge the consequences that your opponents say flow from these submissions. Counsel for both sides will present a positive case within their submissions on each ground of appeal. Following a normal speaking order in a moot, counsel for the Appellant will not have heard the Respondent's submissions by the time they speak. As a result, counsel for the Appellant should generally limit their negative case to the rebuttal portion of the moot. In contrast, counsel for the Respondent will have heard the Appellant's submissions by the time they speak. They should, therefore, rebut these submissions *within* their own main submissions on each ground of appeal.

(1) **Making your positive case within your submissions (counsel for the Appellant and counsel for the Respondent)**: Counsel for the Appellant and counsel for the Respondent will both assert what they say are the legal principles applicable to the moot, based on the authorities relied on:

- counsel for the Appellant must use the law to demonstrate that the appeal should be allowed; and
- counsel for the Respondent must use the law to demonstrate that the appeal should be dismissed.

The substance of your positive case on each ground of appeal will align closely with the submissions made in your memorial (as your memorial will only have dealt with your positive case). To make submissions within your positive case, you may choose to follow the 'ILAC' method: (1) signpost the legal Issue in dispute by stating your submission on that issue; (2) outline the applicable Law; (3) Apply the legal principle established by the authorities to the facts of the moot; and (4) Conclude your submission and signpost the beginning of your next submission. Following this method, therefore, for each submission:

(a) *Signpost the legal Issue in dispute by stating your submission on that issue*: You will already have outlined each submission earlier in your oral submissions. Nevertheless, re-state each submission as you come to it to act as a signpost.

Example:

Counsel 2 for the Respondent:

'If it pleases the court, I shall begin with my first submission, which is that in the course of the negotiations between the parties, there was a variation of the terms of the original contract, not the creation of a new contract.'

(b) *Outline the applicable Law*: Refer to the applicable legal principle underpinning your submission and the authorities that you are relying on to support your submission. This will be the most substantial part of each of your submissions. As was the case for your written submissions, you must demonstrate the legal correctness of your submission with reference to authority that the moot court is either bound by, or is likely to be persuaded by, never with reference to your opinion.

In a logical manner, take the moot judges through the authorities that you say support your submission. Ensure that you have considered the authoritative weight the moot judges are likely to give each authority and present authorities in an order that respects the hierarchy of sources of Irish law (starting with the most influential authority first):

I. **Cite the authority correctly:** The first time an authority is referred to in oral submissions, provide the moot judges with that authority's full citation. Make sure that you refer to your notes when providing the moot judges with this citation, rather than trying to memorise it.

   (i) **EU law, the Constitution, legislation or secondary sources**: These authorities are generally cited orally as you would write them, with any acronyms cited in full. For example: 'Companies (Accounting) Act 2017' becomes: 'the Companies Accounting Act two thousand and seventeen'.

   (ii) **Cases:** The manner in which you cite cases orally is different from how you cite them in writing.

   • The 'v' between the parties' names is cited orally as 'and', not 'vee' or 'versus'. If there is more than one party on either side of the 'v' in a written citation, the 'v' is cited orally as 'against'.

- For English criminal cases, the 'R' is cited orally as 'the Crown'. For Privy Council cases, the 'R' is cited orally as 'the Queen' or 'the King', depending on the reigning monarch at the time the case was decided.
- Orally cite law reports by their full name, rather than by their acronyms. For old cases or cases from foreign courts where you are unsure about the full name of the law report, look at the transcript of the case itself—this will usually contain the full name of the law report. Alternatively, you can search for the meaning of many legal acronyms in the Cardiff Index to Legal Abbreviations.[12]
- Set out below are examples of how written citations are cited orally.

Written citation	Oral citation
Irish Law Reports Monthly: *Tansey v College of Occupational Therapists Ltd* [1995] 2 ILRM 601.	'Tansey and College of Occupational Therapists Limited, reported in the second volume of the Irish Law Reports Monthly for nineteen ninety-five at page six hundred and one.'
Irish Reports: *O'Neill v Ryan* (No. 3) [1992] 1 IR 166.	'O'Neill and Ryan number three, reported in the first volume of the Irish Reports for nineteen ninety-two at page one hundred and sixty-six.'
Neutral Citation: *Moorview Development Ltd v First Active Plc* [2018] IESC 33.	'Moorview Development Limited and First Active Plc, which was the thirty-third judgment issued by the Supreme Court in two thousand and eighteen.'
English Criminal Case *R v Waterfield* [1963] 3 All ER 659	'The Crown and Waterfield, reported in the third volume of the All England Reports for nineteen sixty-three at page six hundred and fifty-nine.'

Once an authority has been cited in full by either party, you do not need to provide its citation again. Subsequent references can be to the case's full or shortened name (so long as the case can still be identified by the moot judges), for example:

---

[12] The Cardiff Index to Legal Abbreviations can be downloaded at: <www.legalabbrevs.cardiff.ac.uk> accessed 1 December 2018.

Tansey v College of Occupational Therapists Ltd could subsequently be referred to as 'the *Tansey* case, previously cited by Mr Delany'.

If you are relying on a citation already given by another mooter, make sure that mooter provided the moot court with the correct citation.

Practical Tip:

Be alert to the moot judges' responses to your citations. If a moot judge notes that you can dispense with formal citations, then from that point onwards you do not need to give the full citation of authorities. Instead, simply provide the full or shortened name of each authority and a pinpoint reference (such as a page or paragraph number) when you are quoting, or referring to a specific passage, from an authority.

After citing your first authority in full, you may also ask the moot judges for leave to dispense with formal citations for subsequent authorities as follows: '[May it please the Court]/[Judge], might I dispense with formal citations?' If the moot judges grant you leave to dispense with formal citations, continue to provide the full or shortened name of your authorities and any necessary pinpoint references.

II. **Offer a summary of the facts of any case referred to:** If the authority that you refer to is a case, ask the moot judges if a summary of the facts of that case would be helpful. The moot judges may or may not want a summary, but be prepared to provide one for every case that you refer to in your oral submissions. In order to provide this summary, and to answer judicial questions on the case, you should know the following information for each case that you refer to:
   - the material facts of the case;
   - the legal principle for which the case is authority (what was the ratio decidendi and what was said obiter?);
   - the court that handed down the judgment in the case and the extent to which the moot judges are bound by that judgment;
   - whether the case has been considered in subsequent cases and, if so, what did those cases say about it; and
   - the judges in the case and whether the judgment was unanimous or by majority (know which judges delivered the majority and dissenting

judgments and what these respective judgments were).[13]

When offering to provide a summary of the facts of a case, do not ask the moot judges if they are familiar with the facts of the case (you should assume that they are) but rather offer to remind them of those facts.

Example:

- 'Would it assist the Court to be reminded of the facts of this case?' or
- 'Would the Court like a brief summary of the facts of this case?'

Once a case has been introduced by either party, and the moot judges have either heard a summary of its facts or have confirmed they do not want a summary, you do not need to enquire again if they would like one.

III. **Explain the relevance of the authority:** When you refer to an authority, explain the relevance of the authority with respect to the submission you are making. It is not enough to make a passing reference to a case or piece of legislation—the moot judges need to know what legal principle the authority establishes or confirms and why it is relevant to your submission.

IV. **Take the moot judges to the specific passage or section of the authority:** In order to explain the legal principle that an authority establishes or confirms, and the relevance of that authority to your submissions, you will generally need to take the moot judges to a specific passage or section of that authority. This could involve quoting directly from the authority or summarising a passage where a legal principle is discussed. In doing so, pinpoint where in the authority you are referring the moot judges to by citing the relevant page, paragraph number, section or article.

When you refer to a passage in an authority,

---

[13] Particularly at competition level, moot judges may press you to summarise the judgments handed down by *each* judge in a particular case. It is prudent to know this information.

make sure that you do not take the passage out of context—this is where reading the whole case or reading around a legislative provision during your research is important.

V. **Read the relevant quotation:** Quotations, particular those from cases, can be very effective in your oral submissions.

If the moot involves the preparation of bundles or the particular quotation has been set out in your memorial, you should explain how the moot judges can find this quotation in the documents that you have provided to the moot court. Once you have identified how the moot judges can find the relevant quotation, wait until they have found it before reading the passage. If the passage that you want to refer to is short (less than seven lines long), you can read it out for the moot judges. If the passage is more than seven lines long and the moot judges have the text in front of them, ask the moot judges whether they would like you to read it or if they would prefer to read it themselves. If they indicate that they would prefer to read it themselves, allow them to do so and do not begin speaking until they have indicated that they have all finished.

Because of the time that it takes to read aloud (or to allow the moot judges to read for themselves) lengthy quotations, use these sparingly. If the quotation can be shortened without changing its meaning or taking it out of context, then consider using the shortened text.

VI. **Avoid referring to too many authorities:** The authorities to which you refer in your oral submissions should already have been set out in your team's written submissions. As is the case for your written submissions, it is important to focus on quality of authorities, rather than quantity. Your goal should be to find the strongest authority or authorities that you can to support your submissions.

> **Example:**
>
> Counsel 2 for the Respondent:
>
> 'When parties carry out negotiations, it may be difficult to say exactly when an offer has been made and accepted. Where there is a disagreement as to what was agreed, the Court must then look at the whole correspondence and decide whether, on its true construction, the parties had agreed to the same terms. May I refer the Court to the case of O'Mahony and Promontoria Gem DAC, which was the sixty-third judgment issued by the High Court in two thousand and eighteen. While this judgment is not binding on this Court, it is of persuasive authority and I refer the Court to a particularly relevant statement of Mr Justice Haughton. Judge, this judgment has no page or paragraph numbers, but the relevant statement is set out in paragraph two of page three of the Respondent's memorial ... [*wait for the moot judges to find it, then read out the relevant paragraph*]'

(c) *Apply the legal principle established by the authorities to the facts of the moot*: Once you have set out the legal principle underpinning your submission and you have referred to supporting authority, apply the law to the facts of the moot. Do this explicitly, rather than expecting the moot judges to connect the law and the facts simply from your discussion about the relevant authorities. As was the case for your written submissions, your explanation of how an authority applies to your client's case can be based on deductive or inductive reasoning. Deductive and inductive reasoning are discussed in more detail in Chapter 1.[14]

> **Example:**
>
> Counsel 2 for the Respondent:
>
> 'As a result, following the Respondent's variation of the original contractual terms, the Appellant accepted these varied terms through its conduct. Based on the communication between the parties as a whole, at the point the network was calibrated following negotiations between the parties, the parties were in agreement as to the same varied terms of the contract.'

---

[14] See Chapter 1 (Section 1.2) for a discussion of deductive and inductive reasoning in a moot.

(d) _Conclude your submission and signpost the beginning of your next submission_: Signpost the end of a submission and state what the outcome should be on the relevant legal issue. If you have further submissions to make, signpost that you are moving to your next submission.

Example:

Counsel 2 for the Respondent:

'That concludes my first submission. There was no new contract agreed between the parties and the parties are bound by the varied terms of the only contract at issue. If the court has no further questions, I shall proceed with my second submission ...'.

Repeat the above process for each submission that you are making on a ground of appeal.

(2) **Making your negative case within your submissions (Counsel for the Respondent only)**: As counsel for the Appellant typically does not make their negative case until the rebuttal portion of the moot, only counsel for the Respondent will be making a negative case within their submissions. Section 5.4 discusses how you rebut your opponents' submissions.

The issue for counsel for the Respondent is determining when during their submissions they should address and rebut the Appellant's submissions. As a general rule, it is most effective to present your positive case first, and then to deal with your negative case, either by weaving it through your submissions at appropriate points or by dealing with it at the end of your submissions. In both situations, you are opening your submissions strongly by asserting the correctness of the Respondent's position. Ultimately, however, this is not a strict rule. You may find that rebutting one of the Appellant's submissions on a particularly central legal issue at the beginning of your submissions destabilises their whole argument and clears the way for you to present submissions from the Respondent's perspective.

> **Example:**
>
> (before beginning your submissions) 'Before I turn to my first submission, I would like to address an important issue raised by Mr Brown in his submissions with respect to the law established by the case of ...'.
>
> (within your submissions) 'While Mr Brown noted in his submissions that the case of Tansey and College of Occupational Therapists Limited provides that acceptance must be clearly and unconditionally communicated, case law has shown that a party may accept an offer through conduct ...'.

(3) **Order of Submissions**: Your submissions on each ground of appeal should be presented in a logical order that is easy for the moot judges to follow. As a result, while you should generally try to address each ground of appeal in the order it appears in the moot problem question or in the order of the moot judge's findings, you can decide the most effective arrangement for your submissions within each ground of appeal. As was the case for your written submissions, you may find that your submissions are most persuasive when presented in a particular sequence, even if this means that your strongest submission will not be your first submission. This approach is most effective if later submissions build on earlier submissions. Alternatively, you may choose to lead with your strongest submission first. This catches the attention of the moot judges from the beginning of your submissions. This approach is particularly effective if you are presenting your submissions as alternatives. If starting with a strong submission, it may also be effective to reiterate it in your conclusion so that it remains in the minds of the moot judges once you have sat down.

5.3.3 Conclusion on your ground(s) of appeal

The overall conclusion to your submissions does not need a detailed summary of all of these submissions. If you have time, use your conclusion to tie all of your submissions together to demonstrate how these support your client's position with respect to the ground or grounds of appeal that you have addressed. Counsel 2 for each team will also use the conclusion to close that team's moot and to reiterate what their client wants.

As with every other part of your submissions, signpost the beginning and end of your conclusion. Always make a final offer of assistance to the moot judges and wait for their response before you sit down.

Example:

Counsel 1 for the Appellant:

'To conclude, the Appellant never accepted the Respondent's offer of part-payment and instead made a counter-offer to the Respondent, thereby rejecting the offer of part-payment. Even if the Court finds that the Respondent's offer was accepted, part-payment of a debt is not valid consideration for waiving the balance of that debt. There was, therefore, no concluded agreement between the parties with respect to part-payment of the amount due. Unless I can be of any further assistance to the Court, those are my submissions.' [*wait until the moot judges respond to you before you sit down*]

Counsel 2 for the Respondent:

'To conclude, the parties agreed to vary the terms of the original contract and acted on the basis that these terms had been varied as agreed. The Appellant is now estopped from seeking to enforce the contract's original terms. For the reasons explained in our submissions, we invite the Court to dismiss the appeal. Unless I can be of any further assistance to the Court, those are my submissions.' [*wait until the moot judges respond to you before you sit down*]

5.4 Rebuttal

The focus of your research and submissions will be on developing your positive case. However, it is important to remember that your submissions do not take place in a vacuum — you must engage with submissions made by your opponents as part of your negative case.

Responding to your opponents' submissions is referred to as rebuttal. If you have an opportunity for rebuttal in a moot, make sure you take it. As discussed above, the timing of your rebuttal will depend on whether you represent the Appellant or the Respondent:

- counsel for the Appellant will normally be allocated a specific length of time for rebuttal following the conclusion of the main submissions;
- counsel for the Respondent should rebut the Appellant's submissions as part of their own submissions; and
- some moots also provide for a separate surrebuttal by counsel for the Respondent. This follows the

Appellant's rebuttal, but can only be used to respond to points raised in the Appellant's rebuttal. Any rebuttal of the Appellant's submissions themselves must still be addressed in the Respondent's main submissions on each ground of appeal.

Try not to go into a moot having given no consideration to your opponents' likely submissions and how you are going to rebut them. As discussed in Chapter 3, as you conduct your research and construct your submissions, consider submissions your opponents are likely to make and the authorities they are likely to rely on. Keep a running list of these, together with a note of any inadequacies that you think exist in these arguments and authorities. Once you receive your opponents' written submissions, consider their submissions and list of authorities carefully and determine how you can most appropriately rebut these. By preparing for your rebuttal ahead of your oral submissions, you give yourself the best opportunity to respond effectively on the day of the moot.

5.4.1 Rebutting your opponents' submissions

Your goal when rebutting your opponents' submissions is to minimise or even neutralise the impact these have on the effectiveness of your own submissions. It is essential that you use your rebuttal to actually engage with your opponents' submissions and the consequences they say flow from these, rather than simply restating your own submissions. An effective way of doing this is by challenging the authorities that your opponents have used to underpin their submissions.

(1) **An authority relied on is distinguishable**: If your opponents rely on a case that appears to support one of their submission, consider whether the case can be distinguished from the facts of the moot. Cases can be distinguishable in law or on their facts. Cases are distinguishable in law if:

- a legal principle considered in an earlier case is sufficiently different to a legal principle that arises in the moot;
- the discussion of that legal principle was part of the obiter dictum of the earlier judgment; or
- when read in light of the facts of the earlier case, the ratio decidendi of that case should be given a narrower meaning than your opponents have given it.[15]

---

[15] James Louis Montrose, 'Distinguishing Cases and the Limits of Ratio Decidendi' (1956) 19(5) Modern Law Review 525, 525.

If you can successfully argue that any of these features is present, the moot judges may agree that they are not bound to follow the earlier case.

Cases are distinguishable on their facts if the facts of the moot are materially different from those of an earlier case. Facts are materially different if their presence would have resulted in the earlier case being decided differently. If a case is distinguishable on its facts, the moot judges may agree that they are not bound to follow it, even though the doctrine of precedent means that they would otherwise be required to.[16]

(2) **An authority was relied on incorrectly**: If your opponents rely on an authority, but they have misread this authority, you may be able argue that the moot judges should not be bound by it. Carefully consider each authority relied on by your opponents and determine whether they have misunderstood the legal principle articulated in the authority or they have relied on statements in the authority that were made obiter.

(3) **The authorities relied on do not represent the law**: You may be able to argue that an authority that your opponents are relying on does not represent the law as it currently stands. This would be the case if:

- the authority has subsequently been overruled or reversed by a later case, or is no longer relevant in light of legislation. This is where the legal databases discussed in Chapter 3 can be extremely useful;[17]
- the authority is not binding on the moot judges because it originates from another country or from a source that sits below the moot court in the hierarchy of sources;
- your opponents are relying on a statement in a case that was made obiter; or
- the authority was made without reference to an inconsistent statutory provision or binding authority that should have been taken into account (the decision is said to have been made '*per incuriam*').

Remember, a case remains good law until it is overruled, reversed or is no longer authority for a legal principle as a result of legislative developments. There is, therefore, nothing

---

[16] *DPP v Morgan* [2015] IECA 50 [85] (Edwards J), noting that '[i]n this Court's view the judgment in the McGrath case is of no relevance to the issue raised, and it is in any case readily distinguishable on its own very peculiar and unusual facts.'

[17] See Chapter 3 (Section 3.3.2).

to stop your opponents from relying on extremely old cases in their submissions. In such circumstances, you may still be able to argue that the moot judges should depart from an earlier case if a more recent decision could be said to more accurately reflect the law in a modern context, even if the older case was never explicitly overruled, reversed or superseded by legislation.[18]

If your opponents call on the moot court to change the existing common law position, consider the arguments against such an assumption of power by the moot judges discussed in Section 2.3.

5.4.2 Structure of rebuttal

If you represent the Respondent, you will address each point of rebuttal at the appropriate stage of your submissions. When doing so, explain what it is in the Appellant's submissions that you are rebutting and explain the reason for your rebuttal.

If you represent the Appellant, your rebuttal will generally be restricted to the amount of time allocated for rebuttal at the end of the moot. This rebuttal should be structured to have an introduction, middle and conclusion with signposts for the moot judges to show where you are in your rebuttal and to identify which of your opponents' submissions you are rebutting.

> **Example:**
>
> Counsel 1 for the Appellant:
>
> (Introduction): 'I have two points to make in rebuttal. First, Ms Byrne relied on a Canadian case, when there is a more recent Irish case that supports the Appellant's submissions. Second, Ms Byrne incorrectly suggested that the English case of Williams and Roffey is authority in Ireland for a submission that an additional practical benefit is sufficient consideration for a promise regarding part-payment of a debt.'

---

[18] *Maloney v O'Connor* [2015] IEHC 678 [31] (Barrett J) noting that 'the problem with citing a more-than-one-century-old case is that a lot of legal water has passed under the jurisprudential bridge in the hundred years or so since.'

(Substance of rebuttal): 'I shall proceed to my first point of rebuttal. Ms Byrne relied on the Canadian case of Saint John Tug Boat Company and Irving Refinery Limited as binding authority for the submission that the Appellant's conduct constituted acceptance of the Respondent's offer of part-payment of a debt. As it is a Canadian case, Saint John Tug Boat Company and Irving Refinery Limited is not binding on this Court. The more recent Irish case of O'Mahony and Promontoria Gem DAC, discussed in the Appellant's submissions, indicates that a clear counter-offer cannot amount to acceptance. In the instant appeal, the Appellant made a counter-offer to the Respondent, thereby rejecting the offer of part-payment. I shall now proceed to my second point of rebuttal ...'

(Conclusion): 'Unless I can be of any further assistance to the Court, my co-counsel, Ms Smith, will continue with the Appellant's rebuttal.'

(Conclusion if you are Counsel 2 for the Appellant, or if only one mooter is presenting rebuttal on behalf of the Appellant): 'Unless I can be of any further assistance to the Court, that concludes the Appellant's rebuttal.'

5.4.3 Rebuttal: points to remember

(1) **Pay attention**: While you may have tried to pre-empt your opponents' submissions in order to prepare responses to these, rebuttal must be a response to the submissions your opponents actually make in their oral submissions. Because you will not know for certain what your opponents will say in their oral submissions until you have heard these, make sure that you remain alert while your opponents are speaking. Have a system in place where you can tick or circle submissions that they do make and cross off submissions that they do not make. Also keep a note of any submissions that your opponents have presented in a way that you had not previously anticipated. Implementing a system to keep track of your opponents' submissions should help you to structure your rebuttal in a coherent and effective manner. As your opponents progress through their submissions, identify submissions that you want to rebut, determine the substance of your rebuttal and the legal basis for this rebuttal.

Pay attention to any comments or questions from the moot judges during your opponents' submissions. A moot judge may actually have picked up on a point that you want to deal with in your rebuttal. So long as you can explain why you are rebutting a particular submission, this rebuttal can be reinforced by referring back to a relevant statement made by a moot judge (for example: 'As the Court has pointed out, the authority relied on by Mr Byrne in the Respondent's submissions is not binding on this Court …').

(2) **Rebut your opponents' submissions, rather than repeating your own submissions or introducing new material**: It can be tempting to use your rebuttal time to repeat your submissions or to introduce new material. There is nothing wrong with reiterating your submissions where you are doing so to rebut something specifically raised by your opponents or to correct a misrepresentation of your submissions by your opponents. However, unless you are responding directly to your opponents' submissions, you should not repeat your submissions. You should also not raise new submissions.

(3) **Surrebuttal**: Some moots give counsel for the Respondent an opportunity to respond to the Appellant's rebuttal. This surrebuttal should only be used to respond to points raised in the Appellant's rebuttal. It should not be used to rebut the Appellant's main submissions.

(4) **Address the moot judges, not your opponents**: While your rebuttal may be a response to points raised by your opponents, you are still addressing the moot judges. Maintain eye contact with the moot judges and avoid turning to speak directly to your opponents.

(5) **Remain courteous and professional**: It is never appropriate in a moot to slam your hands on your desk and shout 'objection', to tut or to shake your head in disagreement. If you disagree with something that your opponents have said in their submissions, raise this in rebuttal and explain why you disagree. Throughout your rebuttal, continue to remain courteous to your opponents and avoid attacking them personally or using inflammatory language.

5.5 Template: oral submissions

This template is designed to provide you with a guide to the expressions used in a moot court. You do not need to repeat each one of these expressions verbatim. Guidance notes are included in italics.

Counsel 1 for the Appellant

Opening remarks

1. May it please the Court, my name is [Ms/Mr] [*surname or full name*] and, together with my co-counsel, [Ms/Mr] [*surname or full name*], I appear in this matter for the Appellant, [*full name of Appellant, including Ms/Mr/Limited etc.*].

2. [Ms/Mr] [*surname or full name*] and [Ms/Mr] [*surname or full name*] will appear in this matter for the Respondent, [*full name of Respondent, including Ms/Mr/Limited etc.*].

3. This is an appeal by the Appellant against the decision of [Ms/Mr Justice]/[Judge] [*judge's surname*] sitting in the [*trial court*], where it was held that [*refer to the findings of the trial judge*].

4. The Appellant appeals against the decision of the trial judge on [*number of grounds of appeal*] grounds [*amend number of grounds of appeal as necessary*]. The first is that [*brief outline of first ground of appeal*]. The second is that [*brief outline of second ground of appeal*] [*continue for more grounds of appeal as necessary*].

5. I shall be addressing the Court on the first ground of appeal. My co-counsel [Ms/Mr] [*surname*], will be addressing the Court on the second ground of appeal [*adjust for more grounds of appeal as necessary*].

6. Would the Court find a brief summary of the facts of the case helpful? [*if the moot judges say yes: make sure the moot judges are given a good overview. You can highlight facts that are most favourable to your client, but never distort these*]/[*if the moot judges say no: thank the moot judge that confirms this:* Judge, I am obliged.]

7. Before I move onto my submissions, may I confirm that the Court has received a copy of the Appellant's [written submissions] [bundle]? [*if the moot judges say yes: thank the moot judge that confirms this:* Judge, I am obliged]/[*if the moot judges say no: hand them the material.*]

Submissions on first ground of appeal

8. [If the Court has no [further] questions on the facts of the case] [*if the facts are summarised*]/[If it pleases the Court] [*if the facts are not summarised*], I shall proceed to my submissions with respect to the first ground of appeal.

9. I shall be making [*number of submissions being made with respect to the ground of appeal*] submissions: first [*briefly outline your first submission*] and second [*briefly outline your second submission*] [*add in any more submissions that you may have*].

10. If it pleases the Court, I shall begin with my first submission ... [*go through submission in detail using method agreed as a team, eg ILAC*].

11. That concludes my first submission ... [*outline what outcome should be*]. If the Court has no further questions, I shall proceed with my second submission ... [*go through submission in detail using method agreed as a team, eg ILAC*]. That concludes my second submission ... [*outline what outcome should be*].

12. [*Continue for any further submissions that you are making on a ground of appeal*].

13. [*If you are addressing more than one ground of appeal, repeat stages 8 to 12 for the next ground of appeal*].

Conclusion

14. To conclude ... [*tie submissions together summing up how they support your client's position on the ground of appeal*].

15. Unless I can be of any further assistance to the Court, those are my submissions.

Rebuttal

16. I have [*number of points*] points to make in rebuttal. First, ... Second, ...

17. I shall proceed to my first point of rebuttal [*provide details of rebuttal, together with an explanation as to why you are rebutting your opponents' submissions*].

18. I shall now proceed to my second point of rebuttal [*provide details of rebuttal, together with an explanation as to why you are rebutting your opponents' submissions*].

19. [*Continue for any further points of rebuttal*].

20. Unless I can be of any further assistance to the Court, my co-counsel, [Ms/Mr][*surname*], will continue with the Appellant's rebuttal.

Counsel 2 for the Appellant

Opening remarks

1. May it please the Court, my name is [Ms/Mr] [*surname or full name*].

2. My co-counsel [Ms/Mr] [*surname*], has addressed the Court on the first ground of appeal.

3. I shall be addressing the Court on the second ground of appeal that [*brief outline of second ground of appeal*] [*adjust for more grounds of appeal as necessary*].

Submissions on second ground of appeal

4. If it pleases the Court, I shall proceed to my submissions with respect to the second ground of appeal.

5. I shall be making [*number of submissions being made with respect to the ground of appeal*] submissions: first, [*briefly outline your first submission*] and second, [*briefly outline your second submission*] [*add in any more submissions that you may have*].

6. If it pleases the Court, I shall begin with my first submission ... [*go through submission in detail using method agreed as a team, eg ILAC*].

7. That concludes my first submission ... [*outline what outcome should be*]. If the Court has no further questions, I shall proceed with my second submission ... [*go through submission in detail using method agreed as a team, eg ILAC*]. That concludes my second submission ... [*outline what outcome should be*].

8. [*Continue for any further submissions that you are making on a ground of appeal*].

9. [*If you are addressing more than one ground of appeal, repeat stages 4 to 8 for the next ground of appeal*].

Conclusion

10. To conclude ... [*tie submissions together summing up how they support your client's position on the ground of appeal*].

11. For the reasons explained in our submissions, we invite the Court to allow the appeal.

12. Unless I can be of any further assistance to the Court, those are my submissions.

Rebuttal

13. I have [*number of points*] points to make in rebuttal. First, ... Second, ...

14. I shall proceed to my first point of rebuttal [*provide details of rebuttal, together with an explanation as to why you are rebutting your opponents' submissions*].

15. I shall now proceed to my second point of rebuttal [*provide details of rebuttal, together with an explanation as to why you are rebutting your opponents' submissions*].

16. [*Continue for any further points of rebuttal*].

17. Unless I can be of any further assistance to the Court, that concludes the Appellant's rebuttal.

Counsel 1 for the Respondent

Opening remarks

1. May it please the Court, as has already been stated, my name is [Ms/ Mr] [*surname or full name*] and, together with my co-counsel, [Ms/Mr] [*surname or full name*] I appear in this matter for the Respondent, [*full name of respondent client including Ms/Mr/Limited etc.*].

2. I shall be addressing the Court on the first ground of appeal; that is, whether [*brief outline of first ground of appeal—frame this as something that needs to be proven*]. My co-counsel [Ms/Mr] [*surname or full name*], will be addressing the Court on the second ground of appeal; that is, whether [*brief outline of second ground of appeal—frame this as something that needs to be proven*] [*adjust for more grounds of appeal as necessary*].

3. Before I move onto my submissions, may I confirm that the Court has received a copy of the Respondent's [written submissions][bundle]? [*if the moot judges say yes: thank the moot judge that confirms this:* Judge, I am obliged]/[*if the moot judges say no: hand them the material.*]

Submissions on first ground of appeal

4. If it pleases the Court, I shall proceed to my submissions with respect to the first ground of appeal.

5. I shall be making [*number of submissions being made with respect to the ground of appeal*] submissions: first [*briefly outline your first submission*] and second, [*briefly outline your second submission*] [*add in any more submissions that you may have*].

6. If it pleases the Court, I shall begin with my first submission … [*go through submission in detail using method agreed as a team, eg ILAC. Rebut Appellant's submissions on first ground of appeal*].

7. That concludes my first submission … [*outline what outcome should be*]. If the Court has no further questions, I shall proceed with my second submission … [*go through submission in detail using method agreed as a team, eg ILAC. Rebut Appellant's submissions on first ground of appeal*]. That concludes my second submission … [*outline what outcome should be*].

8. [*Continue for any further submissions that you are making on a ground of appeal*].

9. [*If you are addressing more than one ground of appeal, repeat stages 4 to 8 for the next ground of appeal*].

Conclusion

10. To conclude … [*tie submissions together summing up how they support your client's position on the ground of appeal*].

11. Unless I can be of any further assistance to the Court, those are my submissions.

Counsel 2 for the Respondent

Opening remarks

1. May it please the Court, my name is [Ms/Mr] [*surname or full name*].

2. My co-counsel [Ms/Mr] [*surname*], has addressed the Court on the first ground of appeal.

3. I shall be addressing the Court on the second ground of appeal, that is, whether [*very brief outline of second ground of appeal*] [*adjust for more grounds of appeal as necessary*].

Submissions on second ground of appeal

4. If it pleases the Court, I shall proceed to my submissions with respect to the second ground of appeal.

5. I shall be making [*number of submissions being made with respect to the ground of appeal*] submissions: first [*briefly outline your first submission*] and second, [*briefly outline your second submission*] [*add in any more submissions that you may have*].

6. If it pleases the Court, I shall begin with my first submission ... [*go through submission in detail using method agreed as a team, eg ILAC. Rebut Appellant's submissions on second ground of appeal*].

7. That concludes my first submission ... [*outline what outcome should be*]. If the Court has no further questions, I shall proceed with my second submission ... [*go through submission in detail using method agreed as a team, eg ILAC. Rebut Appellant's submissions on second ground of appeal*]. That concludes my second submission ... [*outline what outcome should be*].

8. [*Continue for any further submissions that you are making on a ground of appeal*].

9. [*If you are addressing more than one ground of appeal, repeat stages 4 to 8 for the next ground of appeal*].

Conclusion

10. To conclude ... [*tie submissions together summing up how they support your client's position on the ground of appeal*].

11. For the reasons explained in our submissions, we invite the Court to dismiss the appeal.

12. Unless I can be of any further assistance to the Court, those are my submissions.

5.6 Chapter summary

1. A mooter's role will determine the structure and content of his or her oral submissions.

2. Being good at time management is an important element of being a good mooter—make sure that you are clear about timing aspects of any moot that you participate in.

3. Moot judges must be able to follow your submissions. To assist moot judges with this, consider: creating a roadmap of your submissions and signposting points on this roadmap; making the relationship between points clear; and preparing a bundle of authorities.

4. Spoken conventions in a moot may seem formulaic. However, try to follow these conventions at each stage of your oral submissions.

5. Remember, while there are certain spoken conventions that apply across a moot, other spoken conventions will depend on who you represent and whether you are the first or second mooter to speak on behalf of your client.

6. Plan your rebuttal—this should help you to present a more effective negative case during the moot.

Chapter 6

Oral Submissions: in the Moot Court

6.1 Introduction

6.1.1 In the moot court

A good mooter's oral submissions will be a combination of substance and delivery. The first five chapters of this book focused primarily on the substance of your submissions, how to research and structure them, and how to use them to persuade the moot judges to reach the conclusion that your client wants. This chapter concentrates on the day of the moot itself and the different aspects of your delivery. It is important to remember that while you may not be able to control everything in a moot, you are in control of your performance and your conduct on the day.

6.1.2 Practise, practise, practise

Practising your oral submissions should help you to improve your delivery in a moot.[1] As soon as you have prepared your written submissions (discussed in Chapter 4) and structured your oral submissions (discussed in Chapter 5), you should begin practising these oral submissions. Practise as much as you can. The more you practise, the more comfortable you will become in your delivery. Practice will also give you an opportunity to time and then adjust the length of your submissions, depending on whether you are over or significantly under the allotted speaking time (remember to factor in the relevant timing margin discussed in Chapter 5).[2]

There are a number of different ways in which you can practise, all of which you should try to do in the lead up to a moot.

(a) The easiest way of practising is by yourself, but out loud. You may find it easiest to start with this style of practising as you familiarise yourself with your submissions and authorities. Practising by yourself in front of a mirror is an effective way of catching distracting mannerisms that

---

[1]   Iain Morley, *The Devil's Advocate* (3rd edn, Sweet & Maxwell 2015) 12–13.
[2]   See Chapter 5 (Section 5.1.3).

you may have when speaking (such as flicking your hair or fidgeting with your sleeves).

(b) The next stage is to practise in front of your teammate. This will help to build your confidence when speaking in front of another person and is a good opportunity for you both to consider how your oral submissions fit together. You should each act as a moot judge while the other is speaking and intervene with questions and comments that may come from the moot judges. This will allow you to practise reacting and responding to judicial interventions.

(c) If you have time, you and your teammate should practise in front of a third person. Ask the third person to act as a moot judge and to intervene with questions and comments during your submissions.

(d) Finally, once you and your teammate are comfortable with your respective oral submissions, record (as an audio or video recording) your complete oral submissions. Listen to or watch this recording—consider your delivery and catch excessive use of vocalised pauses (such as 'um'). If you have a video recording, also consider your non-verbal communication and how you come across as a speaker.[3]

6.2 Judicial interventions

One aspect of oral submissions where a mooter's delivery may falter is in response to judicial interventions. Some moot judges periodically intervene as you proceed through your submissions, others wait until you have finished your submissions and intervene before you sit down. How you respond to these interventions will demonstrate how well you know your submissions and authorities, whether you are able to think on your feet and your level of professionalism. These interventions are, therefore, something that you will need to deal with effectively if you want to succeed as a mooter.

Judicial interventions generally fall within two broad categories: comments, where a moot judge gives you some sort of direction; and questions, where a moot judge wants an answer. It is impossible to determine in advance how many and what types of judicial interventions you will receive. Your best weapons to defend your submissions from being weakened by these interventions are

---

[3] Iain Morley, *The Devil's Advocate* (3rd edn, Sweet & Maxwell 2015) 422.

preparation and practice. If you have prepared thoroughly for the moot and you have practised your submissions, you should have the knowledge and confidence needed to deal with the judicial interventions you receive.

6.2.1 Anticipating judicial interventions

Preparing rebuttal of your opponents' submissions ahead of a moot is made easier by the fact that you will usually receive either your opponents' memorial, their list of authorities, or both, ahead of the moot. This type of pre-warning is not something you will receive from the moot judges. As a result, it is more difficult to anticipate and prepare for specific judicial interventions in advance. Instead, try to focus on the aspects of your oral submissions that the moot judges may concentrate on.

First, prepare responses to common judicial interventions (examples of which are set out below). This is particularly relevant for judicial questions.

Second, consider whether there are any weaknesses in your submissions that the moot judges might query. Go through your submissions with your teammate and work out if there are any aspects of your arguments or any of your authorities that are not quite as robust as you would ideally like. Work out how you will respond to a judicial query on these weaknesses. Also make sure that you understand how your submissions fit together (for example, are they alternatives or do they build on each other?), how they work with each other in support of your client's position on a ground of appeal and the relationship between your submissions and those of your teammate.

Third, consider your opponents' submissions and authorities. These are likely to be at odds with your submissions and authorities. Be prepared to explain to the moot judges why your submissions and authorities should be preferred over those of your opponents. This is something that you are likely to already have considered when preparing your rebuttal.

As part of your practice sessions, ask your teammate or a third party to act as a moot judge and to intervene while you are speaking. This could be a useful exercise for determining how you respond to interventions and for drawing out comments and questions that you had not previously considered.

6.2.2 Golden rules for responding to judicial interventions

Whatever the type, content or timing of a judicial intervention, there are certain golden rules that you should respect.

(1) **When a moot judge starts talking, you stop**: Judicial interventions can come at any time during your submissions. While some moot judges may wait for a natural pause in your submissions before they intervene, others may interrupt you mid-sentence. Regardless of when a moot judge intervenes, as soon as the moot judge starts talking, you must stop. Never speak over a moot judge, even if you are just trying to finish a point.

If you maintain eye contact with the moot judges during your oral submissions, you may be able to pre-empt the start of an intervention from a moot judge's body language. This could help you to bring a sentence to a natural end before a moot judge starts to speak.

(2) **When a moot judge is talking, you are listening**: Closely tied to the first golden rule is the second — whenever a moot judge is talking, you are listening. Do not start to speak again until the moot judge has completely finished his or her intervention, even if you know your response to the intervention almost as soon as the moot judge starts speaking. Speaking before the moot judge has finished is not only rude, but it increases the risk that you may miss part of the intervention or not fully understand it. Listen closely to any judicial intervention. While you can ask for clarification if a judicial intervention is not clear, you should still pay attention to whatever the moot judge is saying to avoid missing an important element.

(3) **Do not ask the moot judges questions, subject to exceptions**: As a general rule, only a moot judge asks questions in a moot. You should not, therefore, ask the moot judges questions. There are a number of exceptions to this rule:

- asking for clarification if you have not understood a judicial intervention (for example: 'Thank you, Judge. I am afraid that I did not quite follow your question. I would be very grateful if you could kindly clarify the second part of your question' or 'Thank you, Judge. Would you kindly repeat the question?');
- asking the moot judges if you can consult your

teammate or your notes when you do not know the answer to a question;[4]

- asking the moot judges if they would like a summary of the facts of the moot or any authorities to which you refer;
- asking the moot judges if they have received a copy of your client's written submissions or bundle;
- asking the moot judges if you can dispense with formal citation;
- asking the moot judges if they have found a quotation that you have directed them to in your memorial or bundle and asking them if they would like you to read longer quotations;
- asking the moot judges for more time to finish your submissions;[5] and
- asking the moot judges if you can provide them with any further assistance before you sit down.

(4) Never lose your temper or indicate that you think an intervention is unnecessary: This final golden rule is obvious, but is worth emphasising—avoid displaying annoyance at a judicial intervention or giving any indication that you think an intervention is unnecessary. The moot judge has clearly thought that the intervention was justified or else he or she would not have intervened. If you do find yourself becoming irritated during a moot, try to remain calm and respond as politely as possible. Similarly, if you are unlucky enough to be faced with a moot judge who is rude, be patient, remain calm and present your submissions as planned—do not retaliate by being rude yourself.

This is not to say, however, that you cannot disagree with a moot judge—you must simply do so in the appropriate manner. If you disagree with a moot judge's comment or question, politely voice this disagreement before explaining why your submissions are correct. Whenever possible, draw your response back to your submissions and any authorities that you have relied on.

---

4   See Section 6.6.2 for a discussion of what to do if you cannot answer a moot judge's question.
5   See Section 6.6.1 for a discussion of what to do if you are running out of time in your oral submissions.

> **Example:**
>
> 'Judge, I am grateful for your comment. However, in the more recent case of Barge Inn Limited and Quinn Hospitality Ireland Operations Three Limited, the Irish High Court refused to follow the approach adopted by the Court of Appeal in Williams and Roffey in the context of part-payment of a debt and instead followed the Selectmove case, cited in the Appellant's submissions.'

6.2.3 Judicial comments

Judicial comments often take the form of a direction asking you to do something. As a result, while they will not necessarily require a response from you, they do require you to react appropriately. Being comfortable with your submissions will allow you to more confidently react to these comments.

View judicial comments as a moot judge's attempt to help you, rather than to catch you out. Set out below are examples of some common judicial comments and appropriate responses. This is not, of course, the complete list of judicial comments, but should give you an idea of the types of judicial comments you may receive.

Judicial Comment	Appropriate Response and Discussion
'It would be helpful if you could deal with your second submission first.'	'Certainly, Judge.' You should be comfortable enough with your submissions that you can swap the order of them.
'Yes, thank you, I get the point.'	'Judge, I am obliged … [*and move on*].' The moot judge is asking you to move on with your submissions. Make sure that you do just that.
'I did not catch your last point.'	'Thank you, Judge [*and repeat your point*].' Repeat the point you just made, but consider slowing down the pace of your voice slightly.
'You can take it that I am familiar with the facts of the instant appeal.'	'Judge, I am obliged.' Here the moot judge is confirming that he or she does not need a summary of the facts of the moot. Proceed with your opening remarks without offering to provide a summary of the facts.

Judicial Comment	Appropriate Response and Discussion
'You can take it that I am familiar with the facts of the cases noted in your list of authorities.'	'Judge, I am obliged.' This is a more unusual comment as the moot judge is indicating that he or she does not want a summary of the facts of any of the cases being used as authority. Proceed with your submissions without offering to provide a summary of the facts of any cases. If you think the facts of a case are particularly relevant, subtly try to weave these into your submissions (for example: 'As the Court is aware, this was a case where the facts were very similar/ different to those of the instant appeal ...').
'I cannot accept that submission.'	If you are very confident that your submission is legally sound and that the moot judge has simply misunderstood your point, you may want to restate it in a slightly different manner: 'Judge, I am obliged. Perhaps I could draw the Court's attention to an alternative authority, in which the legal principle was expressed slightly differently...' If the moot judge is correct, move on: 'Judge, I am obliged. I shall now move onto my next submission ...' Be cautious about challenging a moot judge's assessment of your submissions. Unless he or she has misunderstood you, it may be best to move on.

6.2.4 Judicial questions

Judicial questions often probe your knowledge of relevant legal principles and authorities.

A. *General guidelines for responding to judicial questions*

While preparation and practice will put you in the best position to respond to judicial questions, there are some general guidelines that you can follow to help you to make those responses as effective as possible.

(1) **Listen**: As discussed above, it is essential that when the moot judge is speaking, you are listening. You do not want to be in a situation where you miss part of a moot judge's question

because you start crafting a response (or worse still, interrupt the moot judge) before he or she has finished speaking.

(2) **Ask for clarification if necessary**: If you do not understand the moot judge's question, ask for clarification. See Section 6.2.2(3) for examples of how you can ask a moot judge for clarification.

(3) **Think before you speak**: When a moot judge asks you a question, you may think that it looks impressive if you launch into an answer as soon as the moot judge stops talking. In practice, this approach actually suggests that this is a question that you have prepared for and could lead a moot judge to test you with a harder question next. If, however, you pause briefly before answering a question, it gives you time to collect your thoughts into a coherent answer and signals to the moot judges that you are giving their question due consideration. This pause should not be too long, just a breath or two.

(4) **Try to avoid putting off answering**: A moot judge may ask you a question that relates to a point you had planned on dealing with later in your submissions. Try to avoid putting off an answer by suggesting that you will deal with it later—the moot judge has asked the question now and wants an answer now. This situation can be addressed in a number of ways:

- by answering the question now and then noting that you will be dealing with the point in more detail later in your submissions (for example: 'Judge, this is a point that I intend to address in detail later in my submissions; however, in response to your question ...'); or
- by bringing forward your later submission and dealing with it in full now (in which case you should not repeat the submission again at the point you had originally intended to deal with it); or
- if you think delaying your answer is appropriate in the circumstances, by giving the moot judges the option of receiving a response now, or in the place in your submissions that you had originally intended to deal with the point (for example: 'Judge, this is a point that I intend to address in detail later in my submissions, I can provide a response to your question now if the Court would prefer, but it may be more helpful to the Court if I address it in the context of my second submission.'). If you do delay your answer in this manner, make sure that you actually provide an answer later in your submissions.

Each approach requires that you are comfortable with your submissions and flexible in your delivery.

(5) **Actually answer the question asked**: Do not avoid a judicial question you do not like by not really answering it. The moot judges will pick up on this.

(6) **Be succinct and professional**: Try not to waffle in your response to a judicial question. Instead, respond as succinctly as you can, while still providing the moot judges with a coherent and comprehensive response. When you respond to judicial questions, maintain your level of professionalism and continue to be courteous and deferential to the moot judges.

(7) **Admit you cannot answer the question**: You should try to answer judicial questions. However, if you cannot answer a particular question, Section 6.2.4(C) discusses your options.

> **Practical Tip:**
>
> When you respond to a moot judge's question, wait until it is clear that the moot judge is happy with your response before you return to your submissions. This should usually be clear from what the moot judge says, or from his or her body language. If you are not sure, however, politely check (for example: 'Judge, could I confirm whether this response addresses your question, and whether you are happy for me to proceed with my submissions?').

B. Sample judicial questions

Set out below are examples of common judicial questions and appropriate responses or reactions. These examples are divided into easier and more difficult judicial questions.

Easier Judicial Questions	
Judicial Question	**Appropriate Response/Reaction and Discussion**
'In what court was this case heard?'	This is information that you should know about any case that you are relying on as an authority. Explain which court delivered the judgment, and indicate whether the case is binding on the moot judges or just of persuasive authority.
'Am I/the Court bound by this authority?'	This is similar to the question above and is information that you should know. Explain where the authority sits in the hierarchy of sources of Irish law and the extent to which the moot judges are bound by it.

Easier Judicial Questions	
Judicial Question	**Appropriate Response/Reaction and Discussion**
'In what year was this case decided?'	This information should be clear from the case's citation. Briefly check this citation before providing the moot judge with the relevant information.
'Why should I follow the views of a dissenting judge?'	Try to answer this question in your submissions to avoid a moot judge having to ask it. If a moot judge does ask this question, you should have an answer to it— for example, the views of the majority judges may not be relevant to your submissions or the dissenting judge may have agreed with the majority on the particular legal principle to which you are referring.
'Was this case decided unanimously?'	This is information that you should ideally have noted when preparing for your submissions.
'Has this case subsequently been considered by the courts?'	This is a slightly harder question, but one that you should be able to answer if you have prepared. To prepare for this question, search available legal databases (discussed in Chapter 3) to check the status of each case that you rely on and whether a case has subsequently been considered by the courts.[6]
'So, your submission is that ...'	Here the moot judge is trying to help you. If the moot judge has summarised your submission correctly, confirm this. If he or she has not summarised your submission correctly, clarify it.
'What is the legal principle that can be derived from this authority?'	In your submissions, make sure that you explain the legal principle that each authority that you rely on establishes or supports. A moot judge may ask you to explain this if you have not made it clear in your submissions. If a moot judge does ask you for this information, be able to explain why you are relying on an authority.

---

[6] See Chapter 3 (Section 3.3.2).

More Difficult Judicial Questions	
Judicial Question	**Appropriate Response/Reaction and Discussion**
'Do you not agree that your opponents have made a compelling argument on this point?'	As part of your research and when preparing for your rebuttal, you should have considered how to neutralise your opponents' submissions. In response to this question, provide reasons why the moot court should prefer your submissions to those of your opponents.
'Why should I prefer the authorities that you have relied on over those of your opponents?'	As with the question above, you should already have considered why the moot court should prefer the authorities that you are relying to those of your opponents. In response to this question, try to challenge the correctness of your opponents' reliance on particular authorities in the same way that you would in rebuttal.
'Both you and your opponents have relied on the same authority, but have interpreted this authority differently. Why should I prefer your interpretation?'	Consider why you are giving an authority a particular interpretation and why this is to be preferred to the interpretation your opponents have given it (for example, did they rely on a statement that was made obiter?)
'Are there any broader policy considerations raised by your submissions?'	To prepare for a question of this nature, consider the implications of your submissions beyond the moot court. For example, if you are asking the court to overrule a line of cases, outline the wider potential implications of this.
'Would your submission be the same if ... ?'	This is a difficult question, as it requires you to apply your submission to a different fact pattern. Go back to the core of a submission and determine the legal principle that underpins it, then try to work through the different fact pattern presented by the moot judge to determine how the legal principle would apply. Answering this question requires strong familiarity with the relevant law and authorities.

More Difficult Judicial Questions	
Judicial Question	**Appropriate Response/Reaction and Discussion**
'But what about the case of ...?'	Hopefully you will have researched the law relating to the moot problem question in sufficient detail that you will not be faced with a situation where a moot judge raises an authority that you have never heard of. In such circumstances, acknowledge that you are not aware of the authority, but reiterate particularly strong authorities that you are relying on and note that the authority mentioned by the moot judge has not been raised by your opponents in their submissions, or (if you are the Appellant) included in their list of authorities. If the moot judge has given you some information about the authority (for example, the court a case was heard in) try to emphasise aspects of your own authorities that make them superior.

C. What to do when you cannot respond to a judicial question

Even with preparation and practice, you may still receive a judicial question that you simply cannot answer. In such circumstances, it is important not to panic—remember, it is just one question within the whole of your team's submissions. If you find yourself without an answer to a question, consider one or more of the following options:

(1) **Consult your notes**: You may receive a judicial question that you cannot immediately answer, but you think it is covered in your memorial, bundle or other notes. If it would refresh your memory to briefly consult your notes, ask the moot judge for permission to do so.

> **Example:**
>
> 'Judge, might I have a brief moment to consult my notes?'

If the moot judge allows you to do so, thank them and refer to your notes. You should only consult your notes if you can do so briefly—do not take up valuable time leafing through all of the paper in front of you to try to find an answer. Try not to use this option too often.

Even if you have not prepared a bundle for the moot judge, you may find that having a printed copy of your written submissions, the full text of your authorities and/or a sheet of key phrases in front of you is helpful for these situations.

(2) **Consult your teammate**: If you think your teammate may be able to help you in answering a judicial question, ask the moot judge for permission to consult him or her.

> **Example:**
>
> 'Judge, might I have a brief moment to consult my co-counsel, Mr Delany?'

Wait until the moot judge has confirmed that you can consult your teammate before doing so. Use this option only exceptionally and avoid using it as an obvious method of stalling.

> **Practical Tip:**
>
> If your teammate is struggling to answer a judicial question that you know the answer to, but it looks like he or she will not ask for permission to consult you, subtly place a note on the desk either communicating the answer to the question or telling your teammate that he or she should ask to consult you.

(3) **Let your teammate answer during his or her submissions**: If a judicial question relates more closely to your teammate's submissions (and your teammate is still to speak), then you may consider asking the moot judge if he or she is happy for your teammate to answer the question.

> **Example:**
>
> 'Judge, my co-counsel, Mr Delany, will be dealing with the issue of estoppel in some detail in his submissions and, if it pleases the Court, Mr Delany might be best placed to provide the Court with an answer on this point.'

If you use this option, you should be confident that your teammate can actually answer the question.

(4) **As a last resort, admit you do not know the answer and move on**: If none of the above options has worked and you still cannot answer a judicial question, admit this and move on.

> **Example:**
>
> 'Judge, I am afraid that I cannot be of assistance on this particular point.' or
>
> 'Judge, that is my submission, and I am afraid that I am unable to take the point further.'

Wait until the moot judge acknowledges that he or she is happy for you to return to your submissions before you begin talking again.

6.3 Speaking techniques

Your effectiveness as an advocate is about more than simply saying your submissions out loud. Good delivery in oral submissions will make it easier for you to communicate your arguments to the moot judges. This section will look in more detail at *how* you deliver your oral submissions, rather than the content of these submissions.

6.3.1 Scripts and speaking notes

It can be tempting to type out your oral submissions word for word, bring a printout to the moot and then read the text to the moot judges. By setting out everything that you want to say, a script can work as a form of reassurance that you will not miss anything out or lose your place in your submissions.

However, reading from a rigid pre-prepared script could hinder your performance in a moot. An effective mooter engages with the moot judges, is animated, speaks fluently and is able to respond to moot judges' interventions with ease. A script can obstruct these aspects of oral submissions. At the same time, unless you are very confident in the content of your oral submissions, taking part in a moot with minimal or no notes could be equally unhelpful, particularly if you find yourself tongue-tied in the middle of your submissions or you want to quote from, or provide a citation for, an authority. A middle ground between reading verbatim from a script and having no notes at all is likely to be most effective—you just need to work out what approach works best for you.

A. Use of scripts

Commentary on mooting often advocates not using a script in oral submissions. In practice, there is nothing wrong with using a script, so long as you use it sensibly.

The key thing to avoid in oral submissions is standing in front of the moot judges and simply reading your script to them. This approach to advocacy may cause you either to look down at your script during the moot or to hold your script up in front of your face. There is also a greater risk that you will deliver your oral submissions in a monotone, boring fashion, and will become flustered if a moot judge's intervention requires you to move your submissions around.[7]

If, however, you feel most comfortable having a script, you can do so, but as a memory aid that you refer to only occasionally. This will require that you know your submissions and have practised delivering them. There are a few techniques that you can implement to reduce your dependence on a script:

(1) **Know your submissions**: You should avoid learning your entire speech, as this will be time-consuming and may prevent you from sounding natural in your delivery. However, you may find it helpful to learn key sections of your submissions, so that you can deliver these unaided, without the need to read your script. In particular, know your introduction and conclusion well so that you can start and end your submissions confidently. You should also know the overall structure of your submissions and the points that you need to cover in each section.

(2) **Implement an identification system**: Highlight, underline or mark in some other way important phrases, quotes or authorities used in your script. This may help you to more easily pick these points out of your script without needing to search the full text for them. This technique can be particularly effective if you use the headings of sections in your submissions or the names of key authorities as prompts.

(3) **Separate submissions**: Consider printing each of your submissions on a separate page with coloured tabs indicating which page deals with which submission. This should make it easier for you to move the order of your submissions around or to refer to another submission in response to a judicial intervention.

(4) **Keep your place**: If you are using a script, know where you are in your script as you deliver your submissions, even though you are not actually reading from that script. This way, if a moot judge intervenes or you need a prompt, you will not have to leaf through your script to find your place. Develop a

---

[7] Iain Morley, *The Devil's Advocate* (3rd edn, Sweet & Maxwell 2015) 182.

system that works for you, such as subtly running your finger along the script as you deliver your submissions or marking your place in your script with a pen or marker each time a moot judge intervenes.

(5) Practise: If you have not practised your oral submissions in advance, using a script may mean that you simply read it to the moot judges. If you want to use a script, make sure that you have practised your oral submissions and are able to deliver them fluently and persuasively.

> **Practical Tip:**
>
> The exceptions to the rule that you should avoid reading your submissions are quotations and citations. If you are quoting a passage of an authority to the moot judges, or are citing an authority, you should read from your notes so that you can accurately deliver the relevant information.

B. Other types of speaking notes

Rather than a complete script of your oral submissions, you may prefer to prepare speaking notes that are more outline in nature. These can take a variety of forms, such as flashcards with prompts, bullet points in a notebook or a mind map. Speaking notes encourage you to look at the moot judges. They may also help you to speak in a more engaging, and therefore potentially more persuasive, manner as you are coming up with the words to fill in the details of your outline as you go along. As speaking notes can be shuffled more easily than a script, they also lend themselves to flexible delivery of submissions.

The level of information that you include in your outline will depend on how detailed you want your speaking notes to be. You may find it helpful to include indented bullet points covering the following:

- each of your submissions;
- the main arguments that you are making with respect to each submission;
- authorities and citations that relate to each submission;
- key information on each authority; and
- any phrases that you want to say or quotes that you will read out to the moot judges.

If you are using speaking notes, consider the following points:

(1) **Choose an approach that is effective and not distracting**: Whether you choose to use flashcards, a notebook or some other approach, it is important that it is not distracting for you or the moot judges. For example, a pile of tiny notecards that you are constantly changing, or a large notebook that you cling on to, could distract the moot judges or make you look nervous. Make sure that your speaking notes can be kept unobtrusively in front of you and discreetly navigated through.

(2) **Know your submissions**: Avoid learning your entire speech and then simply repeating this to the moot judges. However, know key sections of your submissions, such as your introduction and conclusion, so that these can be delivered fluently. Make sure that you are confident in the overall structure of your submissions and the points that you need to cover in each section.

(3) **Separate submissions**: Consider including the outline for each of your submissions on a separate flashcard or page. You can then swap the order of these if necessary as you deliver your submissions.

(4) **Include helpful information**: Your speaking notes should act as prompts when you are delivering your oral submissions. Make sure that any information included in them is actually helpful to you and that you include all information that you will need in order to be able to deliver your oral submissions.

(5) **Set out quotations, citations and other phrases in full**: Set out in full any quotations that you want to read to the moot judges, any citations of authorities or any phrases that you want to use. Do not try to memorise these.

(6) **Practise**: Practise your oral submissions in advance to make sure that your outline is helpful as a prompt, that you know your material well enough to be able to speak fluently without a script and that you can confidently move between submissions.

> **Practical Tip:**
>
> Whether you prepare a script or speaking notes, leave enough space on the page beside your submissions to make notes during the moot. These notes may be points of rebuttal that you want to raise or adjustments to your submissions in response to your opponents' submissions.

C. Adaptability and Responsiveness

Adaptability and responsiveness are important attributes of a good mooter and you should try to respond to judicial interventions without becoming flustered or getting lost in your submissions. If, for example, a moot judge asks you to deal with your second submission first, you should be comfortable enough with your material that a change in the order of your submissions does not cause you to panic or become tongue-tied.

Practice is the most effective way of ensuring that you can adapt your submissions as necessary during the moot. Your script or speaking notes should also be structured so that they help you to be responsive and flexible in your delivery.

D. Voice

As part of preparing for your oral submissions, consider how you are using your voice to convey your submissions to the moot judges. Rushed or inaudible submissions may be difficult for the moot judges to follow.

> **Practical Tip:**
>
> You and your teammate can help each other during oral submissions by agreeing in advance subtle signals that can be used to communicate messages to the teammate who is speaking. These signals could include inconspicuous hand gestures that tell the speaker to slow down, to speak louder or to move on to the next submission. Ensure that these signals are not distracting for the speaking mooter or the moot judges.

(1) **Tone**: If you deliver your oral submissions in a monotone voice, there is a risk that the moot judges will drift off and not follow what you are saying. On the other hand, oral submissions where you unnaturally modulate the tone of your voice (such as raising the tone of your voice at the end of every sentence or being overly theatrical) can be distracting. Try to vary the tone of your voice in a natural way, emphasising the most important words or points in your submissions.

(2) **Volume**: It is essential that the moot judges and your opponents can hear your submissions. At the same time, there is no need to shout your submissions. You just need to be conscious of the volume at which you are speaking, and adjust this volume according to the size of the moot courtroom and whether you are given a microphone. Watch the moot judges for any hint that they are struggling to hear you.

(3) **Pace**: Mooters frequently have difficulty controlling the pace at which they speak. The difficulty of judging for yourself how quickly you are speaking, combined with nerves, mean that mooters often speak too quickly. The problem with this is that you are less likely to be persuasive if the moot judges are struggling to keep up with you. By practising and recording your oral submissions, you will have a better idea of the pace at which you speak and be able to adjust this ahead of the moot.

Do not be afraid to include pauses in your oral submissions. They can be a very effective way of emphasising a point. They also give the moot judges a chance to catch up and to reflect on what you have just said. Practise building these pauses into your submissions.

(4) **Vocalised Pauses**: While pauses in oral submissions can be an effective technique for focusing the minds of the moot judges, try to minimise the extent to which you include vocalised pauses, such as 'um', 'like' and 'ah' in your submissions. Practice, slowing down the pace of your delivery and including deliberate pauses will all help you to increase the fluency of your delivery.

(5) **Enunciation**: Speak clearly throughout your submissions. If you mumble, the moot judges may have trouble following you.

(6) **Pronunciation**: You should try to pronounce case names, the names of judges and the names of your opponents correctly. Mispronouncing names is a mistake that you can generally avoid by preparing thoroughly for your oral submissions. If you have trouble pronouncing any names (or other words) that you will be using in your submissions, check the correct pronunciation with your teammate, or with a lecturer or tutor. During the course of oral submissions, listen carefully to the moot judges when they refer to authorities or other judges— try (within reason) to reflect the pronunciations that they use.

(7) **Accent**: Your accent should be irrelevant in a moot. Try not to adjust your accent to emulate the other mooters or the moot judges as this could be distracting for everyone, including yourself. All that is important is that your submissions can be clearly heard and understood by those in the moot courtroom.

> **Practical Tip:**
>
> While it is important to be aware of how you verbalise your submissions, try not to get overly tied up with trying to fit into a mould of how you think a mooter should sound. You want to come across as natural and sincere, not forced and contrived. So long as your submissions can be heard and followed, you can work on developing your own personal style of delivery.

6.4 Presentation and performance

The moot judges are assessing you from the moment you walk into the moot courtroom to the moment you leave it. Do not think that the only time that the moot judges are looking at you is when you are actually speaking. Instead, be conscious of your demeanour and behaviour for the duration of the moot and maintain your professionalism throughout.

6.4.1 Non-verbal communication

A. Body language

Your body language should reflect the professional nature of a moot.

(1) **When addressing the moot court**: Even if you are nervous, try to look self-assured when addressing the moot court. If you look nervous or bored this may undermine the moot judges' confidence in you. Stand up straight or lean slightly forward, keep your shoulders back, your head up and your hands out of your pockets. As discussed above, you should avoid reading verbatim from a script and should instead merely be glancing down at your notes occasionally.

If you plan to hold your notes, hold them down towards the table or lectern, rather than out in front of you. If you have notes, but are not holding them, rest your notes on the table or lectern in front of you, and keep your arms down and reasonably still.

It is important that you do not fidget with your hair, your notes or anything else during your submissions. Fidgeting is distracting and potentially annoying for the moot judges.

(2) **When sitting**: Maintain your professional demeanour when you are sitting. Sit up reasonably straight in your chair, take notes as necessary and look interested in what is happening in the moot. Avoid slouching over your desk, swinging on your

chair or doing anything potentially distracting or annoying (like fidgeting).

B. Eye contact

Eye contact is an important aspect of mooting as it allows you to engage directly with the moot judges.

(1) **When addressing the moot court**: Direct eye contact with each of the moot judges demonstrates that you are confident in your submissions and may help you to more convincingly make these submissions than if you were looking only at your notes. Looking at the moot judges also helps you to pick up on their body language. If the moot judges look lost or as though they are struggling to hear your submissions, you can remedy this immediately. A moot judge's body language could also indicate when he or she is about to speak; this gives you an opportunity to bring your sentence to a natural end.

Your level of eye contact with the moot judges should not, of course, be unnatural or amount to staring. You should also avoid fixating on one moot judge to the exclusion of all others. Keep your eye contact natural, in the same way that you would when speaking to a group of friends.

(2) **When sitting**: While you may not be looking at the moot judges directly when you are sitting, try to avoid staring into space or looking out of the window. When you are not speaking in a moot, you should be listening to the person that is speaking and taking notes as necessary.

C. Gestures

(1) **When addressing the moot court**: Lawyers on television shows often gesticulate wildly when addressing a court. In the context of a moot, the key is to keep your gestures natural — try not to look wooden, but also avoid gesturing excessively.

A brief movement of your hands as you come to a particularly important point in your submissions can be effective in emphasising the importance of that point. Think about your gestures when you are practising your oral submissions and ask your teammate for feedback on whether your gestures are helpful or distracting.

(2) **When sitting**: When you are not addressing the court, keep all gestures to a minimum. Never try to catch the attention of a moot judge and avoid conveying your feelings about

your opponents' submissions by shaking your head, rolling your eyes or throwing your hands up in exasperation. If your opponents are speaking and you want to communicate with your teammate, do so by way of note, rather than leaning over and whispering in his or her ear.

6.4.2 Etiquette

Moots are formal proceedings and certain rules of etiquette apply. Many of these rules are common sense, but can easily be forgotten in the context of a moot.

A. Politeness

General rules of good manners should prevail in a moot. These rules include the following:

(1) **Address the moot judges, your opponents and your teammate correctly**: Chapter 5 discusses how to address those participating in a moot.[8] You should learn these modes of address and try to use them consistently throughout the moot.

(2) **Turn off and put away your mobile phone**: It goes without saying that you should not be looking at your mobile phone during a moot (and avoid using it as a stopwatch during your submissions). Turn off your mobile phone before you enter the moot courtroom and keep it in your bag until you leave the moot courtroom at the end of the moot.

(3) **Do not interrupt anyone while they are speaking**: It is impolite to interrupt anyone during a moot—when someone else is speaking, you should be listening. This is particularly relevant during judicial interventions.

(4) **Remain silent, but attentive, when you are not speaking**: As noted above, when someone is speaking, you should be listening. If you do not listen to the submissions of your teammate or your opponents, you may miss something important that a moot judge refers to later or that you could have addressed in rebuttal. If you disagree with your opponents' submissions, remain silent and controlled—save points of disagreement for your rebuttal.

(5) **Never raise your voice in anger**: Extremes of emotion should be avoided in a moot. Even if you feel yourself becoming

---

8   See Chapter 5 (Section 5.2).

annoyed at your opponents or a moot judge, remain calm and respond in a polite manner.

(6) **Do not look bored**: The moot judges will expect you to take the moot seriously. If you look bored during a moot, the moot judges may view this as disrespectful. Try to look interested in what is happening in the moot and avoid staring into space.

(7) **Avoid eating, drinking (other than water from a glass) or chewing gum.**

(8) **Do not leave the moot court unless it is an emergency**: While the moot court is in session, you should remain at your desk.

(9) **Be grateful for any feedback that you receive**: Judicial feedback should be accepted graciously, not defensively—use it as an opportunity to learn.

B. Dress code

When deciding what you will wear on the day of the moot, you should first check the rules of the moot for any guidance on the dress code. If the rules of the moot are silent with respect to the dress code, assume that you should dress in business attire or at least as smartly as you can.

Your goal when getting dressed for a moot is to wear something that the moot judges will not be distracted by. If you enter the moot courtroom looking scruffy or inappropriate, you risk creating a negative impression with the moot judges before you have even begun to speak. Conforming to the appropriate dress code demonstrates to the moot judges that you are treating the moot court with respect, and that you are taking the moot seriously. It will also help you to feel more authentic and professional, something that can build your confidence in a moot.

While the scope of 'business attire' is open to interpretation, there are a few broad principles to bear in mind:

- **Men:**
    o wear a two or three-piece navy, dark grey or black suit. If you do not have a suit, a jacket and smart trousers with a belt can be worn;
    o a crisp (well-ironed) white, light blue or light pink shirt looks smart. Make sure that you keep this tucked into your trousers throughout the moot;
    o if possible, wear a tie. Make sure that the design of your tie is muted and professional; and

o your shoes should be clean, polished and dark-coloured.

- **Women**:
  o wear a suit in navy, dark grey or black. If you do not have a suit, a smart skirt or trousers and co-ordinating jacket can be worn. Avoid wearing skirts that are significantly above the knee;
  o like men, a crisp (well-ironed) shirt in a muted colour looks smart. Alternatively, a smart blouse with a modest neckline can be worn; and
  o your shoes should be clean, polished and of an appropriate colour. These can be flat or with a heel (as long as you can comfortably walk and stand in them).

For both men and women, gowns are worn in some, but not all, Irish moots. If gowns are to be worn in a moot that you are participating in, you are likely to be provided with a gown before the start of the moot.

Practical Tip:

Make sure that you are appropriately dressed before you enter the moot courtroom and continue to adhere to the dress code throughout the moot. Once you have finished speaking, avoid the temptation to loosen your tie or undo the top button of your shirt.

C. When to stand and when to sit

There is a defined etiquette governing when you should stand and when you should sit in a moot.

(1) At the start of the moot

- If you are sitting at your desk before the moot judges enter the moot courtroom, stand when the moot judges enter the room. Once the moot judges reach their seats and sit down, you should bow slightly towards the bench and sit down.
- If the moot judges are already seated before you enter the moot courtroom, enter the room quietly, go directly to your desk and bow slightly towards the bench. Only sit down when the moot judges have confirmed that you can do so.

(2) During the moot

- The only time that you should be standing during the moot is when you are speaking. Once you have finished speaking, and the moot judges have indicated that they have nothing further, sit down. At all other times, you should be sitting at your desk.
- If a moot judge asks a non-speaking mooter a question during the moot, the mooter that has been asked the question should stand up before responding and any other mooter that is standing up should sit down. Once the moot judges have indicated that they have nothing further, the mooter should sit down and the original mooter should stand up and resume his or her submissions.

(3) At the end of the moot

- If the moot judges leave the moot courtroom before you, stand up and remain standing until all moot judges have left the room. If a moot judge bows as he or she leaves the room, return this bow.
- If you leave the moot courtroom before the moot judges, stand up, bow slightly towards the bench and leave the room quietly. Do not begin dissecting the moot with your teammate until the door to the moot courtroom has been firmly closed.

D. Humour in a moot

Connected with the professional environment of a moot, it is generally not advisable to deliberately build humour into your submissions (particularly humour that could be interpreted as being in poor taste). This is not to say that a spontaneous comment or observation during a moot cannot be humorous, but any such comments or observations should be included sparingly.

6.5 Controlling your nerves

Mooting can be nerve-racking, particularly when you first begin participating in moots. However, it can also be exhilarating. If you are able to calm your nerves and channel the adrenaline rush that you get, you may find that you enjoy the experience.

6.5.1 Preparation and practice

The best way to control your nerves is to have thoroughly prepared for the moot and to have practised your submissions.

(1) **Read and understand the rules of the moot and the facts of the moot**: Even the most confident of mooters can get anxious if, on the day of the moot, they realise that they have misunderstood the rules or facts of the moot. These should be the first things that you read when you decide to participate in a moot.[9]

(2) **Prepare**: In the lead up to the moot, thoroughly research the law underpinning the moot problem question, consider and prepare for your opponents' likely arguments and authorities, and try to anticipate possible judicial questions. Armed with this knowledge, you should feel more confident when you enter the moot courtroom.

(3) **Practise**: The more you practise your submissions, the more confident you are likely to become with your material. This should improve your delivery, your adaptability and your ability to respond to judicial interventions. Practise in front of your mirror, your teammate and anyone else who is willing to listen. Make an audio or video recording of a practice session to hear and/or see how you come across.

(4) **Familiarise yourself with the moot courtroom**: Particularly if you have never mooted before, you may find it helpful to familiarise yourself with the layout of the moot courtroom. This is discussed in more detail in Chapter 1.[10] If you can, try to visit the room where the moot will be held in advance. If there is an opportunity for you to watch other moots taking place in the same moot courtroom, you should try to avail of this.

6.5.2 Breathing

If you are nervous, you may hold your breath or take quick, shallow breaths. Both of these could increase your anxiety. Controlling your breathing may therefore help you to control your nerves.

Before you enter the moot courtroom, take a moment to just breathe deeply several times. When you are speaking in a moot, remember to breathe. Including pauses in your submissions gives you a

---

[9] See Chapter 3 (Section 3.2.2) for a discussion on how to read a moot problem question.

[10] See Chapter 1 (Section 1.5.2).

moment to catch your breath before you resume your submissions. Similarly, when a moot judge asks you a question, take a breath or two before you respond. This allows you to collect your thoughts.

6.5.3 Projecting confidence

Even if you are nervous before a moot, try to project confidence. You are of limited help to your client if you are frozen with fear. Know what you are going to say in your introduction so that the first impression you give the moot judges is one of poise and control. After that, if you know your material and understand the relevant law, you may find that as you begin speaking, your nervousness dissipates.

6.5.4 Learning

Every moot that you participate in is an opportunity to learn. If you lose a moot, or you are unhappy with your performance, remember that it is not the end of the world. Instead, reflect on the things that you can improve. This may help you to be more confident when you participate in your next moot.

Always make sure that you listen to, and take on board, any feedback that you receive from the moot judges.

6.6 What to do if something goes wrong

Sometimes things go wrong. It is important that whatever happens, you remain calm and in control of your emotions. Set out below are some potential areas for anxiety during a moot and how you may want to respond to these.

6.6.1 You are running out of time

Make sure that you know in advance your allotted speaking time during the moot (including rebuttal time, if any), whether the timer will or will not be stopped for judicial interventions and whether you will receive warnings as you approach and reach your allotted speaking time.

If you find that you are running out of time during your oral submissions, take measures to address this—do not proceed in the hope that you will definitely be allowed extra time to finish your submissions.

(1) **Adjust your submissions**: If you are running out of time, avoid speaking faster to try to squeeze everything you had previously planned to say into a shorter amount of time. Instead, consider paring down the detail you include in some of your final submissions. In order to do this successfully, consider in advance whether there are any submissions or authorities that you would like to discuss, but which are less important, weaker or which could be presented in a way that requires less detail. Decide how you can shorten your presentation on these submissions or authorities, if necessary. By ranking your submissions and authorities in order of strength and importance, and thinking in advance how you can deal with these when time is running out, you may find it easier to make a quick decision during the moot on what can be shortened or even omitted from your submissions.

Remember, only you and your teammate know what you had actually planned to say in your oral submissions. If you do not deal with a submission in as much detail as you had intended, no one else will know. If, however, you become flustered and begin rushing through your submissions, it will be clear to the moot judges that your submissions have not gone as planned.

(2) **Ask for permission to finish your submissions**: If you receive a signal that your allotted speaking time has come to an end, but you are not quite finished with a submission, consider asking for permission from the moot judges to finish the submission or point that you are making.

> **Example:**
>
> • 'Judge, I note that my time has now expired. May I have a short extension to conclude this submission?'
> • 'Judge, I am mindful that my time has now expired. I would be obliged if I could have a short extension to conclude my submission.'

Do not use an extension as permission to launch into a new submission or to continue talking for another 10 minutes— only use this extra time to succinctly finish the point that you are making.

6.6.2 You cannot answer a judicial question

Section 6.2.4(C) discusses your options when you cannot answer a judicial question.

6.6.3 You get tongue-tied

With all of the work and practice that you have put into preparing for a moot, you will hopefully not get tongue-tied when you stand up to make your submissions. If this does happen, consider your options, which include the following:

(1) **Scan your notes**: While you should not be reading a script verbatim to the moot judges, you should still prepare any notes that you have so that a brief glance at these will remind you of what you need to say next. If you are using a script, this could be done by highlighting the heading or key words of each submission. If you are using speaking notes, you could include a phrase or word that relates to a specific section of your submissions.

(2) **Take a few deep breaths and have a sip of water**: Sometimes all you need to do is calm down before you proceed with your submissions. Take a few deep breaths and a sip of water to give you a moment to collect your thoughts before you resume.

(3) **Ask the moot judges if you can have a moment**: If you simply cannot remember what you need to say, ask the moot judges if you may have a brief moment to consult your notes. Use this time to look at your memorial or notes to try to jog your memory.

6.7 The day of the moot

6.7.1 Arrive early

Arrive at the location of the moot at least 15 minutes before the moot is due to start. Particularly if you are driving or using public transport to get to the moot, make sure you know where you are going in advance and build in sufficient travel time. Arriving at a moot just as it is starting or worse still, after it has started, is likely to leave most mooters flustered and stressed.

Use the time between when you arrive at the location of the moot and the start of the moot to go over your submissions one last time or to take a few deep breaths to calm your nerves.

6.7.2 Arrive prepared

The night before the moot, make sure that you have everything that you need for the moot. You would typically want to bring some or all of the following:

- a copy of the rules of the moot;
- your script or speaking notes;
- a copy of your teammate's script or speaking notes (in case there is any need for you to make, or assist with, his or her submissions);
- at least three copies of your memorial and list of authorities (in case the moot judges did not receive a copy);
- your opponents' memorial and list of authorities (if you have received these in advance);
- any extra notes that you may want to refer to, such as a list of citations or potential points of rebuttal based on your opponents' memorial and list of authorities;
- a copy of each of your authorities (if you have prepared a bundle, bring enough copies of your bundle so that one can be given to each of the moot judges and, if required, to your opponents);
- at least two pens or pencils, a highlighter, a notebook and an eraser;
- sticky notes (in case you need to communicate with your teammate or mark a section of a document); and
- something to use as a timer (such as a stopwatch—remember, your mobile phone should not be used as your timer).

6.7.3 Layout of the moot courtroom

The moot courtroom should have been set up before you enter. It could be set up in a lecture theatre, a specially designed moot courtroom or a real courtroom. The layout of a typical moot courtroom in Ireland is discussed in Chapter 1.[11] Keep this layout in mind when you enter the moot courtroom as you should proceed directly and quietly to the correct desk without needing to check where you should be sitting.

6.8 Chapter summary

1. Practice is an essential element in your preparation for a moot—it will improve your confidence and delivery.

2. Try to anticipate judicial interventions and plan your responses to these.

---

[11] See Chapter 1 (Section 1.5.2).

3. If you cannot answer a moot judge's question, consider your options.

4. Decide whether you will use a script or speaking notes during oral submissions—avoid reading your notes to the moot judges.

5. Consider how you deliver your oral submissions—aspects of these submissions, such as the tone and pace of your voice, will influence your persuasiveness.

6. Remember, the impression that you create is based on more than what you say—non-verbal communication may influence the moot judges.

7. If something goes wrong in a moot, it is important not to panic—remain calm and consider your options.

Chapter 7

Organising a Moot

7.1 Introduction

Organising a moot can be frustrating and satisfying in equal measure. The planning and organisation needed to run a moot successfully will appeal to those who enjoy project management. At the same time, organising a moot can be a lot of work, and may require management of a large number of people, not all of whom are as committed to the process as you are.

How you organise a moot will depend on the size of the moot, whether it is a competition or part of students' legal studies and whether or not you inherited the moot from a previous organiser. While every moot will bring with it unique organisational issues, this chapter discusses key considerations for a moot's organiser before, during and after a moot. Where relevant, it separately addresses these considerations in the context of a mooting competition and a mooting module.

7.2 Before the moot

When you organise a moot, the majority of your work will take place before the day of the moot. Set out below is a list of considerations for the pre-moot period.

7.2.1 Structure of the moot

A. Mooting competition

Mooting competitions typically involve several rounds, with one team declared the winner at the end of the competition. Depending on the size of the mooting competition, rounds may take place over several weeks or be held back-to-back over one or two days.

There are two main ways of structuring a mooting competition: as a knockout; or as a league.[1] A 'knockout' moot is organised as a pyramid. All teams compete in the first round, with each team mooting against another team picked in a draw. The winning team

---

[1] These terms are used by Baskind in Eric Baskind, *Mooting: The Definitive Guide* (Routledge 2017) 211.

from each of the first round moots progresses to the second round. This process repeats until two remaining teams compete in the final and the winning team is declared. Knockout moots are relatively simple to structure and require fewer resources (such as rooms and moot judges) as the rounds progress. However, the nature of these moots means that teams who are knocked out in the first round may not have a chance to compete again in the competition—this could be disheartening for a mooter who wants to gain more experience or who was unhappy with his or her first round performance. The pyramid structure of a knockout moot also means that exactly the right number of teams must compete in the first round. This issue can be addressed by: (1) readjusting the size of the pyramid to reflect the final number of teams; (2) making it clear in the rules of the moot that only a specific number of teams will be accepted on a first-come, first-served basis; or (3) giving any extra teams a 'bye' into the second round and so allowing them to progress without having mooted in the first round.

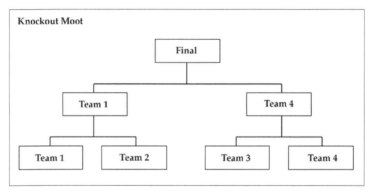

A 'league' moot is organised as a series of preliminary rounds that progress to a knockout. During the preliminary rounds, each team is placed into a group with other teams. Each team then moots against each of the other teams in their group. The team within each group that wins the largest number of moots, or receives the highest number of points, progresses to a knockout stage against the winning teams from the other groups. At the conclusion of the knockout stage, the two remaining teams compete in the final and the winning team is declared. A league moot is helpful for mooters who want to gain experience mooting or who feel that they perform best after having completed their first moot in a competition. However, league moots require more resources than knockout moots during the preliminary rounds and more structuring by the moot's organiser in order to avoid the same teams mooting against each other multiple times. They also require an equal number of teams within each group, as the bye method will not work. This issue could be addressed: (1) by determining the number of groups only once the final number of participating teams has been confirmed; or (2) if you have a relatively small number of participating teams, by forming one group with these teams so that each team can then moot against each of the other participating teams. The two teams with the most number of wins or the highest number of points could then compete in the final of the competition.

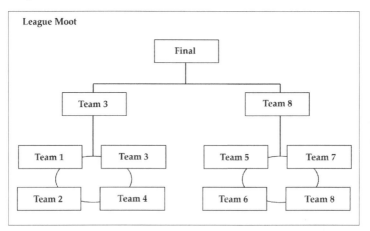

Whatever structure you adopt, you must decide what aspects of the moot will be assessed for the purpose of determining the winning team of each round. The approach that you choose will depend on the resources available and whether written submissions are exchanged ahead of, or only on the day of, the moot:

- you may decide that written submissions will be exchanged, but that these are not marked and do not count towards a team's overall chances of winning;
- alternatively, you may decide that a team's performance will be based on both their written submissions and their oral submissions;[2] or
- you may decide that while written submissions will be exchanged and marked, these marks will not impact on a team's chances of winning, except in a tie-break situation.[3]

B. Mooting module

In a mooting module, your primary aim is to assess and mark

---

[2]   This approach has been adopted in the preliminary rounds of the ELSA Ireland National Moot Court Competition.

[3]   This final approach has been adopted in the National Moot Court Competition.

students, rather than to declare an overall winning team. If marks are assigned to students based on their written and oral submissions, then all students must be marked based on the same round or rounds of moots. In a large class, this may mean that only one round of assessed moots is conducted, with each team mooting against one other team picked in a draw. There is, of course, nothing to prevent a mooting module being organised so that after the preliminary round, the two or four teams with the highest marks compete in a knockout competition. However, these knockout moots should not be relevant to the students' overall mark in the module.

Unlike mooting competitions, mooting modules will almost certainly allocate marks to students based both on their team's written submissions and on their individual performance in oral submissions. You will need to determine how marks will be divided between written and oral submissions, and whether students are marked as a team or individually on these submissions. As written submissions are typically prepared by each team as a single document, there is a logic to assigning all students within a team the same mark for their written submissions. In contrast, a student presents his or her oral submissions individually and so each student could receive an individual mark for this part of the moot. Marks for written and oral submissions would then be collated to give each student a final mark for the moot.

7.2.2 Eligibility to moot

A. Mooting competition

The rules of a mooting competition may specify who can enter that competition. The aim of reducing the pool of people who can participate in a mooting competition is to ensure some level of equality between mooters in terms of knowledge or experience and to keep the competition to a manageable size based on available resources.

As organiser, you will need to decide what type of mooters you want participating in the competition and how big you want the competition to be. If, for example, you want to organise a mooting competition for mooters with limited mooting experience, you may decide that only law students in their first or second year of undergraduate study can participate. If you want to limit the size of the mooting competition, you could restrict the number of teams from each institution that can participate[4] or the geographic location of any participants.[5]

You will also need to decide whether mooters should enter the mooting competition as teams or as individuals who are then paired off into teams once all participants have entered. It is more common for mooters to apply as a team and is logistically easier for you as organiser.

B. Mooting module

Eligibility to participate in a mooting module will be more straightforward than it is for mooting competitions, as all participating students are likely to be at the same level of study. It is inevitable that there will be differences in mooting experience between students, but in the context of a mooting module, such differences are less relevant.

7.2.3 Which party the mooters represent

A. Mooting competition

It is not uncommon for the rules of a mooting competition to require mooters to submit written submissions for both the Appellant and the Respondent. Before each moot in the competition, teams will be assigned the role of either counsel for the Appellant or counsel for the Respondent. As a team progresses to the next round of the competition, try to swap the identity of that team's client. This rotation between clients gives mooters an opportunity to present submissions on both sides of the moot.

B. Mooting module

The number of students in a mooting module and the resources available will determine whether there will be only one or several rounds of moots that count towards a student's mark. Where there is only one round, you will need to determine which teams represent the Appellant and which teams represent the Respondent. If resources permit more than one round of moots, each team should

---

[4]   This approach has been adopted in the Silken Thomas National Moot Court Competition, which limited entries for its 2018 competition to four teams from any one institution.

[5]   This approach has been adopted in the European Human Rights Moot Court Competition, which is open to participants studying law at a third level institution located in a member state of ELSA or of the Council of Europe.

ideally have an opportunity to represent the Appellant and the Respondent in alternate rounds.

7.2.4 Rules of the moot

As organiser, you will need to prepare rules of the moot. These rules explain how the moot will be run. They also act as a handbook for moot participants when determining what they need to prepare and when they need to submit documents. If you have inherited a moot from a previous organiser, you may already have a set of rules that you can update. Alternatively, Section 7.5.1 sets out an abridged template for these rules.

A. *Mooting competition*

(1) **Eligibility criteria and registration fee**: If you have decided to place restrictions on who is eligible to participate in the moot, any eligibility criteria must be clearly stated at the beginning of the rules. These rules should also state how prospective teams can register, whether a registration fee is payable and, if so, how this is paid and whether it is refundable. Intervarsity mooting competitions frequently charge a registration fee. This is a good way of ensuring that only teams that are serious about participating in the competition actually register. A non-refundable registration fee also reduces the likelihood of last minute dropouts.

> **Practical Tip:**
>
> In intervarsity mooting competitions, it is common for mooters to be prohibited from indicating (in their written and oral submissions) which institution they are affiliated with. If this prohibition applies to the mooting competition that you are organising, make it clear in the rules of the moot.

(2) **Number of mooters**: If mooters enter the competition as teams, you should specify the minimum and maximum number of members each team can have. While there will usually be two members of each team speaking during a moot, a team may have more than two members. In such circumstances, one or more members may alternate between a speaking and a non-speaking role during the competition or may assume a non-speaking role for the duration of the competition. Non-speaking members undertake a role similar to a solicitor in a real court and help with research, case preparation and document management. This provides an opportunity for

team members to experience a moot, without having to participate in all or any of the advocacy portion.

(3) **Memorials, authorities and bundles**: The rules of the moot should specify whether mooters must prepare a memorial (or similar document). If mooters are required to prepare a memorial, the rules should set out details of this, including: whether mooters should prepare a memorial for both the Appellant and Respondent or just for one party; the length of any memorial; its format (font, text size etc.); the deadline for exchange; and the process for exchange.

The rules of the moot should also set out details of any list of authorities that the teams are to prepare, including its format, the deadline for exchange and the process for exchange. You may decide to impose a limit on the number of authorities that can be relied on by each team. If a limit is imposed, it should be clearly stated and sensible (for example, a limit of two authorities is likely to be unrealistic). Make it clear whether the limit includes only cases or all types of authorities, whether authorities specifically cited in the moot problem question will be counted in the limit (as a general rule, they are not) and whether extracts from authorities that are contained in authorities relied on by the teams will be counted in the limit.

Decide at the outset whether teams should prepare bundles or whether you will leave this to each team's discretion. If teams are required to prepare bundles, state this in the rules of the moot, together with the number of copies needed.

(4) **Competition structure, timetable and timing**: Set out whether the mooting competition will follow a knockout or league structure. It is important to then set out a timetable specifying the date of release of the moot problem question (if this is not simultaneous with release of the rules of the moot), the date or dates on which each round of moots will be held and the deadline for exchange of documents. This will allow prospective mooters to determine in advance whether they will be available to take part at each stage of the mooting competition.

To ensure that mooters have all the information that they need with respect to timing in their oral submissions, the rules of the moot should specify: (1) the allotted speaking time for each mooter; (2) whether time will be allocated for rebuttal and surrebuttal, and if so, how long; (3) whether the timer will or will not be stopped for judicial interventions; and (4) whether timing warnings will be provided at intervals during each mooter's submissions.

(5) Communication and objections: Provide details of how prospective mooters can contact you for more information. The easiest method of communication is by email, although you may also want to include details of any social media accounts that you have set up for the purpose of publicising the mooting competition. If you anticipate receiving a large number of emails relating to the mooting competition, you may find it helpful to set up a dedicated email address, rather than having mooters contact you through your personal institutional email address.

The rules of the moot should also specify whether there is any scope for objecting to the moot problem question and if so, by when and how these objections should be communicated.

B. Mooting module

The rules of a mooting module will be shorter than the rules of a mooting competition. There will be no need to specify eligibility criteria for taking part or the need for a registration fee. Make sure, however, that you set out details of how you expect students to structure their memorials and lists of authorities, the method that will be used when exchanging written submissions, whether students must submit their written submissions via plagiarism software and the date on which each stage of the process will take place. It may also be helpful for students if you include details of how each student's final mark will be calculated.

7.2.5 Moot problem question

The complexity of a moot problem question and the areas of law covered by it will be determined by the nature of the moot. A mooting competition could, for example, be subject-specific or aimed at mooters with a specific level of experience. Similarly, the problem question used in a mooting module may be drafted to cover areas of law that students have studied as part of their degree.

Moot problem questions should preferably be drafted so that logical arguments can be made on both sides. Because of this, you will need to put some thought into the problem question that you select. When doing so, work out whether you will be able to use or modify an existing problem question or whether you will need to draft a problem question from scratch.

(1) **Existing moot problem questions**: There are a number of sources of existing moot problem questions. If your institution has previously run a moot, there may be a collection of moot problem questions that a previous organiser has gathered or drafted. While you should avoid using exactly the same moot problem question twice in mooting competitions, you can take previous problem questions and modify the facts or the trial judge's findings. Always make sure that you conduct your own research of any areas of law raised by an existing moot problem question to make sure that recent case law or legislation has not made the moot easier or more difficult for one side to argue.

There are several books and websites that include example moot problem questions. While these sources can be helpful when selecting a moot problem question, they are almost all drafted from a non-Irish law perspective.[6] Do your own research before selecting one of these moot problem questions to make sure that any relevant areas of law have not been dealt with by the Irish courts or legislature in a way that unbalances the moot problem question in one party's favour. Chapter 8 of this book includes a range of Irish law-specific moot problem questions.

(2) **Drafting your own moot problem question**: Drafting a moot problem question from scratch can be surprisingly difficult as you need to focus on areas of law that have not been definitively settled by the courts or legislature. A good place to start is recent cases in the Court of Appeal and Supreme Court. In particular, look for cases where a judge has noted that an area of law is unsettled, but does not make a determination on that area of law in the context of the case at hand. Alternatively, a Court of Appeal or Supreme Court case where there is a particularly strong dissenting judgment could also be useful. In both situations, weave facts referred to by the judges as being relevant to the area of legal uncertainty into your moot problem question.

---

[6] See, for example: Books: Eric Baskind, *Mooting: The Definitive Guide* (Routledge 2017) ch 10; Jeffrey Hill, *A Practical Guide to Mooting* (Palgrave Macmillan 2009) appendix 1; David Pope and Dan Hill, *Mooting and Advocacy Skills* (3rd edn, Sweet & Maxwell 2015) ch 15. Websites: MootingNet, 'Mooting problems', <www.mootingnet.org.uk/problems/index.html> accessed 1 December 2018.

7.2.6 Sponsorship and publicity

Sponsorship and publicity are likely to be more relevant to mooting competitions than to mooting modules.

(1) **Sponsorship**: Sponsorship of mooting competitions is beneficial for sponsors and organisers. For a sponsor, it increases that sponsor's visible presence on campus. For a moot's organiser, a sponsor could provide funding for the mooting competition, moot judges for later rounds and/or prizes for the winning team or the best individual mooter. In Ireland, ideal sponsors are solicitors' firms and domestic or international organisations that have a connection with law.[7] Consult your institution's department of law and its student law society to check whether they have any existing relationships with solicitors' firms or other organisations.

To increase your chances of obtaining sponsorship, make sure that you are thoroughly prepared before you approach any potential sponsor. You should be able to explain: (1) how the mooting competition will be structured and what type of mooters it is aimed at; (2) what you need from a sponsor (for example, is it funding, moot judges, prizes?); and (3) how sponsorship would be beneficial for the potential sponsor.

(2) **Publicity**: Publicising a mooting competition is important for three reasons: (1) it informs potential mooters about the upcoming competition; (2) it encourages people to attend as spectators; and (3) it provides publicity for any sponsors. Discuss options for publicising your mooting competition with your institution's department of law, its student law society and lecturers. You may, for example, be able to upload a poster on the department of law's social media channels or on your institution's intranet. Lecturers may also be able to announce the mooting competition in their lectures. Repeat these publicity efforts in the days prior to the mooting competition to encourage spectators to attend.

If the mooting competition is sponsored, check whether any sponsor wants to approve publicity material prior to its release.

7.2.7 Moot judges

One of the most difficult aspects of organising a moot is finding

---

[7] In England and Wales, barristers' chambers frequently sponsor mooting competitions. There is less scope for sponsorship by barristers in Ireland due to the structure of the profession here.

willing moot judges. People are busy and judging a moot can be time-consuming. As a result, you may struggle to convince enough people to help with judging. The best approach is to start recruiting moot judges early in your organisation timetable. Before the start of a moot, you will also need to provide moot judges with a thorough briefing. This is discussed in more detail in Section 7.2.8.

A. Mooting competition

A league-based mooting competition will usually require more moot judges than one based on a knockout structure. Once you have decided what structure you will be using, and have an estimate of how many teams will be participating in the moot, you can then consider how many moot judges you will need. When making this determination, consider:

- whether moot judges will judge each round of moots for the whole competition or if each moot judge will only judge a specific number of moots;
- when the moots will be held and whether any moots will take place in the evenings or on weekends (this is something that you will need to highlight to potential moot judges at the outset);
- how many moot judges you would ideally like to judge each moot (this may be one for preliminary rounds and three to five for the final); and
- whether there is anyone that you would particularly like to judge the final of the mooting competition (such as a real judge or the head of the department of law at your institution).

Once you know how many moot judges you will need, consider who you should approach. Depending on the size or character of the mooting competition, ideal moot judges are practitioners (such as real judges, solicitors and barristers), judges provided by a sponsor, lecturers from your institution's department of law and postgraduate students. Particularly if you have already finished your degree, friends from university who now work as legal professionals can be a very helpful source of moot judges.

B. Mooting module

Finding judges for mooting modules can be particularly difficult as a mooting module may not have an external sponsor who can provide moot judges.

Consider potential moot judges in your social and professional networks. Graduates, postgraduate students and lecturers from your institution can make excellent judges for mooting modules, as they may have a wide breadth of legal knowledge and understand your institution's marking scales. If your moot deals with an area of law that is taught as a module at your institution, the lecturer of that module may seem like an obvious choice as a moot judge. However, students may find this lecturer's presence stressful and may worry that their performance in the moot will somehow influence their mark for the other module. This should not discourage you from approaching any such lecturer, but is simply something to consider.

Finally, before you approach potential moot judges, speak to your institution's department of law or finance department about whether moot judges can claim additional payment for judging moots that are classified as an examination.

7.2.8 Judges' briefing and guide

It is important to fully brief your moot judges to ensure that they understand their role. Ideally, you should try to speak to moot judges in person prior to the moot to discuss your expectations and to answer any questions that they have. A written judges' guide should accompany this briefing. What you include in your judges' guide will be specific to the moot that you are organising, but it must align with the rules of the moot that you have circulated to mooters. Within your judges' guide, consider addressing the following:

(1) **Moot problem question**: Set out the moot problem question in full so that all moot judges have it to hand during the moot. It is also helpful if you include a brief discussion of the current legal position relevant to the moot problem question and a summary of any relevant authorities. This should make it easier for moot judges to assess the quality of each mooter's submissions. Make it clear whether the moot judges are required to mark the mooters' written and oral submissions, or only their oral submissions.

(2) **Details of mooters**: Provide a brief explanation of the types of mooters participating in the moot, such as their level of study. Encourage moot judges to bear this information in mind so that they manage their expectations and interventions accordingly.

(3) **Rules of the moot**: Draw the moot judges' attention to the most important rules of the moot. These are rules such as the

allotted speaking time for each mooter, whether the timer will or will not be stopped for judicial interventions and any restriction on the number of authorities that each team can rely on. You could also include information about how moot judges should deal with infractions of these rules (for example, whether they should allow a mooter's request for a timing extension).

(4) Judging the moot: Mooters should feel like the moot judges have treated them equally and fairly. While moot judges will naturally adopt their own personal style of judging, it is important to encourage a general level of consistency. This can be done by creating a judges' score sheet that identifies aspects of a mooter's submissions that the moot judges are required to assess. Provide a scale of the marks that you would expect the moot judges to award for an excellent, good, average and poor performance. A template of a judges' score sheet for oral submissions is set out in Section 7.5.2.

(5) Judicial interventions: Moot judges will require guidance on interventions, particularly if they have not judged a moot before. It is important that moot judges adopt a measured approach to interventions, particularly interventions in the form of questions—too many will make it difficult for a mooter to get through his or her submissions (particularly if the timer is not stopped during these interventions), too few may prevent a moot judge from adequately testing a mooter's competence and knowledge. You may, therefore, want to provide moot judges with a rough estimate of how many times they should intervene during each mooter's submissions. Depending on the allotted speaking time for each mooter, two or three questions per mooter in the preliminary rounds is usually adequate (although this will depend on the nature of the moot, the experience of the mooters and the content of the moot problem question). This number could then increase in later rounds.

As part of the judges' guide, moot judges may also find it helpful if you provide them with examples of questions that they could ask mooters. This should help the moot judges to understand the nature and difficulty of appropriate questions.

Finally, while judicial interventions should be designed to test mooters, highlight to moot judges that they should avoid labouring a point if a mooter is clearly struggling. Instead, moot judges should encourage the mooter to move on and return to his or her submissions.

(6) **Giving a judgment**: At the conclusion of a moot, a judgment may be given on the law and on the winner of the moot—the team that wins from a legal perspective may not be the team that wins the moot. This is because the team that wins the moot will be determined by how persuasively and effectively that team argues their client's case in light of the available facts and law, rather than being based on the legal merits of the case alone.

(a) If you have structured your mooting competition as a knockout, moot judges will generally give a judgment on the law and the winning team after each moot.

(b) If you have structured your mooting competition as a league, you may decide that while the moot judges can give a judgment on the law and provide mooters with feedback on their performance, they should not give a judgment on the winners of the moot. This is because each team will need to moot against each other team in their group before deciding who will progress to the knockout stage.

(c) In the context of a mooting module, it is advisable that moot judges either give no judgment at all, or only give a judgment on the law and do not pass comment on the winning team or on the performance of individual mooters. Announcing the winning team of each moot may cause students to start speculating on their overall mark before this has been officially collated and released.

(7) **Giving feedback**: When giving a judgment on the law, moot judges should explain the rationale for this judgment. Similarly, when giving a judgment on the moot's winning team, moot judges should provide feedback to mooters. This can be done individually or in front of others in the moot courtroom.

Moot judges should try to provide mooters with constructive feedback. A mooter should be able to take a moot judge's feedback and address problem areas when preparing for his or her next moot. As a result, moot judges should highlight both positive and negative aspects of a mooter's performance. Any discussion of negative aspects should be accompanied by recommendations as to how a mooter can address the relevant issue. Providing mooters with both positive and constructive negative feedback gives those mooters guidance on how to improve their performance going forwards.

In the context of a mooting module, feedback is likely to be given individually and may be in written form after final marks have been released.

7.2.9 Logistics

When organising a moot, there are certain tasks that need to be managed. Set out below is a non-exhaustive list of these tasks. As you deal with each task, work with your institution's department of law and campus services. Depending on the size of the moot, you may also find it helpful to create smaller sub-committees of students who can help you with logistics—each sub-committee could be responsible for one or a number of these tasks.

(1) **Timing**: If you are organising a mooting competition, try to avoid scheduling moots or submission deadlines for times of the year when students are likely to have assignments due or examinations. This can be particularly difficult if you are organising an intervarsity moot. When you do decide on key dates, include them in the moot's publicity material. Students can then check these dates against their institution's own academic calendar.

As moots conducted in the context of a mooting module will form part of a student's examination for the module, you may need to schedule these moots towards the end of the module. There is, therefore, the risk that these moots will clash with students' study for other examinations. If timing permits, it may be easiest for both students and moot judges if any moots are scheduled for just prior to the start of your institution's examination period.

(2) **Rooms**: Make sure that you book rooms to use as moot courtrooms in advance. Create a spreadsheet where you input room numbers, together with the dates and times of the bookings.

When booking each room, try to book it for slightly longer than you anticipate will be needed for the moot, to cater for any delays. Also make sure that any rooms that you book are appropriately sized to fit the mooters, moot judges, court clerk and (in the case of a mooting competition) any audience members. Check in advance that each room will include enough tables and chairs to set up a moot courtroom correctly and any audio equipment (such as microphones) that you plan on using. A moot courtroom should also ideally have at least one lectern that mooters can use when speaking.

(3) **Court clerk**: In mooting competitions (and, depending on

resources, in moots held for mooting modules) you may have a court clerk sitting in each moot courtroom. Court clerks are typically law students and their role is to assist the moot judges by:

- instructing those in the courtroom to rise when the moot judges enter and leave the moot courtroom;
- announcing the case;
- keeping time and warning mooters as they approach the end of their allotted speaking time; and
- handling documents before, during and after the moot.

Court clerks can also assist the moot's organiser by setting up and maintaining the layout of the moot courtroom and directing the moot's participants to the right venues. Ensure that you have secured a commitment to participate from a sufficient number of court clerks and that you have briefed them prior to the moot.

(4) **Pens and paper**: Provide moot judges with pens, paper and a copy of the judges' guide. While mooters should bring their own stationery, it is a good idea to have a small surplus available.

(5) **Refreshments**:

(a) **In-moot refreshments**: At a minimum, provide moot judges with a jug or glass bottle of water and a sufficient number of glasses. In a mooting competition, also provide mooters with glasses of water.

(b) **Post-round refreshments**: If multiple rounds of a moot are being conducted on the same day, organise post-round refreshments in a common area.

(c) **Post-moot refreshments**: At the end of a mooting competition, you should consider providing more substantial refreshments. A post-moot event can be difficult to organise if your available budget is small. However, particularly after a full day of mooting, those involved in the moot may welcome a drinks or dinner event. It is also a good opportunity for mooters and moot judges to network outside of the moot courtroom. In order to manage the size of any such event, consider limiting your invitation only to mooters and moot judges and asking people to confirm in advance whether they will be attending.

(6) **Accommodation**: Accommodation for mooters and moot judges may be needed in a mooting competition if there is any

significant travel involved in attending the moot. Consider whether your budget for the moot is large enough to pay for this accommodation, or whether you will need to ask participants to pay for it themselves (in which case, you should provide them with a list of nearby accommodation options).

7.2.10 Moot timetable

A lot of planning goes into a successful moot. In order to keep on top of this planning, you may find it helpful to create a detailed timetable that covers the period prior to the moot and the day of the moot itself. Within this timetable, list every task that needs to be completed, together with the person (or sub-committee) responsible for the task and the task's anticipated completion date. Try to adhere to this timetable—this should help to avoid things getting forgotten or delayed.

7.3 The day of the moot

On the day of the moot (or, in a moot with multiple rounds, on the day of each round of moots), you and your sub-committees should try to arrive at the venue early to complete the final tasks.

(1) **Setting up the moot courtroom(s)**: Even if someone else has set up the moot courtrooms for you, try to go to each room to make sure that:

- the tables and chairs have been correctly set up;
- any lecterns and audio equipment have been installed;
- there is seating for the audience (if there is to be one);
- the moot judges have been provided with water, stationery and a copy of the judges' guide; and
- in a mooting competition, the mooters have also been provided with water.

It is advisable to also place a notice outside any moot courtroom explaining the times that the room will be in use, the names of the mooters and moot judges that will be using the room, and asking for silence.

(2) **Briefing court clerks**: If court clerks will be present in the moot courtrooms, meet these court clerks before the start of any moots. Make sure that these court clerks are aware of:

- their assigned moot courtroom;
- the allotted speaking time for each mooter;
- the points during each mooter's submissions (and

rebuttal) when a court clerk is to provide the mooter with a timing warning; and

- the nature of these warnings.

> **Practical Tip:**
>
> When and how court clerks provide timing warnings is for you to decide. These timing warnings should be useful and not overly intrusive. For example, it is not helpful to provide mooters with their only timing warning when they have ten seconds left in their submissions or for any warning to be so distracting that it flusters the mooters. Instead, consider asking court clerks to provide the first timing warning when mooters still have enough time left to adjust their submissions, if necessary. Similarly, holding up cards with the number of minutes or seconds that a mooter has left and then rapping on the table when the mooter's allotted speaking time has elapsed, are informative without being off-putting.

Make sure that court clerks are provided with any timers and timing cards that they need. Court clerks should also be told if they are expected to distribute and collect the judges' score sheets.

(3) **Meeting and briefing moot judges**: Try to arrange for moot judges to arrive 15 to 20 minutes before the start of the moot. This should give you time to meet each moot judge, to answer any final questions that the moot judges have and to brief them on the moot (if this has not already been done). Depending on the number of moot judges, you may be able to show each of them to the moot courtroom where they will be judging. Alternatively, ask court clerks to direct the moot judges to their moot courtroom.

(4) **Providing ongoing assistance during the moot**: As organiser, you will ideally not also be acting as a moot judge during a moot. Instead, try to be available for any questions that moot judges or mooters may have.

7.4 After the moot

7.4.1 Mooting competition

At the end of each round of a mooting competition, you must collect the judges' score sheets. Rather than asking the moot judges to bring these to you, it may be easier to task the court clerks with collecting all of the judges' score sheets from the moot courtroom and bringing these to you. Keep an up-to-date list of winning teams and pair up teams that are progressing to the next round of the competition. As soon as you can after the end of each round, provide information about the next round to any teams that are competing, moot judges and court clerks.

After the final of a mooting competition, you should consider giving a brief speech in which you thank any sponsors, moot judges, court clerks and all mooters for taking part. Confirm in advance whether the competition's sponsors would like their representatives to award any prizes, and whether the sponsors require any particular publicity photographs to be taken. If, however, one of the moot judges is a real judge, avoid photographing that judge in front of any branded material (to avoid any (even misplaced) suggestion of partiality in the future).

7.4.2 Mooting module

After the conclusion of the moots for a mooting module, confirm the marks that the moot judges have awarded each mooter. Make sure you collate these marks, together with any written comments from the moot judges.

7.5 Templates

7.5.1 Abridged rules of the moot

Options are included in square brackets and guidance notes are included in italics.
* Refers to information that is more relevant to a mooting competition.
^ Refers to information that is more relevant to a mooting module.

Rules of the [*name of mooting competition/name of institution/code of module*] [Mooting Competition*/Mooting Module^] [*year*]

In these rules, a reference to the 'Moot Court Convenor' shall be a reference to [*organiser's name*] or [his/her] appointed representative.

Eligibility*

1. The mooting competition is open to teams of [*number*] students, each of whom [*any eligibility criteria, such as year of study*].

2. Each institution may enter up to [*number*] teams. If an institution wishes to enter any additional teams, please contact the Moot Court Convenor. Institutions may send an alternative team to compete in any round of the mooting competition only with the express written permission of the Moot Court Convenor, which permission may be withheld at the Moot Court Convenor's absolute discretion.

Registration*

3. All teams participating in the mooting competition must register [online at the following website [*address of any website set up for registration*]]/ [by email to the following email address [*organiser's email address or a general email address for the mooting competition*]] and pay a registration fee of €[*amount*].

4. This registration fee [is non-refundable and] should be paid into the following bank account [*full details of the relevant bank account*]. If paying by bank transfer, please include your institution's name as the reference. Alternatively, teams may pay by cheques made payable to [*name*].

5. The deadline for registration and payment of the registration fee is [*date*].

Structure of the Moot

6. [The mooting competition will follow a [knockout/league] structure, with each round taking place on the following dates: [*insert dates of each round of the mooting competition. Indicate here if all rounds are taking place over one or two days, rather than being spread out.*]]*

7. [There will be one round of moots taking place during the week commencing [*date*]. A timetable will separately be circulated by the Moot Court Convenor indicating the date and timing of each team's moot.]^

8. A moot may only be rescheduled with the express written permission of the Moot Court Convenor, which permission may be withheld at the Moot Court Convenor's absolute discretion.

9. [Each team must be prepared to represent both the Appellant and the Respondent in the appeal. Each team will be informed prior to each round which party that team will represent in the upcoming round.]*

10. [Each team will be informed on [*date*] whether they will represent the Appellant or the Respondent in the appeal.]^

11. The Moot Court Convenor will hold a draw to determine which teams will compete against each other.

12. [Each member of a team will receive the same mark for the team's written submissions, while each student will receive an individual mark for his/ her oral submissions. Your final mark for this module will be determined as follows [*insert formula*].]^

Written Submissions

13. [Each team must submit: one memorial of not more than [*amount*] [words/pages] on behalf of the Appellant; and one memorial of not more than [*amount*] [words/pages] on behalf of the Respondent. Please do not include details of your institution in your memorial.]*

14. [Each team must submit a memorial of not more than [*amount*] [words/ pages] on behalf of that team's client.]^

15. Each memorial must be accompanied by a list of authorities, which list may include no more than [*number*] authorities. Any authority explicitly referred to in the moot problem question and extracts from authorities contained in any authority relied on by a team will not be counted towards that team's maximum number of authorities. The list of authorities will not count towards the maximum [word/page] count allowed for each memorial.

16. Each memorial and list of authorities must:
    a. be typed and printed single-sided on A4 paper;
    b. have numbered pages;
    c. use Times New Roman font size 12;
    d. be 1.5 line spaced; and
    e. use justified alignment and standard margins.

17. Each memorial and list of authorities must be emailed to the following address [*email address*] by [*deadline for submissions*] [*in the case of a mooting module, also include any requirement for memorials and lists of authorities to be submitted via plagiarism software*].

18. [Except with the express written permission of the Moot Court Convenor, which permission may be withheld at the Moot Court Convenor's absolute discretion, only submissions that are contained in a team's memorial can be raised in oral submissions.]

19. [Marks awarded for each team's memorial will not count towards a team's overall mark in the mooting competition, other than in the case of a draw.]*

Oral Submissions

20. Mooters will be notified in advance of the location for each moot's oral submissions. Please arrive at the location before the scheduled start time. If any mooter arrives to a moot's oral submissions late, the moot's judge may, in his or her absolute discretion, decide to begin the moot without the relevant mooter or to disqualify that mooter's team.

21. Each moot will have [*one*] judge. [The final of the mooting competition will have [*three*] judges.]*

22. [At the start of a moot, each team must provide each moot judge (with a copy also provided to the team's opponents) with a bundle containing copies of each authority that the team intends to refer to in oral submissions.]

23. Each mooter shall have [*time*] minutes to present his or her submissions. Warnings will be given when each mooter has [*time*] and [*time*] minutes left to speak and again when each mooter's allotted speaking time has elapsed.

24. The timer [will/will not] be stopped for judicial interventions.

25. [Counsel for the Appellant will have [*time*] minutes for rebuttal following the conclusion of both parties' submissions. [Counsel for the Respondent will have [*time*] minutes for surrebuttal, during which time, only points raised in the Appellant's rebuttal may be addressed.] Each team may waive the right of rebuttal or surrebuttal. However, if counsel for the Appellant waives the right of rebuttal, the Respondent's right of surrebuttal is automatically waived.]

26. There shall be no appeal against a moot judge's judgment.

Moot Problem Question

27. [The moot problem question shall be circulated on [*date*]]/[The moot problem question is set out below].

28. The Moot Court Convenor must receive any objections to the moot problem question at least seven days prior to the date of [the first round of moots].

Contact

29. The Moot Court Convenor can be contacted as follows: [*contact details*].

7.5.2 Judges' score sheet (for oral submissions)

Marking Guide (for each marked aspect of a mooter's oral submissions): • Excellent: 15–20 • Good: 11–14 • Average: 8–10 • Poor: <8		
	Counsel 1	Counsel 2
Name of mooter		
Client of mooter		
(a) **Content of submissions** *Does the mooter display a command of the relevant areas of law? Consider whether the mooter's submissions are legally sound and backed up by appropriate authority. Consider his/her ability to summarise facts, cases and legal principles.*	/20	/20

(b) **Structure and clarity**	/20	/20
Consider whether the mooter's submissions are logical and work together. Consider how the mooter's submissions support those of his/her teammate.		
(c) **Advocacy skills**	/20	/20
Consider the mooter's persuasiveness, clarity, tone of voice and ability to effectively use his/her time.		
(d) **Style and professionalism**	/20	/20
Consider the mooter's use of appropriate language and courtroom etiquette.		
(e) **Ability to respond**	/20	/20
Consider the mooter's ability to respond to judicial interventions and to deal with his/her opponents' arguments in rebuttal.		
Total	/100	/100

7.6 Chapter summary

1. Organising a moot requires planning and organisation.

2. Decide in advance what tasks need to be managed before, during and after the moot—consider whether support is available from your institution's department of law or campus services, or from sub-committees that you have created.

3. The specifics of organising a moot will vary between moots and will depend on whether a moot is a competition or part of a module.

4. Before the moot, confirm the structure of the moot, the type of mooters who can participate in the moot and who those mooters will represent. You may also need to draft (or update) the rules of the moot and the moot problem question and organise logistics, sponsorship, publicity and the selection of moot judges.

5. On the day of the moot, make sure that the moot courtrooms are set up and that all relevant parties are adequately briefed.

6. After the moot, confirm the winning team and organise post-moot refreshments (if relevant).

Chapter 8

Sample Moot Problem Questions

Set out below are sample moot problem questions. Sample question 1 is based on the moot problem question for the 2018 Silken Thomas National Moot Court Competition. If you use any of these sample moot problem questions in a moot that you are organising, you should conduct your own research to update the selected moot problem question if necessary.

CRIMINAL LAW

8.1 Sample question 1 (Criminal law; Evidence)

IN THE COURT OF APPEAL (CRIMINAL DIVISION)

Spotter v Director of Public Prosecutions[1]

On the evening of 5 November 2017, Mr Barry Spotter was summoned to the house of his close friend, Mr Ronald Beasley. When he arrived, he found Ronald waiting for him in a state. Ronald had discovered that his wife, Ann-Marie, had been engaged in an extra-marital affair with a colleague, Mr Drake Malty, and was leaving him to live with Drake. Naturally, Ronald was upset and angry that his wife of twenty years could have done this to him.

Barry spent the next three hours with Ronald helping him to drown his sorrows. At some point Ronald said, 'I'm going to go to Drake's house and rough him up a little, so he thinks again about stealing another man's wife.' Barry tried to talk him out of this idea, as Drake was known to have dealings with criminal gangs in the area, but to no avail. He decided that he would not allow his friend to walk into this confrontation alone and so agreed to accompany him. Barry knew Ronald owned a gun, but could only see that he

---

[1] Based on the moot problem question used in the 2018 Silken Thomas National Moot Court Competition (held in Maynooth University on 13–14 April 2018). This question has been included with the permission of the 2018 Silken Thomas National Moot Court Competition moot court convenor, Ciara McCarthy. It includes minor typographical amendments for consistency with the other sample moot problem questions. This moot problem question is based on the law as it stood in April 2018.

had brought a wooden bat along with him. He decided not to ask whether Ronald had brought the gun with him, as he could tell at this stage Ronald was in a state of rage.

On the way to Drake's house, it was decided that Barry would ensure Ronald's wife, Ann-Marie, was in a separate room so that Ronald could 'teach Drake a lesson' and Barry could assist him to show him what happens when 'you go off with another man's wife'. When they got to the house, Ann-Marie answered the door. Both Barry and Ronald forced her into the kitchen, and closed and blocked the door.

Ronald went into the sitting room where Drake was playing a video game. Barry followed Ronald into the sitting room after first ensuring the door to the kitchen was blocked. They both proceeded to talk to Drake about his actions. However, a violent fight ensued between all of them. Ronald hit Drake twice with the bat on his torso. Barry thought he could hear Ann-Marie in the kitchen attempting to break down the door. Ronald told Barry to go and make sure that Ann-Marie could not leave and to try and calm her down to avoid alerting the neighbours. Barry held the kitchen door closed and tried to calm Ann-Marie down. He could still hear Drake's shouts from the other room. At this point, he entered the other room to get Ronald to leave. However, as he walked into the room he saw Ronald pointing a gun towards Drake. Barry was about to reach for the gun, but a shot went off and hit Drake.

Barry called an ambulance and fled the scene with Ronald. Drake was brought to hospital, but it was confirmed that he had died on arrival from the gunshot wound. Ann-Marie informed the Gardaí what had happened and the following morning, Ronald and Barry were both arrested pursuant to s 4 of the Criminal Law Act 1997 and brought to the local Garda station. They were both detained under s 4 of the Criminal Justice Act 1984 and they both requested to speak to a solicitor. Once Barry's solicitor arrived at the station, he was permitted a five-minute consultation with his solicitor before being brought in for an interview. He requested that his solicitor be present with him during the interview, but this request was refused. Following this, two Gardaí questioned him three times over the course of 24 hours, for a period of three, four and five hours each, respectively. He received a permissible number of breaks between questioning. He made a confession during the final interview as regards his role in the events that had unfolded.

Ronald and Barry were both charged with the murder of Drake, with the Director of Public Prosecutions (the 'DPP') submitting that there was a joint enterprise between the co-accused. They both pleaded not guilty.

During the *voir dire*, it was argued by Barry's legal team that the statement from Barry in which he implicated himself should not be included for the jury to consider as:

1. this statement was made after oppressive questioning in contravention of reg 12(4) of the Criminal Justice Act 1984 (Treatment of Persons in Custody in Garda Síochána Stations) Regulations 1987, SI 1987/119 (the '1987 Regulations'); and
2. Barry was refused the presence of a solicitor during the interviews, something that should have been allowed.

This application was strongly contested by the DPP.

The trial judge, McDougal J decided that as Barry had access to legal advice and she was satisfied that a breach of the 1987 Regulations does not of itself result in the exclusion of evidence, she would allow the statement to be admitted for the jury to consider. McDougal J stated that the non-admittance of the solicitor during questioning was in accordance with the Supreme Court decision in *People (DPP) v Doyle* [2017] IESC 1, [2018] 1 IR 1. Barry's counsel further submitted that the shooting of the deceased was an unauthorised act that went beyond the scope of his agreement with Ronald and that the decision of *People (DPP) v Murray* [1977] 1 IR 360 should be followed. McDougal J disagreed with this submission and favoured *People (DPP) v Doohan* [2002] 4 IR 463.

Following submissions made by both legal teams, McDougal J, in her judge's charge to the jury, included the following:

1. that the jury had to consider whether there was an express or tacit agreement between Ronald and Barry to seriously injure Drake and, if they found this was the case, they could reach the verdict of guilty for both defendants; and
2. in coming to that decision, if the jury found that Barry participated in the joint enterprise with any foresight that Drake could suffer serious bodily injury, it was within the scope of contemplation that Drake may die and was therefore evidence of intention.

The jury found Ronald and Barry both guilty of the murder of Drake under the doctrine of common design.

Barry appealed his conviction to the Court of Appeal (Criminal Division) on the following grounds:

1. that Ronald's actions went beyond the scope of what was agreed and, therefore, Barry was not a party to a common design and the trial judge erred in not directing the jury in accordance with the decision of *People (DPP) v Murray* [1977] 1 IR 360;
2. that the trial judge erred in law on the basis that common design is an agreement and not mere contemplation, and that the court should have followed the cases of *People (DPP) v Cumberton*, unreported, Court of Criminal Appeal, 5 December 1994 and *R v Jogee* [2016] UKSC 8, which ruled that foresight should not be used as a definitive test for common design;
3. that the non-admittance of Barry's solicitor during questioning was in fact a breach and not in accordance with the decision of *Salduz v Turkey* (2008) 49 EHRR 421 and other European Court on Human Rights jurisprudence, distinguishing the decision of *People (DPP) v Doyle* [2017] IESC 1, [2018] 1 IR 1, as Barry had specifically requested a solicitor to be present during questioning and, therefore, the trial judge erred in admitting the statement; and
4. in any event, that the trial judge erred in law in admitting the statement of Barry for the jury to consider, due to the oppressive nature of the questioning.

The DPP submitted that:[2]

1. the trial judge was correct in directing the jury that if there was an express or tacit agreement to seriously injure Drake, they could find Barry guilty in accordance with the decision of *People (DPP) v Doohan* [2002] 4 IR 463;
2. the trial judge was correct in directing that the jury could find any foresight on behalf of Barry as evidence of intention in accordance with the case of *DPP v Costa and Batista* [2008] IECCA 1, which used the foresight test from *R v Uddin* [1999] QB 431;
3. the trial judge was correct in admitting the statement to be

---

[2] Please note that not all moot problem questions include the submissions of both the Appellant and the Respondent.

considered by the jury as to date, Ireland has not opted in
to EU Directive 2013/48 on the right of access to a lawyer
and the decision of *People (DPP) v Doyle* [2017] IESC 1,
[2018] 1 IR 1 is the most recent and binding authority on
this matter; and

4. further, s 7(3) of the Criminal Justice Act 1984 provides
   that a breach of the rules does not automatically result
   in the exclusion of evidence. As a result, the trial judge
   was correct in allowing the statement to be admitted.

8.2 Sample question 2 (Criminal law; Necessity)

IN THE COURT OF APPEAL (CRIMINAL DIVISION)

Smith v Director of Public Prosecution

In June of this year, Henry Johnson and Stephen Smith embarked
on a kayaking trip in Co. Wicklow. They had planned their trip
meticulously and it was supposed to last for seven days. On
day four of their trip, they took a wrong turn. They were then
unexpectedly caught by rapids and were dragged towards a 60-
foot waterfall. Henry fell out of his kayak and began to panic.
Stephen threw out a rope, which Henry grabbed onto. However,
Henry continued to panic—he was thrashing in the water and
pulling Stephen towards the edge of the waterfall. Henry's cries
and movement also startled a nest of bees in a tree next to the edge
of the river. The bees began to swarm around Stephen and Henry.
Stephen is extremely allergic to bee stings.

Stephen tried to calm Henry (while himself trying to stay calm),
but it proved to be futile—Henry was now screaming and pulled
them both towards the waterfall's edge. Stephen called out to
Henry to tell him that he was going to cut the rope as otherwise,
they would both fall over the waterfall. Henry begged him not to,
but they were now rapidly approaching the edge of the waterfall
and the bees were flying around Stephen's head. Stephen cut the
rope and watched Henry fall over the edge of the waterfall. He then
managed to guide his own kayak towards the edge of the river,
where he got out and hid from the bees for six hours.

At nightfall, Stephen staggered through thick woods until he found
a house. He banged on the door until the occupants woke up and let
him in. He told them that his friend, Henry, had died in a kayaking
accident and he had no idea where Henry was.

Unbeknownst to Stephen, Henry had actually survived the fall over the waterfall, but had suffered significant internal injuries. He was discovered by a group of walkers the next morning and was transported by air ambulance to the nearest hospital. There, medical staff immediately administered penicillin, despite the fact that Henry wore an armband that stated that he was allergic to penicillin. Henry died in hospital five days later. Stephen was arrested and charged with murder.

At trial, Stephen pleaded the defence of necessity to the charge of murder. He also argued that the medical staff in the hospital had been negligent in their treatment of Henry.

The trial judge, Francis J, refused to allow the defence of necessity to be put to the jury on the basis that one person's life is not superior to another's. He also directed the jury that if the original injury is an operating cause of death, then the impact of intervening medical treatment should not be taken into account. The jury returned a verdict of guilty.

Stephen appealed his conviction on the following grounds:

1. necessity should have been put to the jury, as it may have provided a defence in the circumstances of the case; and
2. alternatively, the trial judge erred in directing the jury that intervening medical treatment should not be considered when determining whether Stephen was guilty of murder.

CONSTITUTIONAL LAW

8.3 Sample question 3 (Right to earn a livelihood; Inviolability of the dwelling)

IN THE COURT OF APPEAL (CRIMINAL DIVISION)

White v Director of Public Prosecutions

Terence White has a farm in Co. Mayo where he has been growing a plant variety called Happy Spots for nearly 30 years. He is the only farmer in Ireland to grow these plants. The conditions on Terence's farm are perfect for growing Happy Spots plants and last year Terence grew 25 acres of healthy plants.

Happy Spots plants are entirely innocuous when they are growing and when their leaves are green and fresh. When picked and added to food, they add a pleasant nutty flavour to that food. The leaves have always been sold by Terence in compliance with food regulation. However, when the leaves of the Happy Spots plants are dried, mixed with vinegar, sugar and washing-up liquid, they form a paste (colloquially known as 'Happy S') that has strong hallucinogenic qualities. Terence had heard of Happy S, but his life is very busy and he never stopped to make the connection between Happy Spots and Happy S. Neither Happy S nor Happy Spots has yet been declared a controlled drug for the purposes of the Misuse of Drugs Act 1977.

Last month, after reports that a cottage industry producing Happy S had developed, two Gardaí arrived at Terence's front door demanding to see his Happy Spots plants. Alarmed by this demand, Terence asked to see a warrant, which the Gardaí did not have. Terence refused to let them in and asked them to come back when his lawyer was present. The Gardaí left the front door, but set up a visible presence outside Terence's house, with Gardaí patrolling regularly and a marked Garda van parked outside. Three times over the next two days members of the Gardaí knocked on the front door asking to see the Happy Spots plants. Terence repeatedly told the Gardaí that his lawyer was not yet present and asked them to leave. The Garda presence, the sounds of the Garda radios and the repeated visits by Gardaí resulted in Terence becoming shaken by the experience. He started vomiting and became very anxious.

Two days after the Gardaí first showed up at Terence's house, Terence's lawyer arrived. Terence allowed the Gardaí to enter his house so that he could show them his Happy Spots plants. As soon as they saw the plants, the Gardaí arrested Terence and charged him under the Criminal Justice (Psychoactive Substances) Act 2010. All of the Happy Spots plants on his farm were seized and destroyed by the Gardaí.

Following submissions made by both legal teams, Pen J, the trial judge, condemned the evils of profiting from, or living off the proceeds of, iniquity. Pen J noted that: 'Happy S, like marijuana, is different to alcohol. In today's world of political instability and economic stress, a quiet drink with friends is not something to be condemned. On the other hand, substances like Happy S bring nothing but destruction to our country.' Terence was convicted of the supply of a psychoactive substance under the Criminal Justice (Psychoactive Substances) Act 2010.

Terence appealed his conviction to the Court of Appeal (Criminal Division) on the following grounds:

1. his conviction constituted a disproportionate interference with his constitutional right to earn a living; and
2. in the alternative, Pen J erred in law in not considering the Appellant's constitutional right to the inviolability of his dwelling.

THE LAW OF TORTS

8.4 Sample question 4 (Negligence; Duty of care)

IN THE COURT OF APPEAL (CIVIL DIVISION)

O'Sullivan v Bryan

After a day at the library, Jennifer O'Sullivan took the bus home. As she got onto the bus, she noticed that her university tutor, Professor Petch, was sitting towards the front of the bus. Jennifer sat down next to Professor Petch and they spent the rest of the journey chatting about how Jennifer had been finding university, her anxieties about living away from her parents and her extreme worries about her upcoming exams. At her stop, Jennifer exited the bus and waved at Professor Petch as the bus pulled off.

As Jennifer turned the corner next to her apartment, she heard the screeching of tyres and a loud crash. Jennifer ran back around the corner. There she found that a car had crashed into the side of the bus. Professor Petch was seriously injured, as was the bus driver and another passenger. The crash scene was chaotic. An ambulance was called and, once the injured had been taken to the hospital, Jennifer's housemate led her back to her house, where she made Jennifer a cup of tea.

In the coming days, Jennifer found it difficult to come to terms with the accident. Her panic attacks (which she has been having since starting university) intensified, she started having nightmares and soon dropped out of university. Jennifer went to her family doctor, who suggested that Jennifer may be depressed.

Eloise Bryan had been driving the car that crashed into the bus and, at the time of the crash, she had been responding to an email on her phone, rather than looking at the road. Jennifer took an action against Eloise for negligently inflicted psychological harm.

Coffey J in the High Court considered the test established by Hamilton CJ in *Kelly v Hennessy* [1995] 3 IR 253. He found in favour of Eloise on the basis that while Eloise may have been negligent, she could not be held liable for any psychological harm suffered by Jennifer, as she owed no duty of care to Jennifer.

Jennifer appealed to the Court of Appeal (Civil Division) on the following grounds:

1. the trial judge erred in law by finding that Eloise owed no duty of care to Jennifer; and
2. the trial judge erred in law by finding that Eloise could not be held liable for the psychological harm suffered by Jennifer.

8.5 Sample question 5 (Negligence; Causation)

IN THE COURT OF APPEAL (CIVIL DIVISION)

Potts (as a minor suing by his father and next friend, OP) v Short

Sophie Short ran a pottery course for primary school students in Castlebar, Co. Mayo. On the first Sunday of last month, she took three of her best students to the local art gallery to look at the sculptures. While at the gallery, Sophie was discussing a new sculpture with the students. Suddenly, two men in the gallery started shouting threateningly and waving knives. One man grabbed a sculpture near the front door and hurled it at the security guard, while the other man slashed a painting. Sophie and the students hid behind the nearest sculpture, which was big enough to hide them all from the men.

Sophie looked around her. She could see that they were hiding near an open window, which faced the gallery's gardens. While the men were still shouting and grabbing what they could from the gallery, Sophie ushered the three students towards the window. As was doing so, one of the men turned around. He saw what was happening, yelled out and threw the painting that he was holding at those fleeing. The painting narrowly missed Sophie, but its corner hit one of the students (Philip Potts) on the back of the head. Philip fell forward, but managed to get out through the exit into the gallery's gardens. All of the other students and Sophie escaped unhurt. Philip was rushed to hospital. However, he has haemophilia and the excessive bleeding due to the cut on his head caused Philip to suffer brain damage.

Philip (through his father) sued Sophie for negligence. In the High Court, Jackson J found in favour of Sophie on the basis that:

1. notwithstanding any duty of care that may have been owed by Sophie, she is not responsible for the actions of a third party in these circumstances. Quoting from the case of *KBC Ireland Plc v BCM Hanby Wallace (Affirm)* [2013] IESC 32 [84], [2013] 3 IR 759 [84], Jackson J noted that 'the law does not usually recognise a mere *causa sine qua non* (sometimes called "but for" causation) as a sufficient basis for the imposition of liability on a defendant. Many acts, even if negligent, are too remote to provide a just basis for imposition of liability'; and

2. in any event, Sophie appears to be a conscientious teacher who was just trying to protect her students in the way she thought best.

Philip appealed to the Court of Appeal (Civil Division) on the following grounds:

1. Jackson J erred in law in holding that Sophie could not be held liable for the actions of the man in the gallery. The chain of causation was not broken and Sophie is solely or, in the alternative, concurrently, liable for Philip's injuries; and

2. Jackson J erred in law in holding that Sophie's negligence should be determined by a subjective standard.

8.6 Sample question 6 (Tort law; Contract law)

IN THE SUPREME COURT

Glass Houses Ltd v Potter

Sarah Potter purchased a new build house in Dalkey, Co. Dublin from a developer (Glass Houses Ltd). Sarah had heard very positive reports about properties built by Glass Houses Ltd and so she was delighted to find a two-bedroom house for sale for €500,000.

In December 2013, Glass Houses Ltd sent the sale and purchase agreement ('SPA') to Sarah via her solicitors. Her solicitors confirmed that the SPA followed a standard form used by Glass Houses Ltd, and that Glass Houses Ltd had refused to make any amendments to this agreement on the basis that Glass Houses Ltd had previously used the same standard form for the sale of more than 400 houses.

Sarah read the SPA and signed it as requested. When reading the SPA, Sarah did not notice the text included in the footer on the back page. This footer set out in small letters the locations of Glass Houses Ltd's regional offices. It also included the following words: 'This agreement is subject to our terms and conditions, which are available on our website.' While Sarah had previously looked at Glass Houses Ltd's website when trying to decide whether to buy a house, she had not seen the link to their terms and conditions. If Sarah had read the terms and conditions set out on the website, she would have read the following:

> 'Glass Houses Ltd excludes all liability for economic loss suffered by a purchaser, howsoever caused.'

Sarah moved into her brand new house in March 2014 and lived there until January 2018.

In September 2017, the roof of a house built by another developer collapsed, killing the occupants of the house. An official report into the collapsed roof was published on 15 November 2017 and indicated that the collapse had been caused by the buckling of APP Series 2 Beams (a type of load-bearing beam) due to extremely warm outside temperatures.

In 2010, the Government had released a recommendation noting that APP Series 2 Beams were unsuitable for use in residential properties due to their loss of structural integrity in certain conditions. The Government did not actually ban the use of these beams as part of this recommendation.

In October 2017, Sarah received an offer of a new job in New York, which was due to start on 30 January 2018. She decided to sell her house in Dalkey ahead of her move. On 10 November 2017, Sarah listed her house with a number of estate agents for a sale price of €600,000. This sale price was consistent with three independent valuations that Sarah had received in October 2017 as to the correct value of her house. She received an offer of €600,000 on

14 November 2017. However, on 20 November 2017, following a series of checks, Glass Houses Ltd publicly released a statement confirming use of APP Series 2 Beams in all properties that it had built (including Sarah's). As the Government had not banned use of APP Series 2 Beams, Glass Houses Ltd also confirmed in its statement that it would not be undertaking remedial action to replace the APP Series 2 Beams in any of the properties that it had built.

Following Glass Houses Ltd's confirmation that all of its properties contained APP Series 2 Beams and that it would not be replacing these, the prospective purchasers of Sarah's house withdrew their offer of €600,000 citing use of the APP Series 2 Beams in the roof of the house as the reason for this withdrawal. The only other offer that Sarah received for the house was €400,000. Again, the use of APP Series 2 Beams was cited as the reason why the full asking price was not offered. By early January 2018, Sarah was desperate to sell her house and so she accepted the offer of €400,000.

Sarah commenced proceedings for negligence against Glass Houses Ltd in the High Court. She sought recovery of the €200,000 fall in the value of her house. At trial, Glass Houses Ltd confirmed that they had been aware of the 2010 Government recommendation regarding the use of APP Series 2 Beams, but at the time of constructing Sarah's house, they had not made enquiries as to the type of beams that were being installed by their contractors. The High Court found in favour of Sarah. Glass Houses Ltd appealed to the Court of Appeal (Civil Division).

Calms J in the Court of Appeal dismissed the appeal on the basis that:

1. the exclusion clause contained in Glass Houses Ltd's terms and conditions was not incorporated into the SPA between Sarah and Glass Houses Ltd; and
2. Glass Houses Ltd could be held liable for pure economic loss suffered by Sarah.

Glass Houses Ltd appealed to the Supreme Court on the following grounds:

1. Calms J erred in law in finding that the statements in Glass Houses Ltd's terms and conditions were not incorporated into the SPA between Sarah and Glass Houses Ltd; and

2. even if the relevant statements had not been incorporated into the SPA, Calms J erred in law in finding that Glass Houses Ltd could be held liable for pure economic loss.

CONTRACT LAW

8.7 Sample question 7 (Contract law; Intention to create legal relations)

IN THE COURT OF APPEAL (CIVIL DIVISION)

Crystal v Catel

Sarah Crystal decided to sell her exercise bike, as she had never used it. When she was having dinner with her parents last month, she mentioned that she was planning to advertise the exercise bike in the local newspaper in order to find a buyer. Henrietta Catel, Sarah's mother, said that she would pay Sarah €900 for the exercise bike, as she needed a new one. Sarah had hoped that she would receive more for the bike and told her mother that she would sleep on the offer.

After dinner, Henrietta met her son (and Sarah's brother) Steve for a drink. She mentioned that Sarah was selling her exercise bike and that she had already offered Sarah €900 for it. Steve, who had recently broken his exercise bike, decided that he wanted the bike and sent an email to Sarah offering her €1,000. Sarah decided that she would sleep on this offer and so did not reply to Steve that evening.

The next morning, Sarah sent an email to Steve accepting his offer of €1,000, so long as he picked up the exercise bike himself. Sarah then immediately entered into a separate contract with a sports equipment retailer to buy a treadmill with the proceeds that she would receive from the sale of the exercise bike. Steve left his house early that morning to go to the local amusement park and had not yet checked his emails when he bumped into Jon Short, his university friend. Jon mentioned in passing that he had heard Sarah badmouthing Steve's wife. Steve was furious and called Sarah immediately. Sarah confessed and said that she had always hated Steve's wife. Steve was extremely angry that Sarah had acted this way and as soon as he ended the call he decided that he was no longer interested in buying the exercise bike.

When Steve got home that evening, he read the email that Sarah had sent earlier in the day accepting his offer of €1,000 for the exercise bike. He wrote an email back to Sarah telling her to get stuffed as he had no intention of buying the exercise bike now that he had found out about what kind of person Sarah really was. Sarah sued Steve in the High Court for breach of contract.

In the High Court, Betty J found in favour of Steve on the following basis:

1. in line with the statements of Budd J in *Re Rogers (Deceased)*, unreported, Supreme Court, 16 July 1970, there was no intention to create legal relations between the parties; and
2. no enforceable contract existed as there was insufficient agreement between the parties.

Sarah appealed to the Court of Appeal (Civil Division) on the following grounds:

1. the trial judge erred in finding that the statements made in *Re Rogers (Deceased)* applied to this case as there was an intention to create legal relations between the parties. An enforceable contract was, therefore, formed at the point at which Sarah sent the email to Steve accepting his offer; and
2. in the alternative, Steve should be estopped from reneging on his offer.

8.8 Sample question 8 (Contract law; Penalty clauses)

IN THE COURT OF APPEAL (CIVIL DIVISION)

Johnson v Bikes4Rent Ltd

Jeremy Johnson wanted to rent a quad bike to drive around his father's farm while home from university (this was the most effective way of travelling around the farm, which Jeremy worked on during the holidays). On 25 June 2018, Jeremy approached Bikes4Rent Ltd about an offer that they were advertising. Jeremy found the quad bike that he wanted to rent in the Bikes4Rent Ltd showroom and sat down with the sales assistant to go through the relevant contractual documents. The terms of the rental agreement provided that Jeremy would pay Bikes4Rent Ltd €1,000 upfront for one month's rental. The rental agreement also provided (in Clause 5.2) that:

> '5.2 Liquidated Damages: A failure by the Renter to return the Rented Property to the Owner by 2pm on the agreed date of return will result in €400 being charged to the Renter.'

The 'Renter' was defined as Jeremy, the 'Rented Property' was defined as the quad bike that Jeremy had chosen and the 'Owner' was defined as Bikes4Rent Ltd. When Jeremy queried this clause, the sales assistant told him that it was a standard term in all of their rental agreements and represented the average extra cost incurred by Bikes4Rent Ltd when someone failed to return a rented vehicle on time.

Jeremy signed the rental agreement immediately, but Bikes4Rent Ltd's only signatory was sick that day. Jeremy was told to come back first thing the following morning to pick up the countersigned contract containing both Jeremy's and Bikes4Rent Ltd's signatures. Just after signing the rental agreement, Jeremy also arranged for the €1,000 to be transferred into Bikes4Rent Ltd's bank account. This money would appear in Bike4Rent Ltd's bank account on 26 June 2018.

The next day, 26 June 2018, was Jeremy's 18th birthday. He arrived at the Bikes4Rent Ltd showroom at 11.00am, where he took a copy of the fully signed rental agreement (which was dated 26 June 2018) and secured the quad bike on a trailer to drive it to his father's farm.

At the end of the month-long rental, Jeremy brought the quad bike back to Bikes4Rent Ltd's offices. Due to traffic, he did not deliver the quad bike until 4pm. Bikes4Rent Ltd handed Jeremy a bill for €400 due to the late delivery of the quad bike. Jeremy refused to pay. Bikes4Rent Ltd sued Jeremy for the amount due.

At trial, Bikes4Rent Ltd confirmed that due to recent streamlining processes implemented in their offices, the actual additional cost that they had incurred because of Jeremy's failure to return the quad bike on time was actually €100. In the High Court, Duncan J found in favour of Bikes4Rent Ltd on the following basis:

1. the contract between the parties was enforceable; and
2. Clause 5.2 of the sales agreement represented a 'genuine' attempt by the parties to estimate in advance the loss that would result from a breach of the contract. That clause

5.2 was not in practice an accurate pre-estimate of loss did not mean that it was penal.

Jeremy appealed to the Court of Appeal (Civil Division) on the following grounds:

1. Jeremy was not yet 18 years of age when he signed the contract and so could not be bound by its terms; and
2. in the alternative, Clause 5.2 of the rental agreement was an unenforceable penalty clause designed to deter Jeremy from breach of the rental agreement.

LAND LAW

8.9 Sample question 9 (Land law; Lease/Licence)

IN THE COURT OF APPEAL (CIVIL DIVISION)

Wilson v Butler

Stephen Butler owned a large house in Portobello, Dublin 8. Within the house there was a self-contained apartment with its own entryway that was separate from the main entrance to the house. The apartment shared a small garden with the main house, which was accessible by the back door to the apartment. Stephen retained a key to this back door.

In order to earn some money, Stephen put up an online advertisement for an apartment to let. Roger Wilson, a trainee solicitor, met with Stephen and expressed an interest in moving into the apartment. Stephen and Roger entered into an agreement entitled 'Licence Agreement'. Before signing this, Roger looked through the terms of the agreement. He noted that under the terms of this agreement:

1. Roger was required to pay €1,000 per month to a bank account specified in the agreement;
2. the term of the agreement was one year;
3. Roger was only allowed to have overnight guests on Friday and Saturday nights and was not allowed to have more than one overnight guest at a time without prior permission from Stephen;
4. Stephen would not enter the apartment without express permission from Roger other than: (1) to perform

maintenance checks; and (2) if Stephen needed to check the electricity meter for the main house (this meter was located in the kitchen of the apartment). In these circumstances, the agreement provided that Stephen would enter via the back door; and

5. Stephen was entitled, without permission from Roger, to let the apartment above Roger to a third party. That third party would only be able to access his or her apartment through the same entrance as Roger (but would not be able to access the rest of Roger's apartment).

Before he moved into the apartment, Roger received no notice that Stephen has opted out of Part 4 of the Residential Tenancies Act 2004.

Roger lived in the apartment alone for one year (the apartment above Roger was not let during that time). During that year, Stephen entered the apartment once in order to rehang all of the internal doors. He never entered the apartment for the purpose of reading the meter as Roger emailed these readings to him.

At the end of the one-year period of Roger's occupancy in the apartment, Stephen telephoned Roger to ask him what his forwarding address would be once he had vacated the apartment. Roger refused to leave the apartment, stating that the agreement between the parties was a fixed-term tenancy and that Roger had acquired security of tenure pursuant to the Residential Tenancies Act 2004.

Stephen refused to accept this. Stephen went to the Residential Tenancies Board, but was told that it had no jurisdiction in respect of the application. Stephen then sought declaratory relief in the High Court.

In the High Court, Waters J found in favour of Stephen on the following basis:

1. whether something is a lease or a licence is based entirely on the subjective intentions of the parties; and
2. quoting from the judgment of Hunt J in *Board of Management of St. Patrick's School v Eoghan O'Neachtain Ltd* [2018] IEHC 128 [22], Stephen continued to 'exercise dominion' over the property. As a result, there was a licence, not a lease, between the parties and no security of tenure.

Roger appealed to the Court of Appeal (Civil Division) on the following grounds:

1. the intentions of the parties must be determined by looking at the objective circumstances of the arrangement as a whole. The trial judge erred in law in finding that Roger was a licencee and not a tenant; and

2. the trial judge erred in law in finding that Roger had no security of tenure.

Index